LIBRARY INDEXING AND A[illegible]

LIBRARY INDEXING AND ABSTRACTING

By

Deepak Kumar

BLISc, MLISc
Librarian
Sardar Patel Subharti Institute of Law
&
Subharti Institute of
Fine Art & Fashion Design
Subharti University, Meerut (U.P.)
(India)

DISCOVERY PUBLISHING HOUSE PVT. LTD.
NEW DELHI-110 002

Published by:
Namit Wasan
DISCOVERY PUBLISHING HOUSE PVT. LTD.
4383/4B, Ansari Road, Darya Ganj
New Delhi-110 002 (India)
Phone : +91-11-23279245; 23253475; 43596065
E-mail : discoverybooksindia@gmail.com
discoverypublishinghouse@gmail.com
namitwasan9@gmail.com
web : www.discoverypublishinggroup.com

Reprinted: **2019**

First Edition: **2014**

ISBN: 978-93-5056-394-6

Library Indexing and Abstracting

Printed at:
Infinity Imaging Systems
Delhi

Preface

An abstracting service is a service that provides abstracts of publications, often on a subject or group of related subjects, usually on a subscription basis. An indexing service is a service that assigns descriptors and other kinds of access points to documents. The word indexing service is today mostly used about computer programs, but may also cover services providing back-of-the-book indexes, journal indexes and related kinds of indexes. An indexing and abstracting service is a service that provides shortening or summarizing of documents and assigning of descriptors for referencing documents. The emphasis here is not so much on the mechanical practice but on the conceptual understanding of the methodology. The objective is to ensure that the study of this book enables the reader to understand indexing and abstracting in a clearer and better perspective. We hope this book will help the readers to understand and learnt about the different aspects of "*Library Indexing and Abstracting*" in a most comprehensive way.

—Editor

Contents

1

Indexing and Abstracting

INDEXING

According to the British indexing standard, an *index* is a systematic arrangement of entries designed to enable users to locate information in a document. The process of creating an index is called *indexing,* and a person who does it is called an *indexer*. There are many types of indexes, from cumulative indexes for journals to computer database indexes. This discussion concentrates on the back-of-the-book index, found in non-fiction books. Indexes are among those necessary but never spectacular products of hard as well as skilled work that can sometimes make the difference between a book and a good book. index review in *Books Ireland,* February 1994.

The chief purpose of an index is distillation, and in performing that task it can manage to suggest a life's incongruities with a concision that the most powerful biographical stylist will have trouble matching. Thomas Mallon, *New York Times,* 10 March 1991 the ocean flows of online information are all streaming together, and the access tools are becoming absolutely critical. If you don't index it, it doesn't exist. It's out there but you can't find it, so it might as well not be there. Barbara Quint, ASI San Diego Conference, 1994.

WHO DOES INDEXING

In the United States, according to tradition, the index for a non-fiction book is the responsibility of the author. Most authors don't actually do it. While a few publishers have in-house indexers, most indexing is done by freelancers, often working from home, hired by authors, publishers or packagers. More often, the indexer is hired by the publisher, and the fee is deducted from the money due the author. If a packager hires the indexer directly, various payment arrangements can be made. Indexing work is not recommended to those who lack an orderly mind and a capacity for taking pains. A good index is a minor work of art but it is also the product of clear thought and meticulous care.

HOW IS INDEXING DONE

The indexer usually receives a set of *page proofs* for the book, often at the same time as final proofreading is being done by someone else. The indexer reads the page proofs, making a list of *headings* and *subheadings* and the location of each pertinent reference. After completing the rough index the indexer edits it for structure, clarity and consistency, formats it to specifications, proofreads it and submits it to the client in hard-copy form, on disk, by modem, or by e-mail. Since, the indexer is very late in the production process, there can be unreasonable time pressure. As to *how* to index, what goes on between the ear, that's a subject for books, courses, workshops and lifelong learning from experience?

Less time is available for the preparation of the index than for almost any other step in the bookmaking process. For obvious reasons, most indexes cannot be completed until page proofs are available. Typesetters are anxious for those few final pages of copy; printers want to get the job on the press; binders are waiting; salesmen are clamouring for finished books *surely* you can get that index done over the weekend? *Chicago Manual of Style,* 14th ed. Indexers are in effect trying to provide answers to a host of unasked questions.

Indexers therefore need to work as if their audience is present. But there are two snags: *first,* in most cases they do not know who this audience will be; *second,* in most cases they do not receive any feedback as to whether their judgements have been successful. From a communicative point of view, there is probably no more isolated intellectual task than indexing. The twilight howl of the indexer might well be Is there anybody there? David Crystal, editorial, *The Indexer,* April 1995

CAN'T A COMPUTER DO THE INDEXING

The short answer is no. Computers can easily construct a *concordance* but this is not an index, and is not very useful to someone looking for information. The so-called automatic indexing software programmes now appearing on the market are simply not up to the task of indexing a book. Book indexing involves a little bit of manipulating words appearing in a text, which computers can do, and a lot of understanding and organising the ideas and information in the text, which computers cannot do and will not do for many years to come. An example of the difference is that a book on protective gloves for occupational use might have a chapter discussing surgical gloves, how they get punctured and how they are tested for integrity, but might never use the word *holes*.

Yet a user of the book would expect to find this word in the index and be directed to the appropriate chapter. The indexer handles dozens or hundreds of such issues in every book. Where the text is already on computer disk, the indexing features of word processing programmes can ease the handling of page numbers and sorting, but the real indexing work is still done by the human. Powerful dedicated software is also available for personal computers to aid the professional indexer in constructing, sorting, editing and formatting the index, whether from hard-copy text or computer files. Many indexers use one of the programmes listed on the Indexing Software page. Automated indexing was never intended to produce back-of-the-book indexes. As Indexicon demonstrates so well, back-of-the-book indexes cannot be automatically generated.

WHAT SKILLS OR EDUCATION DO INDEXERS NEED

Many publishers and packagers don't ask for specific degrees or credentials unless they are looking for someone with subject matter expertise for a technical book. Skills needed to learn indexing include excellent language skills, high clerical aptitude, accuracy and attention to detail. Once you are indexing professionally, you will find that self-discipline, curiosity, tolerance of isolation and love of books are necessary to keep going.

In addition to all this, of course, there are the business and marketing skills needed to succeed as a self- employed professional. Clients take their cue from you: if you behave in a professional manner, most of them treat you accordingly. Whoever the indexer is, he or she should be intelligent, widely read, and well acquainted with publishing practices also levelheaded, patient, scrupulous in handling detail, and analytically minded. This rare bird must while being intelligent, levelheaded, patient, accurate, and analytical work at top speed to meet an almost impossible deadline. *Chicago Manual of Style*, 13th ed. I wonder whether there is any profession in which a knowledge of one's tongue is of the slightest use.

HOW DO INDEXERS GET CLIENTS

Most people start by sending letters and resumes to publishers. Find their addresses in *Literary Marketplace, Writer's Market* and *Books in Print*, available in your library. It may take hundreds of letters to get a first indexing job. Experienced indexers say they get most jobs through recommendations from satisfied clients and networking, although some still come from marketing efforts. Now, many people interested in indexing are pursuing the apprenticeship model, working with an established indexer to build skills and experience. The three best ways to get work? Network, network, network.

HOW MUCH ARE INDEXERS PAID

.That's the wrong question. A freelance indexer is running a small business; as a businessperson, you are not *paid*, you set prices and charge for a service. You are not an employee; you are an independent contractor. This is an important distinction because of how it changes your thinking. It's also very important for tax purposes, but that's off the subject.

HOW DO INDEXERS PRICE THEIR SERVICES

The two most common ways of quoting book index prices are per page and per entry. Different publishers prefer different methods, and indexes for different media also are priced differently. All the different ways of quoting prices can be reduced to a fee per hour. While experienced indexers come to know what rates per page or per entry they can afford to accept, beginning indexers would be well-advised to focus on the hourly fee when figuring their bids. This enables new indexers to decide what kinds of work are best for them, and to track improvements in skill, efficiency and income as they become experienced.

If you are starting out as a freelance indexer, you won't be able to get the same fee as an indexer with 10 years of experience. This does not mean inviting exploitation by unscrupulous clients. Remember, if you are qualified as an indexer, you are producing a professional product, and you should be fairly compensated. Set yourself a rock-bottom hourly fee for run-of-the-mill indexing, the lowest figure you should ever accept, and stick to it. Remember, no one says you have to take what the prospective client is offering. No one says the client has to pay what you charge. Both parties are free to negotiate or go elsewhere. It is your responsibility to set the fee you charge for indexing, and negotiate to get it. Indexers need to charge for their services according to the time they expect to spend on the work.

On the other hand, many clients want a predictable price since, they are under budget constraints. These clients will not pay by the hour, especially if they don't know your work. How do you quote your prices to get your hourly fee? If the client opens the discussion by saying she wants the index done for $1,200, or for a certain amount per indexable page, a fixed bid is called for. Fixed bids are good for the client but risky for the indexer.

The indexer must be familiar with the book before a reasonable bid can be given, because of wide variations in words per page and complexity of material. The expected number of entries per page or in the whole index should also be specified, since, this is a key factor in the time spent doing the index. Publishers in some fields want to ensure a detailed index, so they use pricing by the entry.

As long as both parties are clear on exactly what constitutes an entry and how they are counted, this has the advantage of compensating the indexer for extra time spent on complex material. Again, the expected number of entries per page should be specified. No matter how the bid is to be figured, start with the hourly fee to make sure you are being compensated according to your set rate.

First, estimate how many hours it will take you to do the index, including editing, proofing and preparing final copy. This estimate is crucial. Actually indexing a representative sample of the book is helpful here, and estimating skills should improve with experience. Then multiply by your hourly fee to get the total amount you expect for indexing the book. If the client wants a lump sum bid, you are done. To prepare a bid or price quote for a client who uses per-page pricing, divide your total estimate by the page count. To prepare a price quote on a per-entry basis, figure the total number of entries in the book and divide this into the total estimate.

In summary, use one of the following methods, where $FEE is the total fee, PAGES the indexable page count of the book, and ENTRIES the total number of entries in the book:

- Fixed price = $FEE
- Per-page rate = $FEE/ PAGES
- Per-entry rate = $FEE/ ENTRIES

If the client has a price or rate in mind, work the numbers backward to figure the hourly fee resulting from the client's number before deciding whether you can afford to accept it. When someone offers you an indexing assignment at $12 per hour, take note of the advice from Dr. Wellisch in the next quote; you could do almost as well at McDonald's! An hourly indexing fee should always be at least four times the wage one can earn by flipping hamburgers at a fast-food emporium.

WHAT KIND OF ANNUAL INCOME CAN I EXPECT FROM INDEXING

Here are some important factors which affect your income from indexing or any other independent service business:

- How you set your prices.
- How much you want to work.
- How skilled you are at finding enough good clients to keep busy.
- How skilled, and fast, you are at indexing.
- How much your business expenses are.

In short, your income depends on your motivation and your business skills as well as your indexing skills. There are indexers who treat it as a relaxing, part-time business; there are indexers who work long hours and support themselves in nice middle-class style as a result. Most probably fall in between. You have to decide what you are looking for. You need to spend time learning how to start and run a business as well as learning to index. Books and magazines on home-based business and entrepreneurship have lots of ideas and advice applicable to freelance indexers.

Seminars and workshops on business skills and sales technique can be quite useful, but be careful with your money. Talk to graduates before signing up. Suppose we look ahead to the future, finding that after gaining some experience, you reach a speed and skill level where the combination of rates paid by clients and the time you spend doing the work results in a good hourly rate. What hourly rate might you expect? ASI regularly surveys freelance and in-house indexers to find out what salaries and fees are being paid.

The latest survey is available on this web site, in the Members Area. If you are an ASI member, you may view and download the survey. In case you don't have access to this information, bear with me as I discuss the mechanics of estimating your self-employment income without using a specific rate. To estimate your annual income from indexing, multiply your hourly rate by the average number of work hours in a year.

Forty hours per week times 52 weeks a year is 2,080. Wait! If you want to index full-time, you need to consider all the time your business takes besides actual indexing. Writing letters and making calls to get work, rushing to the FedEx office before they close, billing, doing your tax return, shopping for supplies, backing up your computer files, meal breaks and occasional holidays and vacations are all unpaid time. Don't forget idle time between jobs; it takes several years of building a client base for most indexers to get full-time work. If you plan to put 40 hours per week into your business, then allowing for all the above within the 40 hours results in a rule of thumb of about 1,200 hours per year of actual paid indexing work. OK, multiply your hourly fee by 1,200. That's your gross revenue. But remember, this is a business; your actual income is much less.

To figure hourly income, self-employment taxes and federal, state and local income taxes come off the top, plus the cost of your supplies, utilities, ASI membership dues and the amortised cost of your office equipment. A good rule of thumb is to take at least 50 per cent off the rate. So, multiply your hourly income by how many hours you can work per year. If this is not enough for you to live on, don't quit the day job yet. Most indexers start indexing as a part-time moonlighting effort, supporting themselves with another job. Once they are sure they want to do this kind of work full-time, and clients are paying well and keeping them so busy it is hard to get everything done, they can make the decision to try full-time indexing.

Once you are well-established, idle periods and time spent marketing diminish, resulting in more paid work hours. You can eventually reach 2,000 hours per year, if you are willing to work more than 40 hours per week. In addition, a very good indexer who works fast can make a higher hourly rate for a given page rate, because it takes fewer hours to do the work. *Money* magazine recently published an article on successful homebased businesses which quoted one experienced freelance indexer who says he averages $50,000 per year. Some indexers are skeptical; others say this is possible after a few years if you work hard and find the right clients. Wealth... is more accurately measured in what you enjoy than in what you possess. Jean Aspen, *Arctic Son*

HOW CAN I LEARN TO INDEX

A local college or university with a Library Science or Information Science department may offer indexing courses. Many people take the indexing correspondence courses offered by the US Department of Agriculture. Assignments are graded by indexing professionals and a certificate of completion can be provided. If you are considering ASI membership, take note of the excellent self-paced course offered to ASI members. Available on interactive CD-ROM, this comprehensive course includes many practical exercises and self-assessments.

A certificate of completion can be obtained by taking the optional exams. Look at the Indexing Courses and Workshops web page for more information about all these options. Before you invest money in an expensive course, check out some books on the subject to gauge your interest and aptitude. Indexing cannot be reduced to a set of steps that can be followed! It is not a mechanical process. Indexing books is a form of writing. Like other types of writing, it is a mixture of art and craft, judgement and selection. With practice and experience, indexers develop their own style as do other writers. The best we can do as teachers of indexing is to present the rules and offer guidance.

DEFINITION OF ABSTRACT

Abstracts, like all summaries, cover the main points of a piece of writing. Unlike executive summaries written for non-specialist audiences, abstracts use the same level of technical language and expertise found in the article itself. And unlike general summaries which can be adapted in many ways to meet various readers' and writers' needs, abstracts are typically 150 to 250 words and follow set patterns. Because readers use abstracts for set purposes, these purposes further define abstracts.

PURPOSES FOR ABSTRACTS

Abstracts typically serve five main goals:

- *Help Readers Decide if they should Read an Entire Article*: Readers use abstracts to see if a piece of writing interests them or relates to a topic they're working on. Rather than tracking down hundreds of articles, readers rely on abstracts to decide quickly if an article is pertinent. Equally important, readers use abstracts to help them gauge the sophistication or complexity of a piece of writing. If the abstract is too technical or too simplistic, readers know that the article will also be too technical or too simplistic.
- *Help Readers and Researchers Remember Key Findings on a Topic*: Even after reading an article, readers often keep abstracts to remind them of which sources support conclusions. Because abstracts include complete bibliographic citations, they are helpful when readers begin writing up their research and citing sources.
- *Help Readers Understand a Text by Acting as a Pre-reading Outline of Key Points*: Like other pre-reading strategies, reading an abstract before reading an article helps readers anticipate what's coming in the text itself. Using an abstract to get an overview of the text makes reading the text easier and more efficient.
- *Index Articles for Quick Recovery and Cross-referencing*: Even before computers made indexing easier, abstracts helped librarians and researchers find information more easily. With so many indexes now available electronically, abstracts with their keywords are even more important because readers can review hundreds of abstracts quickly to find the ones most useful for their research. Moreover, cross-referencing through abstracts opens up new areas of research that readers might not have known about when they started researching a topic.

- *Allow Supervisors to Review Technical Work without becoming Bogged Down in Details*: Although many managers and supervisors will prefer the less technical executive summary, some managers need to keep abreast of technical work. Research shows that only 15 per cent of managers read the complete text of reports or articles. Most managers, then, rely on the executive summary or abstract as the clearest overview of employees' work.

TYPES OF ABSTRACTS

Although you'll see two types of abstracts—informative and descriptive—most writersnow provide informative abstracts of their work.

DESCRIPTIVE ABSTRACT

A descriptive abstract outlines the topics covered in a piece of writing so the reader can decide whether to read the entire document. In many ways, the descriptive abstract is like a table of contents in paragraph form. Unlike reading an informative abstract, reading a descriptive abstract cannot substitute for reading the document because it does not capture the content of the piece. Nor does a descriptive abstract fulfill the other main goals of abstracts as well as informative abstracts do. For all these reasons, descriptive abstracts are less and less common.

SAMPLE DESCRIPTIVE ABSTRACT

We continue to document all major climatic variables in the uplands and floodplains at Bonanza Creek. In addition, we have documented the successional changes in microclimate in 9 successional upland and floodplain stands at Bonanza Creek (BNZ) and in four elevational locations at Caribou-Poker Creek (CPCRW). A sun photometer is operated cooperatively with NASA to estimate high-latitude atmospheric extinction coefficients for remote-sensing images. Electronic data are collected monthly and loaded into a database which produces monthly summaries.

The data are checked for errors, documented, and placed on-line on the BNZ Web page. Climate data for the entire state have been summarised for the period of station records and krieged to produce maps of climate zones for Alaska based on growing-season and annual temperature and precipitation.

INFORMATIVE ABSTRACT

An informative abstract provides detail about the substance of a piece of writing because readers will sometimes rely on the abstract alone for information.

Informative abstracts typically follow this format:

- Identifying information;
- Concise restatement of the main point, including the initial problem or other background;
- Methodology and key findings;
- Major conclusions.

Informative abstracts usually appear in indexes like *Dissertation Abstracts International.*

SAMPLE INFORMATIVE ABSTRACT BASED ON NON-EXPERIMENTAL WORK

Environmental Impact Statement. Federal Register: December 11, 1997. "Endangered and Threatened Wildlife and Plants; Proposed Revision of Special Regulations for the Gray Wolf." Fish and Wildlife Service, Department of the Interior. On November 22, 1994, the U.S. Fish and Wildlife Service published special rules to establish non-essential experimental populations of gray wolves in Yellowstone National Park and central Idaho. The non-essential experimental population areas include all of Wyoming, most of Idaho, and much of central and southern Montana.

A close reading of the special regulations indicates that, unintentionally, the language reads as though wolf control measures apply only outside of the experimental population area. This proposed revision is intended to amend language in the special regulations so that it clearly applies within the Yellowstone non-essential experimental population area and the central Idaho non-essential experimental population area.

This proposed change will not affect any of the assumptions and earlier analysis made in the environmental impact statement or other portions of the special rules.

SAMPLE INFORMATIVE ABSTRACT BASED ON EXPERIMENTAL WORK

Research reported by Daly, Miller, and their colleagues suggests that writing apprehension is related to a number of factors we do not yet fully understand. This study suggests that included among those factors should be the belief that writing ability is a gift. Giftedness, as it is referred to in the study, is roughly equivalent to the Romantic notion of original genius. Results from a survey of 247 postsecondary students enrolled in introductory writing courses at two institutions indicate that higher levels of belief in giftedness are correlated with higher levels of writing apprehension, lower self-assessments of writing ability, lower levels of confidence in achieving proficiency in certain writing activities and genres, and lower self-assessments of prior experience with writing instructors.

Significant differences in levels of belief in giftedness were also found among students who differed in their perceptions of the most important purpose for writing, with students who identified 'to express your own feelings about something' as the most important purpose for writing having the highest mean level of belief in giftedness. Although the validity of the notion that writing ability is a special gift is not directly addressed, the results suggest that belief in giftedness may have deleterious effects on student writers.

A MORE DETAILED COMPARISON OF DESCRIPTIVE *VS.* INFORMATIVE

The typical distinction between descriptive and informative is that the descriptive abstract is like a table of contents whereas the informative abstract lays out the content of the document.

To show the differences as clearly as possible, we compare a shortened Table of Contents for a 100-page legal argument presented by the FDA and an informative abstract of the judge's decision in the case:

- Descriptive Table of Contents of the Argument.
- Informative Abstract of the Decision.

Table of Contents of the Argument

Court Brief Filed Dec. 2, 1996, by the Department of Justice in defence of FDA's determination of jurisdiction over cigarettes and smokeless tobacco products and its regulations restricting those products to protect children and adolescents.

Statement of the matter before the court; statement of material facts:

- The health effects of cigarettes and smokeless tobacco.
- The basis for the assertion of jurisdiction.
  - The evidence that nicotine in cigarettes and smokeless tobacco "affect[s] the structure or any function of the body"
  - The evidence that the pharmacological effects of nicotine in cigarettes and smokeless tobacco are 'intended'.
  - The evidence that cigarettes and smokeless tobacco are 'combination products'.
- The rule.
  - Cigarettes and smokeless tobacco as combination products.
  - The regulatory goal.
  - Youth access restrictions.
  - Advertising and promotion restrictions.

Informative Abstract of the Decision

On April 25, 1997, Judge William Osteen of the Federal District Court in Greensboro, North Carolina, ruled that FDA has jurisdiction under the Federal Food, Drug, and Cosmetic Act to regulate nicotine-containing cigarettes and smokeless tobacco. The Court held that "tobacco products fit within the FDCA's definitions of 'drug' and 'device,'" and that FDA can regulate cigarettes and smokeless tobacco products as drug delivery devices under the combination product and restricted device provisions of the Act.

With respect to the tobacco rule, the Court upheld all restrictions involving youth access and labeling, including two access provisions that went into effect Feb. 28:

- The prohibition on sales of cigarettes and smokeless tobacco products to children and adolescents under 18; and
- The requirement that retailers check photo identification of customers who are under 27 years of age.

The Court also upheld additional access and labeling restrictions originally scheduled to go into effect Aug. 28, 1997, including a prohibition on self-service displays and the placement of vending machines where children have access to them. The Court also upheld the ban on distribution of free samples, the sale of so-called kiddie packs of less than 20 cigarettes, and the sale of individual cigarettes. However, the Court delayed implementation of the provisions that have not yet gone into effect pending further action by the Court.

The Court invalidated on statutory grounds FDA's restrictions on the advertising and promotion of cigarettes and smokeless tobacco. Judge Osteen found that the statutory provision relied on by FDA, section 520(e) of the Act (21 U.S.C. 360j(e)), does not provide FDA with authority to regulate the advertising and promotion of tobacco products. Specifically, the Court found that the authority in that section to set 'such other conditions' on the sale, distribution, or use of a restricted device does not encompass advertising restrictions. Because Judge Osteen based his ruling on the advertising provisions on purely statutory grounds, he declined to consider the First Amendment challenge to those parts of the rule. The government is appealing the advertising portion of the ruling.

BIBLIOGRAPHIC CITATION OR IDENTIFICATION

As more and more databases are stored and accessed electronically, abstracts are more frequently reproduced apart from the entire article or document. In a large corporation or government entity, for instance, an abstract of a progress report might be circulated and stored in a dozen offices or on multiple computers even though the report itself is filed in only one location. Clear identification is crucial so that readers who want to review the entire text can locate it from the information given with the abstract.

Depending on where your writing is printed and stored, you'll need to include different kinds of identifying information with your abstract:

- Bibliographic Citation
- Organisational Identification
- Internet Citation

BIBLIOGRAPHIC CITATION

If your writing will be printed and disseminated as a book, part of a book, or an article in a journal or magazine, give a full bibliographic citation that includes all the publication information so that readers can find print copies of the article.

ORGANISATIONAL IDENTIFICATION

If your abstract is part of a corporate or government document that will not be printed or disseminated outside the organisation, you need only include your name, the title of the document, its completion date, a project name, and an authorisation or organisational number. If your abstract will be circulated outside your organisation: your company or organisation name, the name of the organisation that commissioned the document, a contract number, a security classification, and key words to help in cataloguing your abstract.

INTERNET CITATION

If you're 'publishing' your own work on the World Wide Web or if your writing will appear on the Internet as part of a full-text electronic database, you can save readers time by citing the Internet address for the full text. Typically, writers note both print publication information and the URL —the *http* or *www* address—with the abstract.

PROCESSES FOR WRITING ABSTRACTS

Unless you work for an abstracting service, you'll usually write abstracts of your own finished work. This part explores some strategies for drafting your abstract. Strategies and advice on revising and editing are located in Key Issues in Preparing Abstracts.

CUT AND PASTE METHOD

Beginning with reading may seem odd since, you wrote the paper, but it can frequently be the fastest way to write an abstract because it allows you to 'lift' as much of the abstract from your original paper as possible:

- Guidelines for Using the Cut and Paste Method:
  - As you read through your own paper, highlight or copy sentences which summarise the entire paper or individual sections or sub-points of your main argument.
  - Write a sentence that summarises the main point.
  - Add sentences that summarise sections.
  - If you're writing a descriptive abstract, you're ready to begin revising.
  - If you're writing an informative abstract, look through your paper for details, particularly of key findings or major supporting arguments and major conclusions. Paste these into your abstract and proceed to editing for consistency and length—frequently in the original 'cuts' you will still have more detail than is necessary in an abstract.

OUTLINING METHOD

Frequently, the best place to start writing an abstract is to first make an outline of the paper to serve as a rough draft of your abstract. The most efficient way to do this is to write what Kenneth Bruffee calls a descriptive or 'backwards' outline.

Backwards Outline Instructions

- Read through each paragraph of your paper and write one phrase or sentence that answers the question 'what does this paragraph do?'.
- Take your list of descriptions for each paragraph and look for connections: *i.e.,* do these 3 or 5 paragraphs do something similar? What is it?.
- When you've reduced your outline to 4 or 5 accurate generalisations, you most likely have a descriptive abstract.
- If you're writing an informative abstract, fill in key details about your content.

Detailed Backwards Outline

Because informative abstracts need more detail, the regular backwards outline may not be as useful a strategy for this type of abstract. Instead, do a backwards outline on the lefthand side of a piece of paper. Then, on the right-hand side, answer the question 'what does this paragraph *say?*' for each paragraph in the paper.

Then complete the steps below:

- Take your first column and generalise down to 4-5 sentences about what the paper *does.*
- Use these sentences as topic sentences for the paragraphs in your abstract.
- Now, go to your second column and choose appropriate content for each section you outlined in #2. In other words, use the right-hand column to fill in details about what your paper says on each point outlined in #2.

KEY ISSUES IN PREPARING ABSTRACTS

These are some of the key issues in writing an abstract:

- Concise, Accurate Statement of the Main Idea.
- Organisation of Subpoints.
- Use of Details.
- Revising and Editing.

CONCISE, ACCURATE STATEMENT OF THE MAIN IDEA

Abstracts begin with a one-sentence summary of the main point of your paper and often introduce the problem the paper explores. Especially for papers based on research, the first sentence of the abstract announces the subject and scope of the research as well as the problem and your thesis. That's quite a bit of information to condense into a sentence or two, and so the concise statement of the main idea often takes careful revision.

Choose from these options to read more about preparing a concise statement of the main idea:

- Condensing Information for Non-research Papers
- Condensing Information for Research Papers
- Beware of Focusing too Narrowly
- Test Your Ability to Judge Conciseness

Condensing Information for Non-research Papers

Most non-research papers can be summed up in a nutshell statement—a single sentence that boils down a paper to its essential main point and doesn't aim to capture details, supporting arguments, or types of proof.

One-sentence Summaries for Different Types of Papers

Each of these non-research papers summarises its main point based on its overall purpose:

- This paper argues that the 'saving democracy' rhetoric surrounding the Gulf War was merely a mask for the U.S.'s interest in keeping oil prices down.
- Ethnography and ethnology are the preferred research methods of many anthropologists.

Condensing Information for Research Papers

In addition to stating the main point of the paper, research-based papers often need to set up the context and scope of the research as well. Setting the context includes stating the subject of your work as well as the problem that prompted your research. You might also refer to major researchers who have already done work on your topic as a way of setting the context. Remember, too, that your abstract must always include the main point of your paper, so don't neglect that focus as you work on stating the problem and context.

Example:

- In this example, note that the writer uses the names of key researchers to set the context and then focuses on what researchers don't yet know. After setting up the problem he's addressing in the research, the writer then announces the scope and focus of the paper in the second sentence:
  - Research reported by Daly, Miller, and their colleagues suggests that writing apprehension is related to a number of factors we do not yet fully understand. This study suggests that included among those factors should be the belief that writing ability is a gift....
- In this example, the writer announces the subject and scope of the research although he doesn't set context or suggest the problem that prompted the research. Depending on your ultimate goals for the abstract, you may be more successful with this approach that states the main point of your research paper even without setting context:
  - This report examines the changes in photosynthesis with an energyproducing carnivorous plants, specifically the Venus Fly Trap.

Beware of Focussing Too Narrowly

No one who has ever written a concise restatement of a complex point will claim that the work was easy or straightforward. Usually, a writer needs to work back and forth between revising the restatement and re-reading the paper to be sure the main idea is stated accurately and clearly. Having worked so hard on that point, though, don't assume that you don't need to revise other parts of your abstract. In this example, the writer restates only the main point and dismisses key information from the 15-page document that should be included in the abstract.

Sample Abstract with Overly Narrow Focus

EPA is denying a petition to delete phosphoric acid from the reporting requirements under section 313 of the Emergency Planning and Community Right-to-Know Act of 1986 (EPCRA) and section 6607 of the Pollution Prevention Act of 1990 (PPA). This action is based on EPA's conclusion that phosphoric acid does not meet the deletion criteria of EPCRA section 313(d)(3). Specifically, EPA is denying this petition because EPA's review of the petition and available information resulted in the conclusion that phosphoric acid meets the listing criterion in EPCRA section 313(d)(2)(C) in that the phosphates that result from the neutralisation of phosphoric acid may cause algal blooms. Algal blooms result in deoxygenation of the water and other effects that may ultimately lead to a number of serious adverse effects on ecosystems, including fish kills and changes in the composition of animal and plant life.

Test your Ability to Judge Conciseness

The biggest problem writers run into when beginning an abstract is providing enough accurate information to convey an article's main idea without providing more detail than is needed.

A DETAILED SUMMARY

A summary of: Jaime O'Neill, No Allusions in the Classroom, *Newsweek*, September 23, 1985. Author Jaime O'Neill's article, 'No Allusions in the Classroom,' emphasises the communication problem between teachers and students due to the students' lack of basic knowledge. The author supports this assertion by using a combination of personal experience, evidence obtained from recent polls, other professors' opinions, and the results of an experiment he conducted in his own classroom. The experiment O'Neill conducted was an ungraded eighty-six question 'general knowledge' test issued to students on the first day of classes. On this test, "most students answered incorrectly far more often than they answered correctly."

Incorrect answers included fallacies such as: 'Darwin invented gravity' and 'Leningrad was in Jamaica.' Compounding the problem, students don't ask questions. This means that their teachers assume they know things that they do not. O'Neill shows the scope of this problem by showing that, according to their teachers, this seems to be a typical problem across the United States.

O'Neill feels that common knowledge in a society is essential to communicate. Without this common knowledge, learning is made much more difficult because teacher and student do not have a common body of knowledge from which to draw. The author shows the deterioration of common knowledge through poll results, personal experience, other teachers' opinions, and his own experiment's results.

SAMPLE RESTATEMENTS OF MAIN IDEA

To test your ability to find a balance between insufficient/ inaccurate information and too much information, judge these sample restatements of the main idea of Jaime O'Neill's article:

- In 'No Allusions in the Classroom,' professor Jaime M. O'Neill discusses thefrustrations he had with his students not understanding his allusions. Is this a concise statement of the article's main idea?
  — Yes.
  — No.
- In the article 'No Allusions in the Classroom,' a teacher of 15 years, Jaime M. O'Neill exposes the overall lack of basic knowledge of college students in areas of history, geography, and politics. Is this a concise statement of the article's main idea?
  — Yes.
  — No.
- In the article 'No Allusions in the Classroom,' the author, Jaime M. O'Neill relays his frustrations

resulting from what he finds to be a lack of basic or common knowledge of the American student. He is a professor who has taught at several different colleges in the United States. Through his experiences in the classroom he noticed the fact that students were not catching on to his allusions. He states in the article that this miscommunication is causing a problem in the education process. Is this a concise statement of the article's main idea?

— Yes.

— No.

- In 'No Allusion in the Classroom,' by Jaime M. O'Neill, the problem of ignorance is discussed. Jaime O'Neill says that college students lack common knowledge and it is interfering with education. Is this a concise statement of the article's main idea?

  — Yes.

  — No.
- Author Jaime O'Neill's article 'No Allusions in the Classroom', emphasised the communication problem between teachers and students due to the students' lack of basic knowledge. Is this a concise statement of the article's main idea?

  — Yes.

  — No.

ORGANISATION OF SUBPOINTS

After a summary of the main topic/problem/point of your paper or report, the abstract provides some detail on how you reached this point. The information provided in the abstract should follow the organisation of the paper/report itself, almost like providing an outline for the reader in text form.

ABSTRACTS OF PAPERS WITHOUT HEADINGS

When abstracting a paper that doesn't have headings and sub-headings, you must depend on your sense of major 'chunks' in the text.

Note

The numbers in this abstract are for illustration purposes only. Number 1 designates a concise statement of the main point. Number 2 designates a summary statement of the first major argument and its support.

Number 3 corresponds to a summary of the second major argument, and Number 4 corresponds to the second argument's support:

- This paper argues that the 'saving democracy' rhetoric surrounding the Gulf War was merely a mask for the U.S.'s interest in keeping oil prices down.
- Such an argument is made by *first* describing the ways in which OPEC controlled oil prices by limiting sales, pointing specifically to how Kuwait was producing more oil than allowed by current OPEC agreements.
- *Second,* the paper examines why the U.S., was invested in keeping good relations with the only two OPEC nations—Kuwait and Saudi Arabia—which frequently made trade agreements that benefited the U.S.
- *Finally,* the paper does a close reading of the newspaper coverage of the Gulf War, examining how an early recognition of the monetary incentive changed to a democratic one when Bush ordered troops to Saudi Arabia.

ABSTRACTS OF PAPERS WITH SUB-HEADINGS

When abstracting a paper that has headings and sub-headings, use those to help you identify key parts of the paper for your abstract. The following sample abstract, based on a research paper, uses the introduction, subjects, methods, results, and discussion headings from the original paper.

Note

The numbers in this abstract are for illustration purposes only. Number 1 designates a concise statement of the main point and 'problem' prompting the research. Number 2 designates a summary of the selection of research subjects.

Numbers 3 and 4 correspond to summaries of research methods and results, respectively, and Number 5 designates a summary of conclusions:

- 'Students in networked classrooms' examines the question of whether students in a computer classroom are more likely to engage in peer review than students in traditional classrooms.
- To test this question, two classes in each environment were studied.
- An observer participated in all four classes for the duration of a semester, noting the nature of the interaction between students. Further, the observer interviewed both students and teachers about the nature of peer interaction and review.
- Based on this sample, the study finds that students in computer classrooms are more likely, by a ratio of 2:1, to engage in peer review.
- As a result of this finding, the paper concludes that for this one variable, computer classrooms are a more effective environment in which to teach writing.

USE OF DETAILS

Details should be used judiciously in abstracts. Determining the amount of detail to provide depends a great deal on what type of abstract you are writing, the complexity of the paper, the word limit for the abstract, and the purposes you imagine readers of your abstract have for reading.

COMPLEXITY OF THE PAPER

An abstract of a five-page progress report is likely to be shorter than an abstract for a 100-page Master's thesis, mainly because a long paper will include more main ideas, not just details. Keep in mind your readers and their reasons for reading your abstract. Focus your abstract on main ideas and provide only those details that are crucial for readers to understand your main points.

WORD LIMIT FOR THE ABSTRACT

Some publications limit the length of abstracts to no more than 75 words. Others allow abstracts of complex documents to run up to 350 words. Be sure to check the publication's guidelines. If it has a low word limit, concentrate on capturing only main ideas from your paper. Don't try to cut a 200-word abstract down to 125 words by simply cutting connecting words, articles, etc. Even the shortest abstracts need to be readable, not telegraphic.

READERS' PURPOSES

Some publications limit the length of abstracts to no more than 75 words. Others allow abstracts of complex documents to run up to 350 words. Be sure to check the publication's guidelines. If it has a low word limit, concentrate on capturing only main ideas from your paper. Don't try to cut a 200-word abstract down to 125 words by simply cutting connecting words, articles, etc. Even the shortest abstracts need to be readable, not telegraphic.

REVISING AND EDITING

When you work from your own texts, abstracts are usually easy to draft. After all, most writers begin by cutting and pasting from the text itself. But abstracts can be tricky to revise and edit, particularly if you need to reach a low word count. In this section, we offer some advice on strategies for moving from a first draft of an abstract to a polished finished version.

BEING CONCISE

When you cut and paste parts of your paper into your draft abstract, you may find that you initially include words and phrases that clarify the meaning in the paper but that simply add extra words in the abstract. Read your drafts carefully to cut unnecessary words. Note that the italicised words in the example can be cut without any loss of meaning in the abstract. 'Students in networked classrooms' examines *the question of* whether students in a computer classroom are more likely to engage in peer review than students in traditional classrooms.

To test this question, two classes in each environment were studied. An observer participated in all four classes for the *duration of a* semester, noting *the nature of the* interaction between students. Further, the observer interviewed both students and teachers about *the nature of* peer interaction and review. *Based on this sample,* the study finds that students in computer classrooms are more likely, by a ratio of 2:1, to engage in peer review. *As a result of this finding,* the paper concludes that, for this one variable, computer classrooms are a more effective environment in which to teach writing.

SMOOTHING OUT CONNECTIONS

After you revise for conciseness, you will also want to be sure that each sentence in your abstract leads smoothly into the next. Sometimes you need to add or change transitional words and phrases. Sometimes you need to repeat key words. And sometimes, you need to combine sentences so that the connections between ideas are logically clear.

In our example, we combine what were sentences 2 and 3 and the last two sentences:

- This paper examines whether students in a computer classroom are more likely to engage in peer review than students in a traditional classroom. Two classes in each environment were observed, with the participant observer noting interactions between students. Further, the observer interviewed both students and teachers about peer interaction and review. The study finds that students in computer classrooms are twice as likely to engage in peer review and concludes that, for this one variable, computer classrooms are a more effective environment in which to teach writing.

AVOIDING TELEGRAPHIC ABSTRACTS

A highly condensed style can save money when you send a telegram but can make abstracts too dense. Don't cut articles or connecting words that show relationships among ideas. Do repeat key words that show the content of your paper. Abstracts may be short, but they are meant to be readable.

POLISHING STYLE

A reader looks at a summary for the sole purpose of getting a quick glimpse of the article. As a result, she doesn't want to waste time with a lot of phrases and words that do not further the meaning, nor is she interested in the summary writer's opinion. Accounting for audience needs, there are three generalisable principles about the style of summaries:

USE OF 'I'

Although use of 'I' or 'we' is acceptable in some disciplines, many frown on its use in abstracts. Read several abstracts in the publication you're submitting to or the databases you expect to include your abstract. When in doubt, do not use 'I.' Instead, use the following strategies:

Substitute for 'I'

Most abstracts make the paper/report/study the focus of the abstract and the grammatical subject of sentences in the abstract.

Try these sentence openers:

- This paper explores...
- This study suggests...
- The report investigates....

Passive Voice

In combination with substitutes for 'I,' passive voice helps writers focus on the paper/report/study. Instead of, 'I propose that ethnography is a better research method than case study', the abstract might use: "Ethnography is proposed as a better research method than case study." Be sure to combine substitutes for 'I' with passive voice to avoid overusing the passive.

USE OF QUOTES

When using your own sentences, you don't need to put them in quotation marks. For example, if your methods section begins with "Three methods were used to investigate this question: case study, surveys, and observational research," feel free to repeat the sentence in its entirety in the abstract.

Remember, however, the following points:

- Revise the sentence so it makes sense in the abstract.
- Do not 'lift' sentences which are not your own.

USE OF LITERARY PRESENT TENSE

Abstracts use the present tense because we assume texts speak to the present even if their authors are dead and/or wrote the words in the past. As a result, write about the text and/or author as if they were composing the words at the moment.

For example:

- Hemingway describes Paris as......
- The Declaration of Independence states that all men are created equal.

Caution: This rule varies from discipline to discipline.

SOME DO'S AND DON'TS FOR ABSTRACTOR

	DO's		Don'ts
1.	Scan the document purpose fully for key facts.	1.	Repeat words of the title.
2.	Slant the abstract to the audience.	2.	Change the meaning of the original.
3.	Tell what was found.	3.	Comment on or interpret the document. Do not use adjectives.
4.	Tell why the work was done.	4.	Mention earlier work.
5.	Tell how the work was done.	5.	Include detailed experimental results.
6.	Place findings early in the topical sentence.	6.	Discuss details of conventional apparatus.
7.	Put details in succeeding sentence.	7.	Mention future work.
8.	Place general statements last.	8.	Begin abstract with stock phrases.
9.	Separate relatively independent subjects.	9.	Use uncommon or rare phraseology.

(Contd...)

10.	Differentiat eexperiment from hypothesis.	10.	Use questionable jargon.
11.	Be informative but brief.	11.	Waste words by stating the obvious.
12.	Be exact, concise and unambiguous.	12.	Say the samethings in two days.
13.	Use short, complete sentences.	13.	Use noun forms of verbs.
14.	Use short, simple familiar words.	14.	Over use synonyms.
15.	Avoid unnecessary words.	15.	Use a choppy, telegraphic style.
16.	Employ normal technical English.	16.	It should not be a mere recital of subjects covered. Expressions such as 'is discussed' and 'is described' should never be included!
17.	Use direct statements.	17.	The abstract should be a condensation and concentration of the *essential information* in the paper.
18.	Describe conclusions in the present tense.		
19.	Use abbreviations sparingly.		
20.	Avoid using unusual words or phrases.		
21.	Cite bibliographic data completely.		

2

Indexing Languages

AUTHORITY CONTROL AND SUBJECT INDEXING LANGUAGES

Analogously with natural languages, artificial languages with which the mediation between a collection of documents and its potential users takes place are also made up, as Elaine Svenonius has often explained, of four necessary components:

- Vocabulary, that is, all the elementary expressions used to define individual entities, attributes and relationships semantics, that regards the meaning for which a determined expression is included in the vocabulary and used in the language, that is, the relationships which are derived a priori from that meaning and which define it syntax, that regards the composition, by means of the structure of individual elements taken from the vocabulary, of more complex expressions pragmatics, which concerns the conditions and modalities for language application.

Authority control, or with the term vocabulary control, which Elaine Svenonius considers to be equivalent, involves the first component, vocabulary, and comes about in the second, semantics. This analytical approach to linguistic systems of 'cataloguing' mediation provides the most correct theoretical reference for a series of considerations, from which the properties and functions of authority control should result easier to recognise and consequently once clarified the relationships between authority control and the different cataloguing languages, to mark the subject indexing languages.

- Authority control can not be identified, nor is it advisable that it be identified, with a particular cataloguing language, since, syntax and pragmatic components are extraneous to authority control, which vice versa more than the vocabulary and semantic components characterise and diversify the single languages. This independence in relation to single cataloguing languages, or to particular types of language, constitutes a fundamental property and strong element of authority control. Its efficiency must be preserved and widely extended, with the punctual exclusion of the procedures of vocabulary control of those elements and aspects which, being distinctive of single languages, result reciprocally incompatible and thus do not lead to a process of unitary control. The origins of authority control are easy to locate in the paragraphs of the rules for bibliographic cataloguing by author and title, but it is now time to completely abandon the idea that authority control is a phase in the application of a particular cataloguing language, in order to project and realise a system of an unique and general authority control, which satisfies not only the needs of systems of truly bibliographic mediation, but also of systems of, among others, archival and museum mediation. The more it is general and international, the more vocabulary control is efficient, since, it permits the reduction of the waste of resources produced by the repetition of the same operations of control in different places, times and contexts. That is something particularly appreciated in an epoch in which everything is aimed at economising even on intellectual work. Especially, however, the more it is unique and general, the more authority control is efficient, since, it furnishes the unifying element between different cataloguing systems, indispensable for the realisation of instruments, logicians and informatics, which facilitate, and make coherent to the utmost, the research for information in documentary spheres which are traditionally separated, as for example, that of collections in libraries, archives, museums and those in digital formats accessible only by telematic means.

- Cataloguing languages are different, first of all, because of diverse pragmatics, that is because they are destined for use in distinct circumstances with distinct functions and modalities. But, authority control does not concern pragmatics. This means that the conditions and relationships which depend upon the material, formal and substantial characteristics of the single objects to describe and index, the various contexts in which such objects are described and indexed, the particular purposes for their description and indexing, and which determine the use of specific cataloguing languages, at any rate do not determine a diversification of authority control, either regarding the process or the product of such a process, which will be an univocal normalised expression inserted in a web of relationships. Inserting this consideration into the specific theme of this paper, it is impossible not to observe that the conviction that authority control is distinguishable, and must be distinguished, without ulterior specifications is still widespread, and that it is commonly held regarding 'authors'. This conviction, which is certainly involuntary, and thus not justified, in the normative activity of the IFLA, which on this subject published two distinctive guidelines, one which was formally presented as relating to the 'authority records' and one which was formally presented as relating to the 'subject authority entries' Moreover it is also easy to establish that such a persistent conviction has determined, although with non-identical consequences, the same organisation of two of the most important national systems of vocabulary control, that of the Library of Congress and that of the Bibliothèque Nationale de France. In the search screens the Library of Congress authorities are divided into subject authority headings, name authority headings, title authority headings and name/title authority headings; nevertheless, searching for the same expression either as name, title or name/title or as subject the authority record is retrieved. This demonstrates that the authority file is unique, that the control operations relating to the same expression are carried out only once, and that it is simply considered necessary to adjust the appearance of the control system to the conviction held above, making the 'subjects' seem separate from the rest of the entries. The *Notices d'autorité* of the BNF are analogically presented separated into *personnes physiques, collectivités, titres uniformes* and RAMEAU effectively divided. This means that at the BNF all the management and control operations for the same expression are duplicated, with a waste of resources which does not correspond to an increase of visible efficiency in the system, and which would be sad if it were motivated only by the obligation to conserve some, slightly justifiable formal differences between expressions which are equivalent the most evident case is that of the dates of birth and death, not normally stated in the terms given in the *fichier d'autorité personnes physiques*—which proposes, for example, the preferred form Dante Alighieri—but are present in the RAMEAU *vedettes*—where the preferred form is Dante Alighieri. These solution differences and uncertainties in the authority control systems, from which can be derived only problems and waste, beginning with the error of considering the 'subjects' as semantically distinguishable entities, on the same level as persons, corporate bodies and works. It is therefore indispensable to clarify that it is impossible to identify an entity as a subject if not in relation to the to pragmatics, that is, to the concrete circumstances which have implied in such a case the use of a subject indexing language in the cataloguing record of a document. However since, authority control does not regard those circumstances, it is not theoretically correct, nor practically useful, to perceive and practice a subject authority control as a process in itself. In the FRBR model, which in reality is also reflected in the *Guidelines for authority records and references,* are the classes of entities *work, expression, manifestation, item, person, corporate body, concept, object, event* and *place.* These entities "represents the key objects of interest to users of bibliographic data", and each one having a formal expression as the primary necessary attribute which designates it can be subjected, and it is potentially opportune that they all be subjected, to the authority control procedures. The 'subject' is not an entity in the FRBR model, it is a relationship, which does not rigidly correspond to single classes of entities, but which can involve vice versa entities belonging to each of the classes proposed in the model. It was certainly not indispensable that FRBR remind cataloguers that the name of a person, the corporate body name or the title of a work can be inserted in a cataloguing record in order to realise different functions. However, FRBR goes further since, it suggests the possibility that even the terms which represent these entities for which only the subject function is indicated can be linked to a cataloguing record with a diverse function. If in fact "typically the user will formulate a search query using one or more attributes of the entity for which he or she is searching, and it is through the attribute that the user finds the entity sought", and if, for example, the second and most important attribute of the work, after the title, is the 'form', that is "the class to which the work belongs', how is it possible to allow an efficient search, using this attribute, of a work concretely expressed in a manifestation if not designating this attribute with a controlled term, which cannot but be the same used, in the context of other cataloguing records, for subject access? Putting it very simply, if Walter Scott's *Ivanhoe* is an historic novel, how is it possible to retrieve, by literary genre, the various manifestations of this novel if not directly or indirectly linking the relative cataloguing records to the term 'Historical novel', thus inserting into the search mechanisms of the editions of a work a term presumably also used in the subject indexes, but which in this case does not express the subject of the work? It is true that above all in our catalogues until now, we did not bother to activate retrieval requirements for 'genre' too much, but this has been only a convenient default, seeing as how Cutter already, over a century before the FRBR, had indicated the search by literary genre as one of the requisites of the catalogue. If we then move from the bibliographic context to other cataloguing contexts, the use of potentially expressive subject descriptors in order to indicate something else becomes quite prevalent. 'Etruscan Ceramics' for example, is a term for which the function of a subject is typical in a bibliography, but probably is to be excluded in the catalogue of a museum collection, in which 'Etruscan ceramics' will indicate what the indexed object is, not its theme. That of the 'form of the work' in FRBR is the most relevant, but not the only case of the potential use of an entity *concept, object, event or place* for the purpose of indicating not the subject, but another characteristic of the indexed and described document. Absolutely nothing in the form and the meaning of a term can predetermine the function that the term will play in the single cataloguing record and consequently in a particular index, above all if from the bibliographic context we widen the field to other cataloguing contexts. On the other hand however, to be efficient, unique and general, authority control must leave that function out of this consideration. This further confirms that there is no theoretical or practical justification for continuing to distinguish a subject authority control in the general activity of vocabulary control. It is not by chance that IFLA, having produced the two guidelines on authority records quoted, has nevertheless produced an inevitably unique guideline for the codification of authority records in a readable format for the machine, that is to say *Unimarc. Authorities* in which a specific field for all subject entries alone as such do not exist.

- Semantics is pertinent in authority control, in the three forms described by Elaine Svenonius: referential, relational, category. Referential semantics concerns the uniqueness of meaning of each of the elementary expressions included in the vocabulary: it is the task of authority control to guarantee this uniqueness, supplying each strictly indispensable and sufficient expression of all the formal elements to impede any misunderstanding in use and interpretation. The potential polysemy of an expression is a frequent phenomenon in natural languages, which has no effect on communication, since, normally pragmatic circumstances clarify the meaning for which the polysemic expression is effectively used. But a general authority control, although it is functional in most cataloguing contexts, cannot delegate the referential semantics to the clarifying properties of a single context, nor be conditioned by those properties, and must rather satisfy completely and alone the needs of unambiguousness of the expressions of the vocabulary in all the cataloguing contexts. In this regard, the case that immediately comes to mind is that of those proper names, often called 'geographic', which, in common use, can indicate both a territory and the population of that territory, as well as the corporate body that holds sovereignty over that territory. In some contexts these proper names do not result poysemic: in the context of the author cataloguing 'Italy' is not effectively polysemic, since, the meanings of the territory and of the population are not pertinent to the context; while, certainly but not alone in other contexts, of the subject indexing, those proper names are very polysemic, to the point of sometimes making syntactic relationships ambiguous and the compre-hensive meaning of the entries in which they are inserted doubtful, as well as often making the search and selection of the cataloguing information fastidiously heavy. To be efficient, general authority control must resolve the problems of real polysemy even when not common to all the cataloguing context, and must guarantee the unambiguousness of the expressions in any context in which they are used. The relational semantics concerns the relationship of meaning between all the expressions included in the vocabulary. Among these relationships one is unquestionably considered pertinent to any form of authority control, and that is the equivalence relationship: if in various cataloguing contexts two or more expressions can be used with the same meaning, that is if they indicate the same entity, these two or more expressions are correlated in the authority file, in such a way to guarantee the individualisation of that entity by means of any of these expressions. Traditionally the principle of uniformity was applied to the equivalence relationship, for which one of the expressions was designated as preferred, and became the only one effectively present in the cataloguing records. The informatics management of authority control can offer alternatives to this solution, which allow us to realise a unique and general authority control without imposing the use of the same expression in all contexts, but it must be kept in mind that uniformity has its value as an element of coherence and of predictability in catalogues, and that thus it is opportune to give it up only in the presence of real and fundamental cataloguing needs. The control of equivalence relationships, however, does not exhaust the needs of semantic correlation of any cataloguing language. Author and title bibliographic cataloguing imposes control of some cases of associative relationships in point and of hierarchical relationships. The opportunity of controlling this type of relationship can only increase with the application of the FRBR model. Extended to all categories of entities, the control of associative and hierarchical relationships represents a fundamental need for the subject indexing languages, but it is presumable that it is indispensable or useful for any other cataloguing language too, and certainly advantageous for the interconnection between different languages. It is thus appropriate carried out on the level of general authority control. Obviously on this level of control only hierarchical and associative relationships of universal validity may be expressed, that is those explainable by the typical and essential definition of the entity submitted to authority control, and which thus cannot be contradicted in any particular context. Any entity can then be involved in semantic relationships that are not universally valid, but inherent to the context of application of a determined language. Such relationships must not be expressed on the level of general authority control, but in specific and sectorial vocabulary and classification control instruments, for the elaboration of which the existence of a general semantic control instrument does not necessarily constitute an obstacle, rather a facilitation. Substantially a semantic relationship structure is a classification structure, and thus needs a primary general criteria of subdivision, upon which ulterior articulations can be based. General bibliographic classifications are based upon a primary articulation by subject, which implies the possibility that the same concept, if pertinent to more than one subject, belongs to several classes. This does not correspond to the needs of characteristic semantic structuring of authority control, since, as has been repeated several times in this paper, such a process must leave out of consideration the single context, even when disciplinary, in which the single entities are concretely quoted. With a view to authority control it is therefore necessary to adopt another general criterion of classification which is independent of single contexts, but is valid and useful in all of them and has a secure application. More than a century of studies and of practice in indexing has shown that the criterion of categorical analysis which consists, as regards semantics in the individuation of a limited number of general and universal semantic categories answers these requisites, so that each entity can belong to only one category and in the assigning of each entity, for the single attributes which constitute the typical definition, to one of the individuated categories. The individuation of semantic categories is necessary to avoid incongruities and contradictions in the identification and expression of semantic relationships, but it is also more generally necessary for the normalisation and the informatics management of authority control. It is certainly not a case that upon the citation of general semantic categories is based all of the mentioned *Guidelines for subject authority and reference entries,* nor is it a case that every field of *Unimarc. Authorities,* excluding those of the notes and equipment information, correspond to a semantic category. In the exercise of this general categorial semantics the authority control is however not alone. Even in the FRBR model, in order to control other types of cataloguing relationships, some general semantic categories have been individuated principally usable even in authority control. This shows a convergence of needs and solutions which induce one to hypothesise that the full actuation of the FRBR model make a unique and general authority control realisable, but that even a unique and general authority control is indispensable for the full actuation of the FRBR model.

- Authority control is applied to the single units of vocabulary regarding a priori their characteristics and relationships, those which are constantly valid and for which the single unit is admitted in the comprehensively understood linguistic system. That is, authority control concerns the paradigmatic, not the syntagmatic, side of linguistic communication, and does not thus a posteriori regard the relationships which depend upon connotations of objects to describe and index, and which exist between the unit of vocabulary only when and since, both are present together in a determined statement. Thus the syntax which is the representation of these relationships through the ordering in sequence of correlated units, and which is one of the most distinctive elements between diverse languages cannot be object of a real authority control, but can be object, when necessary, of only a correction verification and of substantial uniformity in the area of the application of a particular cataloguing language. Understanding the syntax of authority control involves a series of inconveniences, which do not appear to be compensated for by any particular advantage. It impedes the realisation of a unique and general vocabulary control which is a connecting factor between different cataloguing languages. This is because syntax is the element for which less compatibility is shown not only between typologically distinct languages, but also between kindred languages which could easily share the same vocabulary. The cases of subject indexing languages are seen as emblematic. The differences between various languages which express a theme in pre-coordinated form, and of those with post coordinated languages, are not so many differences in terminology, but are rather differences in the grade and form of expression of the syntactic relationships, which sometimes makes it impossible to establish the equivalencies not only between index entries expressed by languages which draw from different natural languages, as the MACS project has shown, but even between entries expressed by languages which draw from the same natural language. As an inevitably ulterior consequence, the authority control pretext of syntactic constructions adds a notable heaviness to the entire process to this contraction of its own area of efficiency, with a very useless increase. It does not determine a major expressiveness, since, it is virtually uncontainable of the whole of the forms submitted to control, which contradicts the first requisite of controlled vocabulary which is to be such even regarding its growth. The constant expansion of the vocabulary is a need of cataloguing languages, but it has the condition that the gathering of new forms is always motivated by the need to express new unitary concepts as a general limit, not new concept correlations which can easily be expressed through the combination of pre-existing forms. To create a new authority record for the string Hospitals—Administration—Data processing—Evaluation—Computer programmes, when authority records already exist for each of the single terms that compose it, it is not in any way useful to the expressiveness of the language, but obliges us, at least in theory, to the fulfillment for this entry of all the procedures of control and of semantic correlation. Being in this case particularly articulated and heavy, such procedures were not in the least way effected, which confirms the complete uselessness of this authority record, the creation and measurement of which has nevertheless absorbed resources. And here is one of the motives, certainly the most concrete and practical, for which the authority control of syntactically constructed entries must be avoided. The creation of authority records for this type of entry determines a waste of resources, which are subtracted from the more qualifying aspects of authority control, making the realisation more difficult, if not impossible. Moreover, the problem is noticed even in the Library of Congress and the Bibliothèque Nationale de France since, both institutions, in order to avoid the collapse of their vocabulary control systems, are activating a review of the procedures aimed at limiting the application of authority control to only elementary expressions, at least to the extent that they are compatible with the use of indexing languages which remain substantially enumerative. Inverting the preceding procedure at the Library of Congress a new one has been established to avoid the creation of new phrase headings and the progressive transformation of many pre-existing phrase headings in entries with subdivisions is in course. At the same time the list of free-floating subdivisions has been notably amplified, with the attribution of the qualification of free-floating to many subdivisions which were not previously free-floating, which has offered the eventuality that for a new entry constructed combining pre-existing expressions it will be quite rare that a new authority record will be produced. Analogous interventions are also taking place in RAMEAU, although it is a more recent language conception and thus less enumerative that LCSH. When improperly extended to expressions constructed for syntax authority control results quite weakened and inefficient in its semantic component, which loses the necessary rigour both in individualisation of relationships and in categorial analysis. To give a simple example, what is the entry immediately above, the BT of Hospitals—Administration? Hospitals? Administration? Health facilities—Administration? Health facilities—Organisation? Hospitals—Organisation? And what is the category to which the entry belongs? Is it the category of Hospitals given in the entry in the first position or that of Administration, which is the focus of the corresponding syntax? But above all, can such uncertain semantics ever satisfy the general needs of authority control? Or again, to ask a final question, does it make sense to corrupt to such a point authority control only to extend partially and occasionally syntax to an aspect of cataloguing languages, which is not pertinent to it?

In the articulation of preceding considerations, the sense of the relation between authority control and subject indexing languages is given, but almost hidden behind the closer examination of the single problems. It is well to reassume them here. The existence of subject indexing languages certainly does not call for or imply the existence of a particular authority control exclusively dedicated to subjects. Authority control, being an interconnecting element between different cataloguing languages, must concern all the categories of entities, and in such a way satisfy even the lexical needs of subject indexing languages.

The use of subject indexing languages, as for other cataloguing languages, contributes to the individuation of new expressions to be submitted to authority control, expressions whose ordinary use can not predetermine their possible successive uses, and that thus, once completed the control procedures, can be used in any cataloguing context, either for indicating a subject or for indicating something else. Cataloguing languages, which include among others subject indexing languages, necessitate a verification of the expressions used which are not merely formal, but in addition more completely semantic. Such a verification, since, it sticks to meanings and relationships of universal validity, is appropriate that it be effected at the level of general authority control.

On the other hand, it is not opportune to extend authority control to syntactic constructions, because this reduces the rigour and efficiency of the control process, weighing it down until it becomes unfeasible, and impeding its function of unifying element between diverse cataloguing languages. Each cataloguing language, and thus each subject indexing language, possesses its own syntax and the verification of the correctness of its syntax can only be effected in the circumscribed context of the application of each language. This conception of relationship between authority control and subject indexing languages is born from the meeting, already fertile, but which can become even more so, between technological progress and theoretic reflection.

Informatics has made telematic interconnection between different documentary contexts, virtually simultaneous access to several contexts and deriving of data from one context to another not only possible but technologically easy. However a common logical linguistic instrument is lacking, and this is evident to everyone, but it is not the duty of informatics to furnish it. As concerns subject indexing languages the theoretic reflection has already individuated the principles which are functional in the elaboration of that instrument. Principles which in Italy have already been adapted, diffused and often clearly defined by the Gruppo di ricerca sull'indicizzazione per soggetto, and which can now find application in the project for renewing the *Soggettario*, promoted by the Biblioteca Nazionale Centrale di Firenze.

Among the most important are: the principle of the subject as relationship property, a factor of coherence and pertinence in a text and no longer as a pre-existing entity supplied with a name; the principle of the separation between semantics and syntax, with the control of the first which can leave the proper formal structures out of consideration of the single languages, and thus be potentially unique and general, and the control of the second which is rather the actuation of those structures; the principle of the definable relationship, for which the semantic correlation of the vocabulary unity is exclusively founded on the essential definition of each unity which is universally valid. Authority control being unique and general, and thus adequate for the situation created by technological progress, must make use of the most advanced theoretic reflection on subject indexing languages, and at the same time must satisfy the needs of subject indexing languages much more than it has until now.

EVALUATION OF INDEXING LANGUAGE USED IN COLLECTIVE CATALOGUES OF UNIVERSITY LIBRARIES

It is a fact that the interactivity between thematic representation, indexing language and information retrieval is conducive to continuous evaluations of language performance during search strategies, guiding their refinement and use in the indexing of documents. The studies of Henzler, Betts and Marrable, Fidel and Gil Urdiciain demonstrated this relevance when they evaluated the performance of indexing language and of natural language in automated systems such as online catalogues and specialised databases.

The results obtained revealed that the combination in the use of terms of indexing language and natural language proves to be ideal when devising strategies, affording quality in the retrieval by subject carried out and expected by the user. In addition, Gil Urdiciain observes an increase in relevance in information retrieval with the use of indexing language, inserted in a context of high subject specialisation, placing the precision of database systems before recall.

The indexing languages, characterised as knowledge organisation systems that correspond to the lists of subject headings and thesauruses, are controlled languages built from the principles and meanings stemming from terms that are part of specialised language and natural language, representing the set of terms to recover the indexing information. They should be structured in a multidimensional plan, crossing cultural and geographical boundaries of access and representation, without disregarding the main functions which include eliminating ambiguity, controlling synonyms and establishing semantic relationships.

The primary function of indexing languages is to represent the content of documents in an information retrieval system, according to content, and its second function is to mediate information retrieval by representing the users questions, according to use, hence, playing a key role in the indexing and information retrieval processes and enabling the representation of documented contents, thus facilitating user-search by topic whenever information needs to be accessed quickly and accurately. The considerations of Zeng and Boccato lay out the need for constantly updating the indexing languages used by online catalogues of university libraries, in line with the innate characteristic of scientific progress and the plethora of dynamic and progressive knowledge generated by universities.

The views and comments of librarians and users are collaborative to consolidate these processes, in light of the fact that they should be seen as individuals who interact, understand and interpret their environment and at the same time, share their knowledge with a community of interpreters. On this matter, Hjørland reports that the socio-cognitive views are interested in individual cognition, however, approaching it from a social context. Accordingly, the process of individual knowledge is associated with the historical, social and cultural context of units and information systems responsible for organising and retrieving information. Thus, the objective of this study is to evaluate the use of alphabetical indexing language of online collective catalogues, focusing on technologies of representation and information retrieval from the standpoint of university libraries and within the socio-cognitive context of librarians and users.

THE ALPHABETICAL INDEXING LANGUAGES OF UNIVERSITY LIBRARIES' ONLINE CATALOGUES

Indexing languages are support tools for indexing and information retrieval, which are a fundamental component of automated information systems for organising and disseminating information in specialised scientific areas that require a greater control of terminology. Fernández Molina and Moya Anegón consider online catalogues as automated retrieval systems of information that are more generally available and which are the first to be used by any user when there is a need for information.

In the First Meeting of Experts on an International Cataloguing Code, held in 2003, also known as 'Principles of Frankfurt', the functions of the catalogue were organised, corresponding to the environment of online catalogues, hence, the Paris principles were expanded to the field of bibliographic description by subject and to the conceptual models established by IFLA—International Federation of Library Associations. The evolution of representation and information retrieval, made possible by technological advances, can also be evidenced by the agility of the description activity, through cooperative cataloging that enables importing standard records in other retrieval information systems from various libraries, in accordance with international standards, aiming to interchange them, hence, contributing to the formation of online Bibliographic Database. This process offers advantages in terms of time, as the cataloging of a specific work will be much faster and easier, resulting in a lower cost.

Cooperative cataloging must be carried out carefully and specifically, regarding the thematic processing of the information and considering the guiding principles to conduct quality indexing. This is a result of developing the indexation during cataloguing, according to a defined indexing policy adopted by the system and with the proper use of alphabetical indexing languages as knowledge organisation systems. It can be concluded that the proper use of indexing language is necessary to ensure the implementation of quality indexing and information retrieval processes used by indexers and by users.

The shifts in paradigms within the scope of indexing as a representation process of information for constructing online catalogues, from the proposed use of *FRBRs,* are collaborative in these processes. The construction of online catalogues focused on users and on social context that involves the processing of information must be performed by multidisciplinary and integrated teams: Librarians, users, authors, catalogue designers, systems analysts, among others, valorised by the presence of librarians as promoters in the design of access points, exemplified also by the analytical access of subjects, authors and titles and other resources applicable to the representation and information retrieval. From this perspective, it is important to use relevant indexing language that portrays not only the profile of the catalogue, but also its user communities and, therefore, the evaluation studies of indexing languages to assist in choosing the more suitable knowledge organisation system to meet such purposes.

EVALUATION STUDIES OF INDEXING LANGUAGES IN INFORMATION RETRIEVAL SYSTEMS—METHODOLOGICAL APPROACHES

When discussing the research work and evaluation methods of indexing languages in information retrieval systems, we verify a correlation between these themes and the epistemology of science information that includes independent outlooks to consolidate this scientific field. Several aspects influenced the development of this area, defining different epistemological paradigms, yet interrelated and complementary. They are characterised by the existence of physical views, cognitive views and socio-cognitive views in the process of information retrieval.

The physical paradigm values the information retrieval system and the message transmitting process, and inserted in this context, we consider the online collective catalogue as 'physical' and the bibliographic record as the transmitter, which transmits the information to the user that receives the message. This information will be encoded to be transmitted as a message by the indexing language, which is then decoded by the user, sharing the same code of the bibliographic record. The communication design enables the feedback of the process, which may cause noise or silence in the recovery process of the information recorded on index supports. In contrast, the evaluation studies with a quantitative approach, from the 1970s, illustrate a shift from the physical view to the cognitive view, signaling the development of evaluation studies focussed on the user.

In the cognitive paradigm, the user is placed in an active position to elaborate ideas, concepts, etc. within an individual context. This scenario is viewed through the human dimension outlook, that is, the perspective focussed on the user, because the information retrieval systems should be modelled according to the user, in the framework of their information needs and their behaviour patterns in the search and use of information. However, since, the 1990s, the cognitive approaches have been analysed and criticised by many researchers which, in addition to divulging the cognitive processes of individuals to carry out indexing processes and designing building systems for information retrieval, aggregate 'context' as an important element, emphasising a social-cognitive view, hence, rendering this process effective.

Our view, supported by Capurro, leads us to presume that the construction of a retrieval information system holds users and their information needs as its focal point. The users, in turn, playing an active role in the socio-cultural context, enable the storage and perform the recovery and interpretation of the available bibliographic records. Consequently, the individual is seen as a part of a society and thus, the studies developed from the socio-cognitive approach regard the phenomena as embedded in a social context.

In the research development of information science, especially in the evaluation of indexing language thematic, we see that the theories about the quantitative and qualitative methods are part of this important scientific-theoretical scenario depicted by the physical and cognitive paradigms. This demonstrates the applicability of these approaches in the evaluation studies focussed on the system and on the user and not considering evaluation studies of indexing languages by the socio-cognitive approach based on epistemological ideas resulting from the social paradigm.

The quantitative methodology, representative of the physical paradigm, enables gathering information from a larger number of respondents, statistical analyses and, usually, the comparison and generalisation of results. From this perspective, we emphasise the classical indexing language evaluation studies; the Cranfield I and Cranfield II Projects, which were developed in 1957 and 1963, respectively,; the Lancaster study, which established the parameters and quantitative indices of precision and recall, which are applicable to assessing information retrieval systems exemplified by the MEDLARS system and the Aberystwyth Test.

These were developed in 1970 inscribing the issue of specificity as a substantially important matter in the development of alphabetical indexing languages, in addition to the research of Torres and of Oliveira, the object of whose empirical study was the Subject Headings List of the BIBLIODATA network, the particular interest of our study. The qualitative methodology works with a plethora of interpretations, meanings, beliefs, values and attitudes, establishing close relationships with the theoretical and conceptual foundations arising from the cognitive paradigm in the Information Science area, showing the change from physical view to the cognitive view, and characterising the elaboration of evaluation studies guided by the user.

Qualitative evaluation studies on indexing languages developed by Owens and Cochrane and Toews are examples of this methodology scenario, depicting the importance of using international guidelines and standards in the construction of knowledge organisation systems that are compatible with the users search needs. Qualitative methodology provides direct involvement with individuals, places and interactive processes; starting a descriptive collection guided the accuracy that must exist during the analysis of data interpretation.

It should be noted that in the context of qualitative methodology, the cognitive approach is present in the area of information science when conducting searches on thematic processing and information retrieval, showing the actions undertaken by librarians and users during the development of these processes. Thus, studies using the qualitative-cognitive methodology show the subjectivity of the librarians and users mental activity during their professional activity. This is seen from actions that intend to reveal the implicit aspects in the knowledge structures of these professionals and users.

The studies of Dervin on the sense-making approach, initially applied to the communication sciences area, contributed to developing cognitive approaches. The data collection technique called Focus group was also used in qualitative-cognitive research work, initially in the marketing area and then in social sciences, ergonomics, health sciences, information science, and others. In the field of information science, the research work of Connaway applied the focus group technique to analyse the performance of the online catalogue of the University of Wisconsin-Madison, with emphasis on the evaluation of indexing language adopted by the system from the users perspective.

The introspective technique of the Verbal Protocol or 'Think Aloud' is applied to qualitative evaluation studies where the individuals express, aloud, what they think and what goes on in their minds while performing a task. These statements are recorded, and the individuals behaviour, such as facial expressions are also recorded. Thus, the language of thought performs many cognitive processes such as perception and reasoning. In Brazil, the pioneer research work using the technique, developed by Fujita and Fujita, in observing indexed reading, shows excellent results in the use of the verbal protocol, illustrating new aspects of indexed reading, among other contributions.

By using the verbal protocol technique, users can 'think aloud' by producing opinions and comments about the object being evaluated, hence, carrying out a cooperative and participatory evaluation: The users participate by identifying and understanding problems of information retrieval and by using the system in their own work environment. Thus, Boccato and Fujita developed a research work to evaluate, from the users perspective, indexing language DeCS-Descriptors in

Health Sciences, used for information retrieval in the LILACS system produced by BIREME, in order to obtain indicators to outline language improvement strategies in the area of speech and language therapy. The study led to the consideration of the statements issued by the four participants and the results of the analysis revealed that the DeCS language in speech therapy demonstrated the search had unsatisfactory results on information retrieval.

In summary, regarding research development in the information science area, especially the thematic evaluation of indexing languages, we saw that the quantitative and qualitative methods are part of this important scientific-theoretical scenario portrayed by the physical and cognitive paradigms. This demonstrated the applicability of these approaches in evaluation studies focussed on the system and the user, not considering evaluation studies of indexing languages by the socio-cognitive approach based on the epistemological ideas resulting from the social paradigm that regards users inserted into their social environment.

THE SOCIO-COGNITIVE CONTEXT OF INDEXERS AND USERS IN UNIVERSITY LIBRARIES

The socio-cognitive context concerns representation and information retrieval from the perspective of individuals in their socio-cultural-historical context, on the assumption that the users information needs are constructed from outside to inside, that is, the users environment influence and contribute to constructing this need, which will be represented by their mental models associated with their conception of the world, reflected on their real information interest. Boccato and Fujita The context performs the mediation between the real situation in the library, guided by the analysis concepts used by the indexers, and the linguistic system, the indexed language adopted by the system, characterised by the representation of the indexed documents.

The socio-cognitive context of indexers refers to " a prior knowledge that such professionals have their working tools and the real needs of users". The activity of indexing leads to the indexer adopting a conception of the matter which should be intimately related to their established institutional objectives and to the information retrieval system itself, detailed in the indexing policy. These conceptions of subject analysis, which we believe affect the performance of the indexer, are classified according to Albrechtsen in simplist conception, content-oriented conception and requirements-oriented conception. The users previous knowledge is characterised by the university, by the research groups and by the online collective catalogue, elements that guide and influence the expression of their need for information, concomitant with the cognitive processes to meet this need.

Thus, the socio-cognitive context is a factor to be considered in the indexing process development, from indexing reading, aimed at the analysis and representation of information consistent with the users search needs. Associated with the socio-cognitive aspect, the physical aspects, to which the institution and/or the information system are linked through the mission, objectives, the strategic plans and philosophy, and the psychological aspects are fundamental to form the indexers context, as very significant variables in the construction of this process.

The indexing language seen as the indexers expertise and prior knowledge, should enable highly accurate content matching of the documents and the users information needs expressed by their repertoire, resulting from prior knowledge constituted by the university, the research groups, the curriculum classification of scientific and academic disciplines and by the information retrieval system itself. In this case, the holistic and collective views of indexers and users are favoured, as they contribute to the definition of a thematic processing of information and to the modelling and construction of information retrieval systems.

Based on this concept, the information science area turns to a theoretical dimension brought into focus by interpretive approaches, focused on the semantic factors and the information social context of indexers and users. In this sense, our research work is contextualised between the shift of cognitive paradigm to the social paradigm, which puts the context of indexers and users in the center of the informational processes, characterised by the representation and information retrieval and knowledge. Therefore, this research focuses on the socio-cognitive context of indexers and users, based on the theoretical perspectives of Hjørland, which approves a 'methodological collectivistic approach' for the proposal of conducting an assessment study on the use of indexing language in online catalogues of specialised scientific areas of university libraries, focusing on technologies of representation and information retrieval, using the verbal protocol as a data collection technique.

The verbal protocol technique, viewed by the socio-cognitive approach, focuses on the individual when performing a particular activity and its cognition related to its production context. With regards to the indexers, the interest is the thematic processing of information, specifically the indexing and the use it will make of indexing language when representing the information. From the users perspective, the focus is on information retrieval by subject, by using language to search for information and interacting with their environment.

MATERIALS AND METHODS

The data collections were performed on a sample of nine libraries of the UNESP in the three knowledge areas, exact sciences, humanities and biological sciences, of the civil engineering, education, and dentistry courses. The empirical study objective was the Subject Headings List of the Bibliodata Network used in the processes of indexing and information retrieval in the online collective catalogue ATHENA is demons-trated in table.

The methodology consisted of a three-part diagnostic study:

- Operation and procedures in the processing of indexed information in the UNESP Libraries Network based on the perspective of the General Coordinator of Libraries;

- Operation and procedures in the processing of information in the UNESP Network of Libraries from the cataloguers outlook;
- The users evaluation on access and retrieval of online information.

Table 2.1. Selection of UNESP University Libraries and their Tespective Identifications

Course	Area	Libraries/Brazilian City	Identification
Civil engineering	Exact sciences	Bauru	E1
		Guaratinguetá	E2
		Ilha Solteira	E3
Education	Humanities	Presidente Prudente	H1
		Rio Claro	H2
		São José do Rio Preto	H3
Dentistry	Biological sciences	Araçatuba	B1
		Araraquara	B2
		São José dos Campos	B3

To perform the first part, organisational diagnostic questionnaires were administered to the directors of university libraries. The preparation of the questionnaire was essential for the organisational diagnosis, consisting of a total of twenty-six open, closed and mixed questions.

In the second part, for the operation and procedures for the processing of information in the UNESP Network of Libraries from the cataloguers outlook, we used the cognitive approach with the verbal protocol introspection technique, as follows:

- *Group Verbal Protocol* (GVP) with the heads of libraries, cataloguers, reference librarians, faculty staff users, head researchers and research group staff, and student body users for accessing the participants knowledge on the processing of indexing content of university libraries as a source of qualified data collection in the diagnosis.
- Individual Verbal Protocol was conducted with by Cataloguers to identify the procedures of subject

analysis and representation in cataloguing books, as well as to identify the difficulties and restrictions.

In the third part, regarding the evaluation of user access and retrieval of online information, Individual Verbal Protocols were performed with undergraduate freshmen and senior Users, of the aforementioned courses. In the introspective technique of verbal protocol " the individuals, talk aloud, and express what occurs in their minds during the execution of a task". These statements are recorded and transcribed verbatim to be analysed later through the establishment of categories. In the context of this study, the verbal protocol, seen from the socio-cognitive approach, focuses on the individual at the moment of undertaking a specific activity and his cognition in relation to his context of production.

In addition to this, it should be pointed out that the participation of the cataloguer is evidenced in the development of the indexing in the cataloguing via the use he makes of indexing language during this activity. With respect to the user, the focus is centred on the search and retrieval by subject, by means of the use of language in the satisfaction of his research needs integrated with his environment consisting of the university, research group, syllabus and catalogue.

Individual verbal protocol consists of the recording of the 'think aloud' of a single individual during the undertaking of a task, and group verbal protocol itemises the discussion of a copy-text on the subject that involves the task to be observed and, consequently, collected from the utterances of the individuals and from their cognitions of the theme being dealt with and evaluated. The different modalities of verbal protocols follow similar procedures in their application:

Procedures that Anticipated Application of Verbal Protocol

Definition of the universe of the research:

- *GVP and IVP*: University libraries of the UNESP Library Network Brazil.

Selection of copy-text:

- *GVP*: Passage between pages 205 and 208 of the following article: Dias, EW, Naves, MML, Moura, MA. The information-seeking behaviour of researchers and subject analysis.
- *IVP-C*: The bibliographical record itself to be catalogued for inclusion in the ATHENA catalogue of the UNESP Library Network.
- *IVP-U*: The bibliographical record itself retrieved from the ATHENA catalogue of the UNESP Library Network.

Definition of the task:

- *GVP*: Discussion of the copy-text previously referenced.
- *IVP-C*: Undertaking of the by cataloguers of the indexing for the cataloguing of books on dentistry, civil engineering and education, highlighting the use of the LCARB in the process of the representation of information.
- *IVP-U*: Undertaking by the users of information retrieval on topics determined by them in dentistry, civil engineering and education, in the collective Athena catalogue, by subject field, using the LCARB indexing language.

Selection of the individuals:

- *GVP*: Three librarians, one teacher and one student.
- *IVP-C*: Population of by cataloguers from the three knowledge areas, biological, exact and human sciences, respectively, dentistry, civil engineering and education, amounting to nine individuals from UNESP libraries.
- *IVP-U*: Population of undergraduate users from the first and last year of the dentistry, civil engineering and education courses in nine libraries of UNESP, totaling eighteen participants.

Informal Conversation with the Individuals

In this conversation, the researchers contacted the individuals through the General Coordination of Libraries explaining the objectives of the research, the methodology used and agreeing a date for the collection of data. The anonymity of all the participants was protected.

Procedures Adopted During the Application of Verbal Protocol

- *GVP*: After the reading of the copy-text, a discussion was initiated, in which the researcher made the necessary interventions so as to prompt the participants. The entire discussion was recorded and transcribed verbatim.
- *IVP-C*: Every expression of thought uttered by the cataloguer during the execution of indexing in the cataloguing task and recorded with the aid of an MP3 device.
- *IVP-U*: Every expression of thought uttered by the user during the development of indexing in the bibliographic search and recorded with the aid of an MP3 device.

Procedures Following the Application of the Verbal Protocol

Transcription of the recordings:

- *GVP*: After the recording of the discussion of the text by the individuals, a literal transcription was made with the identification of the sources of the individual statements. This identification was made in the following way: Head of Library, reference librarian, cataloguer, Faculty Staff Users/teachers, Student Body Users.
- *IVP-C*: After the recording of the 'think aloud' during the indexing in the cataloguing, a literal transcription was made of the recordings of the individuals statements.
- *IVP-U*: After the recording of the 'think aloud' during the information retrieval, a literal transcri-ption was made of the recordings of the individuals statements.

Analysis of the Transcriptions

- With the transcriptions ready, a detailed reading of the data was undertaken in search of significant and recurring phenomena for the construction of the categories. Following the construction of the categories, we returned again to the data to extract passages from the transcription that exemplified each category. Thus, the procedures adopted for the organisation diagnosis applications in university libraries, and the individual and group verbal protocols were conducted in order to characterise the organisational/academic context in the UNESP Library Network and to observe the views of cataloguers and users to analyse the actions and opinions of the participating individuals regarding indexing during cataloguing and information retrieval. Thirty-six data collections were held for nine groups of verbal protocols, nine individual verbal protocols with cataloguers and eighteen individual verbal protocols with student body users. The total number of individuals participating in this research was seventy-two persons, with forty five in the group of verbal protocol; nine cataloguers and eighteen students. The collections began in May 2006 and concluded in September 2007; they were conducted in the individuals work or study environments, namely the premises of the nine UNESP Library Networks that were previously scheduled to participate in our study. In addition, we should highlight the difficulty of bringing all the participants together in the same place on the same day and at the same time, since, the execution of the data collection was possible only when all of them were in the same field of observation. The transcripts of the data collection generated a substantial amount of data. Considering the socio-cognitive approach to the interaction of the organisational environment and the different perspectives arising from the different participants involved in the data collection indicated the complexity in analysing these transcripts, thus, the reading in full of the verbal protocols were performed, since, the language used by the individuals is not always the same used in the literature. For the collected data analysis procedures and to meet our study proposals, twelve categories were elaborated based on the theoretical frameworks, the research objectives and the statements made by the participants who contributed to exemplifying each phenomenon; each category was systematised into three themes:

– Indexing language by content: indexing procedures:
  a. Procedures for indexing representation;
  b. Language selection;
  c. Choosing terms;
  d. Performance of language in the indexing representation process;
  e. Indexing language by usage: knowledge/ importance of language;
  f. search strategy;
  g. performance of language in the information retrieval process;
  h. system precision and recall ability;
  i. evaluation of the information retrieval system;
  j. Indexing language by form: procedures for construction, upgrading and maintenance of language;
  k. the role of the librarian in the construction, upgrading and maintenance of language.

RESULTS AND DISCUSSION

The results presented aim to demonstrate the vision of the context in which the by cataloguers and the users are inserted and, consequently, of the use that is made of indexing language in the indexing in the cataloguing and in the information retrieval. To this effect, we analysed the organisational diagnostics questionnaires completed by the heads of libraries and the individual and group verbal protocols.

The analysis of the organisational diagnostics questionnaires revealed a picture of administratively consolidated university libraries, promoting a participative management, many involving the users in the process of the planning of products and services. With regard to the activity of indexing in cataloguing, it was confirmed that the libraries are aware that the LCARB is an instrument of terminological control adopted for the representation and information retrieval in the ATHENA catalogue. In addition, when asked whether the referred indexing language meets the needs of representation, the replies varied between 'does not meet' or 'partially meets'.

In the information retrieval process, almost all the libraries concurred in responding that the language does not meet the needs of users searches by subject, although all of them provide formal and informal training of users which includes the use of the ATHENA catalogue in the information retrieval process by subject field. The qualitative analyses of the data collected with the application of the verbal protocol technique, in the individual and group modalities, were undertaken on the basis of the selection of the statements uttered by the individuals in this study in the choice of twelve categories, systematised in three thematic axes regarding the use of the Subject Headings List of the BIBLIODATA Network.

The indexing language has been widely discussed by cataloguers and users, teachers and students, in group and individual verbal protocols in the three knowledge areas and has given rise to many questions and concerns about the performance and importance of this mediation and communication instrument between indexing and information retrieval in online collective catalogues of the specialised scientific areas of university libraries.

The socio-cognitive context of UNESP Library Network cataloguers, comprised by the university, library, UNESP quality standard for bibliographic records, Subject Headings

List of the BIBLIODATA Network, parallel indexing languages, ATHENA catalogue and the teachers and undergraduate students of specialised scientific areas influenced the indexing, which provided us important results on the use of LCARB for the information representation in the online collective catalogue ATHENA.

Such results arrived from the declarations uttered by the participating individuals in the Group (PVG) and Individual (PVI) Verbal Protocols may also be verified, in their entirety, identified in the following way: Heads of Libraries (HL), by Cataloguer participant in the group verbal protocol (C), by Cataloguer participant in the Individual verbal protocol (C-I), Reference Librarians (RL), Faculty Staff Users/teachers (FS-U) and Student Body Users (SB-U) and accompanied also by the identification of the respective libraries.

In a synthetic analysis, the use of LCARB proved to be a 'required' instrument in the UNESP Network, which was used for confirmation and validation of subject headings to be described in field 650. This important finding is associated with some aspects, also explicit by the obtained results.

As a first aspect, due to the fact that LCARB does not have a specialised and updated vocabulary and as it does not provide a consistent syntactic and semantic structure, it was observed that the use of parallel knowledge organisation systems was a frequent practice in the search for specificity that is required by the thematic processing of information in scientific areas, through the description in field 690, reflecting the plethora of knowledge in which the university library is inserted.

NATURAL-LANGUAGE PROCESSING AND AUTOMATIC INDEXING

Indexed books represent the most common example of a subject information retrieval system. Problems associ ated with both the quality and cost of human intellectual indexing have made automatic indexing an attractive goal. During the 1950s and early 1960s there was great optimism that this goal would be readily achieved. However, many of the ideas proposed for text analysis, indexing, and machine translation have proved to be simplistic; the complexity and richness of natural langu age defeated these workers. The indexing problem can be stated quite simply. It requires a content analysis of documents followed by characterisation of such content by descriptive labels.

This requires the following steps:

- Conceptual analysis of the significant content of a document.
- Expressing the analysis by a set of words or phrases to represent the subject.
- Translating the relevant subject descriptions into standard language.
- Arranging the standardised subject descriptions according to the syntax of the indexing language used in the information system.

The ease with which the problem can be expressed does not imply ease of solution. For example, a human indexer reads a section of text and can determine its subject content without conscious thought—reading the text normally involves understanding, which implies that content analysis has been accomplished. This can best be seen when the smooth flow of this process is interrupted, as may happen when the subject matter of text is both complex and unfamiliar. The indexer then has repeatedly to re read and examine text until understanding is acquired.

Then subject analysis is the relatively easy matter of selecting the most appropriate indexing phrase. For this solution to be a model for a computational approach to indexing, however, it must be expressed in algorithmic form: a major problem. To investigate how it has been tackled, a brief look at some applications of statistical indexing techniques will be followed by a more extensive survey of Natural Language Processing (NLP). No attempt will be made to survey the areas involved in expert systems and of knowledge representation; Walker's Knowledge Systems and Prolog provides a useful introduction to these areas.

DATABASE INDEXING

At present the literature dealing with indexing topics and concepts is mainly concerned with retrieving infor mation from texts stored in databases, whose function is usually to inform the user of some easily quantifiable fact and also to point the user to some relevant document. The pointing function may be either an abstract, or keywords removed from either the orig inal text or the abstract itself. In neither case is the text manipulated by the system similar to a book.

Dealing with such texts is essentially easier than dealing with a book, for the following reasons: the texts normally involve only several sentences as opposed to tens or hundreds of thousands of words; they are usually in the form of abstracted data; and large num bers of significantly different texts are present in the database, and measures of dissimilarity and similarity between texts are thus normally easier to quantify than for a book. Comparisons between manual and automatic indexing systems show further data on the difficulties of indexing books.

Cleverdon noted that:

- 'If two people or groups of people construct thesauri in a given subject area, only 60 per cent of the index terms may be common to both;
- If two experienced indcxers index a given docu ment using a given thesaurus, only 30 per cent of the index terms may be common to the two sets;
- If two intermediaries search the same question on the same database on the same host, only 40 per cent of the output may be common to both searches;
- If two scientists or engineers are asked to judge the relevance of a given set of documents to a given question, the area of agreement may not exceed 60 per cent.'

Although these are generalisations, and there are likely to be areas where the performance will exceed these figures, in others it will be considerably worse. Cleverdon suggested that many of these problems could be solved by eliminating the thesaurus and using instead the title or abstract of the article in free-text form; an approach which has had some success, and results from the work of Salton seem to show that performance exceeding that of manual indexing can regularly be achieved for many users, though Blair and Marron come to very different conclusions with the same data, claiming that fewer than 20 per cent of relevant documents are being retrieved.

ARTIFICIAL INTELLIGENCE (AT) APPROACHES TO INDEXING

Much of this work has been shown to be adequate for abstracts, particularly scientific or technical. Indeed, all current automated text-indexing systems are based largely on such statistical work, and hardly show even moderate sophistication in attempting any form of con tent analysis.

These techniques are less useful when applied to longer texts where keywords may form poor identifiers for the subject matter" and recourse still has to be made to the intellectual indexing process to identify correctly the 'aboutness' of a particular section of text, though even this may prove inadequate for research purposes. For example, when it is necessary to determine whether a particular idea has been put forward by a given researcher it is often found that indexes, to books or to databases, form poor tools for solving this problem."

CONTENT ANALYSIS

Despite the incursions of a variety of non-textual forms requiring indexing, the bulk of the material that indexers are likely to deal with is the precursor of books—galleys and paste-ups. To mimic human intellectual analysis of these texts it is necessary to determine their content by attempting con tent analysis that implies comprehension by the pro gram. It may seem curious that so little progress appears to have been made in content analysis of texts, when human indexers do such analysis with no apparent effort—syntax analysis; semantic analysis; and discourse analysis.

SYNTAX ANALYSIS

If the overall objective is to determine the intellectual content of tne text, then a sub-problem presents itself when we have to determine the meaning of a sentence. In most systems this means that sentence structure must be determined and possibly regularised in order to simplify the subsequent semantic analysis, which can now be designed to work with less rich forms of words—and therefore those that are more amenable to computational processing.

Syntax analysis performs two main functions in analysing natural language input:

- *Determining the Structure of the Input*: Syntax analysis should identify the subject and objects of each verb and determine what each modifying word or phrase modifies. This is most often done by assigning a tree structure to the input, in a process referred to as parsing;
- *Regularising the Syntactic Structure*:4 Subsequent processing can be simplified if we map the large number of possible input structures into a whatsoever, despite the amusing/apocryphal stories of the results of com puterised content analysis—for example, 'the editors of the new Macmillan Guide to Britain's Nature Reserves do realise the mammoth is extinct, even though it appears in the book's index. An over-zealous computer, working though the text, seised upon a sentence beginning: 'This guide is a mammoth work..."

This apparent lack of progress implies lack neither of effort nor of desire to attend to needs expressed by those involved in the literary field. Many of the problems are well known, if not well understood, for it is the challenge of natural-language processing that a text in its entirety may be less ambiguous than its individual parts. So a natural-language processor must resolve this ambiguity by applying context to select from the various possibili ties available, which are governed by the lexicon and grammar. This is hard because the text may contain the information required to resolve ambiguities, or it may be implicit in the shared background of the author and the reader.

To see more clearly the problems that arise when we look for meaning in text, three stages of text analysis will be examined. These are smaller number of structures. Some material in sentences can be, and usually is, omitted without changing the meaning: *e.g.,* 'She earns less than Mary1. By restoring the omitted text, the sentence structure can be regularised. Other transformations can relate sentences with normal word order to passive and cleft constructions: these will allow subsequent processing to concern itself with a much smaller number of structures. Thus, although there is no absolute need for regularisation, its absence will require usage of more complex semantic rules.

To determine whether regularisation, or even syn tactic analysis prior to semantic analysis, is required, computational linguists have looked at the work of psychologists interested in the way people deal with unusual or abnormal sentences, because such sentences may produce errors giving some understanding of how people deal with sentences in real life. It may be argued that people can use syntactically correct material which lacks any meaning; for example: 'Twas brillig, and the slithy toves'. Here syntax is the only factor giving an appearance of intelligibility. This shows that sentence parsing by humans can take place on the syntactic level with no need for semantics.

Sentences which are ungrammatical, but clear in their intended meaning, for instance 'She like go holiday.', show that semantics may drive an adequate interpretation of a sentence when syntax is poor. Thus we have two strategies used to give meaning to sentences: a syntactic-driven strategy which may be used when semantics are weak or non-existent; and a semantic-driven strategy when syntax is weak. Both methods may be used to extract meaning from a sentence if sections are not clear on the first reading.

In other attempts to explore ways of dealing with sentences in real life, psychologists have been interested in sentences where the reader is 'led up the garden path' in assuming that the sentence means one thing, then when the last word or two is read, sees that his assump tions were erroneous.

An example of this is: 'The horse raced past the barn fell.', where the reader thinks the horse was racing past the barn—until the last word is met, then backtracking occurs in an attempt to re analyse the meaning of the sentence, which is interpreted in the sense, 'The horse raced past the barn fell.' Marcus attempts computer-simulation of the human approach to this problem, and hopes to obtain insights into strategies used for sentence parsing. This should give not only an understanding of how people interpret the written word, but also possible strategies to be adopted by a computer/parsing program.

PARSERS

Historically, parsing algorithms can be divided into three sections: context-free parsers; transformational parsers; and augmented context-free parsers such as the augmented transition network.

CONTEXT-FREE PARSERS

A context-free parser attempts to decompose a sentence by successively applying a series of derivations such as:

- Sentence (S) = noun phrase (NP) + verb phrase (VP).
- Noun phrase = article (T) + noun (N).
- Verb phrase = verb (V) + noun phrase.

With 'The girl had a lamb' the mapping would result in:

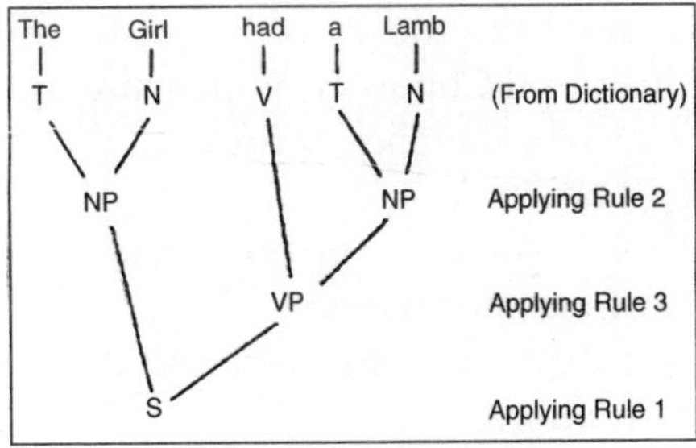

This type of parsing is known as bottom-up; the parse is started at the lowest level, that of individual words, and then built up towards a more complex construction. It could, however, start at the top of the tree and attempt to fit the structure to the sentence. Thus the task is to find a set of rules in the grammar of the language, which, correctly applied, produces the sentence being parsed. This is the top-down approach, always implemented with backtracking as a large number of possible parses at one level of the analysis turn out to be unsuccessful when the next level is attempted. The program must be able to retrace its steps to a previous stage and re-commence an alternative parse. There are advantages and disadvantages in both approaches.

A top-down approach tends to be a poor choice for ambiguous sentences; a bottom-up approach reduces the possible number of interpretations the pro gram has to consider. Thus, if ambiguities arc not a feature of the document, a top-down approach would give a more efficient program. Already many difficulties are manifest in this system; the grammar rules given are too simple for any real life situation, and extensions have to allow for more complex and variable sentence constructions. This may result in an unacceptable number of possible parses: for example, the sentence: 'Gravely concerned with spreading racial violence. President Kennedy used his press conference to issue counsel to both sides in the struggle' produced 136 possible analyses. An excessive number of pos sible solutions leads to the abandonment of this par sing strategy and the adoption of transformational grammars.

TRANSFORMATIONAL PARSERS

Harris proposed the theory of linguistic transformation, elaborated by his pupil Chomsky, which attempts to generate the deep structure of a sentence, representing its syntactic and semantic interpretation.

Thus a sentence such as 'The boy broke the window' can have a number of transformations:

- The window was broken by the boy (passive transformation);

- It was the boy who broke the window (cleft transformation);
- Was it the boy who broke the window? (question transformation).

All these sentences have constituents in common. If this underlying structure—the deep structure—can be uncovered, the difficulty of ascertaining the meaning may be reduced.

In the case of the sentence, 'The boy broke the window', deep structure might be represented as:

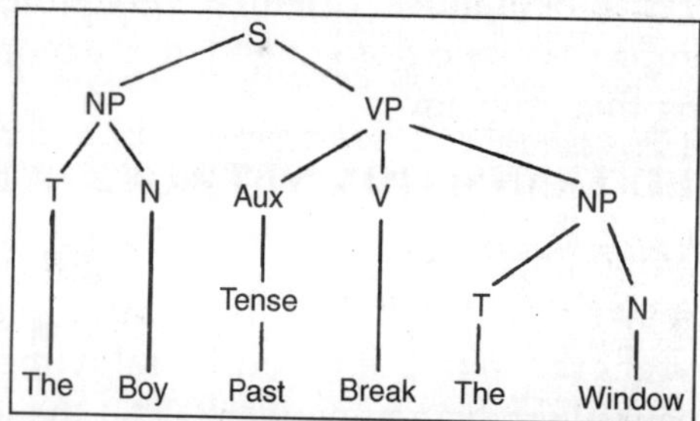

However, though the process of sentence generation from deep to surface structure can be accomplished using only a small number of transformations to produce an acceptable output, the converse does not hold. Hundreds of different reverse transformations apply to each given structure at the analysis step, making this a very ineffi cient process unless extra information is present to guide transformations into paths with a high likelihood of producing the correct deep structure.

Examples of systems which apply a series of reverse transformations may be seen in Petrick "and work by the MITRE group, all done in the 1960s. However, these types of parsers are no longer in common use, as not only were they found computationally inefficient, but a considerable amount of linguistic development has taken place since, the mid-1960s which is reflected in the greater sophistication in both concept and software. Many critiques of transformational grammar are available, but Wilks also postulates the alternative strategy of Preference Semantics," whose core is a system of preferential choice between deep semantic patterns with no conventional grammar analysis or generation.

Wilks argues that transformational grammar was devised independent of considerations of meaning, context and inference, and goes on to 'consider such an even apparently structural-grammatical matter as the ambiguity of prepositions; 'out of', for example, is highly ambiguous, which can be seen from any reflection on such sentences as: I live out of town. I hit her out of anger. I threw the ball out of the window. The statue is made out of marble.... Transformational grammar makes no suggestions whatever as to how the choice should be made.' Preference Semantics, oriented very much towards processing complex sentences, is suggested as a more plausible way of tackling this problem.

AUGMENTED TRANSITION NETWORK (ATM)

The last syntax analyser to be examined is the Aug mented transition network, which has the same power as a transformational grammar, but is considerably more straight forward. In a simple transition network (TN) the grammar is composed of states interconnected by branches specifying transitions between states. Thus a sentence could be represented by: that is, a sentence consists of a sequence of: noun phrase, verb, noun phrase. And a noun phrase consists of: article, adjective, noun.

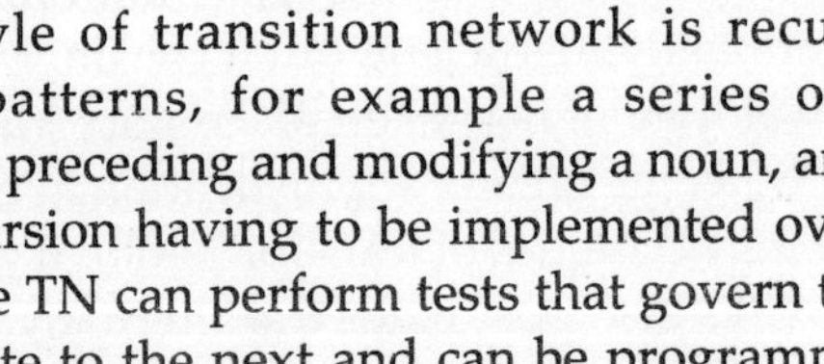

$$S \xrightarrow{NP} S_1 \xrightarrow{V} S_2 \xrightarrow{NP} S_3$$

$$NP \xrightarrow{T} NP_1 \xrightarrow{N} NP_2 \quad (NP_1 \text{ loop: ADJ})$$

This style of transition network is recursive; thus, repetitive patterns, for example a series of adjectives immediately preceding and modifying a noun, are catered for without recursion having to be implemented over the whole network. The TN can perform tests that govern the transition from one state to the next and can be programmed to query sentences where grammar might be suspect. So far, this is simply another variant on a regular grammar, but it has the advantage of recursion and of being represented in the form of a digraph, or directed graph, consisting of nodes joined by arcs.

The arcs are labelled by words or word categories; for example, noun (N) or noun phrase (NP), and it is the task of the parser to traverse the graph from node to node. In this example it can only move from node S, to S2 if the next item in the parse can be identified as a verb. Representing a gram mar as a digraph enables formal mathematical opera tions to be performed on the graph, as well as defining its properties. An augmented transition network (ATN) consists of this system with the addition of a system for generating deep structure and allowing grammatical constraints to be imposed, so that it has the important property of performing both surface and deep analysis simultaneously.

Generally, an ATN parser works in a similar way to the top-down context-free parser and uses the conventional backtracking routines to escape from possible parses which proved untenable. Examples of working grammars based on the ATN model include the Linguistic String Parser, -DIAGRAM, Proto-RELADES, and LAS. A com parison between an ATN and a two-stage parser—known as the sausage machine—may be found in the work of Wanner.

CONTEXT-SENSITIVITY

Despite considerable progress in parsing many major problems still remain, at least a proportion of them requiring context-sensitive grammars for their probable resolution in terms both of parsing and semantic pro cessing. An example of the type of difficulties which have proved hard to resolve can be gained by studying prob lems associated with parsing compound nouns.

The following closely follows Sparck Jones who states that three processes apply to compound nominals: they have to be:

- *Bracketed*: Wicker (bread basket) *vs* (wholemeal bread) basket;
- *Lexically disambiguated*: Bread = loaf vs bread = money;
- *Given a meaning characterisation*: Basket for bread *vs* basket with bread.

She states, 'various strategies, or rather non-strategies, have been adopted to deal with compound nouns. One, for example, is to put compound nouns in the lexicon. A second is to assume that restrictions on the possible interpretations of the constituents, for a specific universe of discourse, will force an appropriate interpretation on the whole. A third is not to attempt a full characteriza tion of the whole. And a fourth is to disregard elements which cannot be processed. These are all unsatisfactory, for obvious reasons. We cannot put all the compounds, even for a limited domain, in the lexicon. We cannot rely on sense restrictions to give us an acceptable interpreta tion. We cannot assume that an explicit characterisation is unnecessary. And we cannot throw parts of the input away.'

Furthermore, even with a considerable quantity of domain-specific knowledge, there must be differences in interpretation of:

- 'These border plants are expensive'—implying that the set of plants being considered are those normally found in a border; and
- These border plants have to be replaced'—that is, these plants in the border have to be replaced. The location of the plants is under consideration irrespective of the actual type of plant found there.

At present no system can cope with such nuances of meaning. We could take the matter still further. If we were to use the same core of words, but applied to a different domain: The IRA have done so much bombing that all the border plants have to be replaced' we have a situation where 'border plants' could apply to plants which grow, but is more likely to apply to factories (= plants) located at the Eire/N Ireland border. Disam biguation here would be a far from straightforward task.

The problem lies in parsing having been syntax-driven; most parsers are based on context-free grammar, whilst the underlying problems of ambiguous structures essen tially need semantic guidance not only from the context but also by using referents from domains of personal experience of the reader.

However, any conclusions formed from considering these facts can only be tentative, and influenced by the domain of discourse of any particular text. For example, much work has been done on the automatic indexing of chemical texts.

M The interest for many potential readers in this field is likely to be bound up with chemical structures, physical processes and chemical reactions. By their nature these are domain-restricted, and, due to the logical way chemical names are built up, eminently suitable for the application of stemming techniques— which in the process of stripping off prefixes and suffixes will be able to identify the structure, elements or con stituent groups of the compound under discussion—followed by statistical analysis. Few other subjects will be so amenable to this type of analysis.

INDEXING QUALITY

One also needs to ask 'How good an index do we need?' These ambiguities may simply be ignored, and reliance placed on other, clearer, sections of the text to fill in the doubtful areas, and/or human intervention for disambiguation. This crucial question could only be answered according to individual needs. Factors to con sider include the costs of checking entries manually for possible errors; of running a program that produces fewer errors than the one currently in use; and of errors—if the error rate is low enough users are likely to be satisfied with the performance. At present, linguistic analysis of text by computer is not far enough advanced for such questions to be answered, but if we draw on results obtained from statistical, non-linguistic, indexing systems, we can surmise that 100 per cent accuracy is not needed for acceptable performance.' The caveat should be added that, as with most research on indexing, these results apply to large databases, and may well be inapplicable to texts such as books.

SEMANTIC AND DISCOURSE ANALYSIS

The object of parsing a sentence is only the first stage in a strategy to attempt to find some way in which the meaning of a sentence and the meanings inherent in a series of sentences could be represented in a computer with the aim of manipulating concepts and ideas inherent in the text with the same facility as the computer can manipulate characters.

It is only when text can be understood by a computer that we can hope to simulate the intellectual actions of a human indexer. As in the case of syntactic analysis, a realistic solution to the problem of semantic analysis must imply simplifi cation—in which case we need to specify a formal language on which to map natural language. Furthermore, in the case of indexing, we must decide also whether any other specialised needs must be met cither in the form of extra semantic information, or, conversely, whether all the information obtained from a full seman tic analysis would be required for our purposes.

It has been suggested that the task is to examine the semantic component of:

- Methods of identifying meaningful units in the input document;
- The derivation of document descriptions from these;
- The construction and use of classifications and other forms of index language organisation.

Unfortunately none of these aims is achievable without the addition of substantial quantities of outside knowledge. Part of this may come from the text itself, but many more assumptions of knowledge common to the author and the intended audience are made than may initially be obvious. Difficulties arising here may be illustrated by reference to a straightforward description: 'Just before dawn, the Valiant sighted the Zwiebel and fired two torpedoes. It sank swiftly, leaving few survivors."

Understanding this simple story is more than under standing the sum of its parts. We have to consider what the 'it' refers to. There are four possible antecedents: dawn; Valiant; Zwiebel; torpedoes. Straightforward syntactic analysis enables us to exclude torpedoes and semantic analysis excludes dawn, but only general world knowledge enables us to surmise that Valiant and Zwiebel must both be ships, and there is a causal relationship between firing torpedoes and sinking another ship. This type of implicit information, inherent in all texts, must be recovered to enable an automated indexing system to make an intelligent assessment of the suit ability of particular phrases or concepts as index entries. This search for meaning is at the root of both semantic analysis and discourse analysis and this aspect of computational linguistics has so far proved intractable.

Most attempts to solve the prob lem have been restricted in their domain as a conse quence of the method used to overcome the problem, which is attempting to assemble all the knowledge needed to answer any particular problem. This knowl edge could be used at the syntactic analysis stage by removing some syntactically plausible but semantically unlikely parses. The organisation of such quantities of knowledge is no trivial undertaking, though it has been attempted. One notable method was that of frames, ' based on the observation that new knowledge tends to be assimilated by identifying at least a portion of it with patterns inherent in pre-existing information.

These frames may be:

- Prototypes, describing classes of objects, actions, or situations: *e.g.*, chairs, running, attending the theatre. They form a general framework of expectations—so whether one goes to a theatre in Edinburgh or Vienna, the general outlines of what one does, how one behaves, and the point of the visit remain broadly the same. Consequently the 'going to the theatre' frame is likely to remain valid;
- Instance frames, describing particular instances of action, etc., *e.g.*, yesterday's visit to the theatre.

There are obvious similarities between frames and context-free grammar: prototype frames correspond to the rules of the grammar itself and instance frames to detailed grammatical knowledge. The concept of frames may also be considered as a context-free description of world knowledge. Some frame-based knowledge representation langu ages have been developed and this type of work has lead to the development of scripts that attempt to contain the metaknowledge needed to understand a given simple narrative. Thus, if a computer program has the appropriate script for a particular scene, it is possible to arrange for it to query anomalous situations, ask apparently intelligent questions and make responses to queries that involve concepts not directly mentioned in the text.

The classic example of a script is that of a restaurant where information is present about the characters, scene and typical actions. Anaphoric resolution thus becomes easier. For example: 'The customer told the waiter that he would like some wine.' We know that waiters serve food and drink, and customers order it, so it is clear that he must refer to the customer, not the waiter; whereas 'The customer told the waiter that he should bring the wine list' would result in he applying to the waiter, as it is the job of the waiter to bring this and similar items. This example shows that scripts cannot be used in novel situations: for these plans can be used, with attempts made to construct a causal chain.

This is no trivial problem: many of the required connections may be implicit, rather than directly stated, in the text. However, a system has been implemented by Wilensky as PAM (plan applier module) and as a simplified system called micro-PAM. These systems produce a complex series of inferences that raise the problem of which inference should be followed. The database of rules and scripts needed is very large even for what would normally be considered as fairly trivial situations, such as the restaurant scenario. A system requires considerable development effort to 'understand' even those episodes which consist of a relatively low number of sentences, even only one sen tence.

Avoiding generalisation, it can be seen that if a large number of sentences deal with essentially the same concept, then processing of the information becomes easier than if rapid changes of content in the sentences necessitated the implementation of a large number of plans in the system. A natural-language indexing system might use semantic analysis of text to produce suitable index entries, but only if the domain of discourse was very restricted. Unfortunately, this is also the area where statistical analysis and word stemming techniques can be quite successfully applied; the more diffuse areas prove intractable both for statistical analysis and discourse analysis.

The former is unsuited to this work, as keyword extraction may have little relevance to the production of useful index entries, and the very vastness of the domain in the latter poses difficult problems despite efforts to produce generalisations of text. One way of dealing with this problem is to develop a system, goal subsumption, which tries to plan for the satisfaction of several goals at the same time. In spite of all these strategies, however, the problem has in essence remained unsolved, particularly in attempts to transfer laboratory results to the domain of ordinary texts.

CONTROLLED VOCABULARY

- An essential process is the joining together of subcultures when a wider common language is needed. Often two groups independently develop very similar concepts, and describing the relation between them brings great benefits... The Semantic Web, in naming every concept simply by a URI, lets anyone express new concepts that they invent with minimal effort. Its unifying logical language will enable these concepts to be progressively linked into a universal Web.

Thus concludes Tim Berners-Lee's seminal 2001 *Scientific American* article on the Semantic Web. The concepts established here are strong ones, and the vision of a thoroughly interconnected Web of data that these concepts suggest, could prove a catalyst for the way we research, develop, interact with, and build upon ideas, culture and knowledge. The idea presented here, of independent groups working with similar concepts, is applicable to the very technologies that can serve as the Semantic Web's underpinnings.

The Semantic Web communities and library communities have both been working towards the same set of goals: naming concepts, naming entities, and bringing different forms of those names together. Semantic Web efforts towards this end are relatively new, whereas libraries have been doing work in this area for hundreds of years. The tools and vocabularies developed in libraries, particularly those developed by the Library of Congress, are sophisticated and advanced. When translated into Semantic Web technologies they will help to realise Berners-Lee's vision.

Semantic Web technologies are now, in their own right, starting to reach a state of maturity. Berners-Lee, the director of the World Wide Web Consortium (W3C) and Eric Miller, W3C Semantic Web Activity Lead, frequently describe these technologies in terms of the Semantic Web Stack. Many of the components depicted as layers in the Semantic Web Stack are already in place, although not nearly as widely implemented as most Semantic Web proselytisers would like.

Development on the various levels depicted in this graphic has been a long time in the making. In a recent interview with Andrew Updegrove in the *Consortium Standards Bulletin*, Berners-Lee identifies one cause of the slow rate of development, implying that each layer is dependant on the layers below it. "We were asked to hold up the query and rules work because people didn't want to start on it until the ontology work had finished, so for some we were in danger of going too fast".

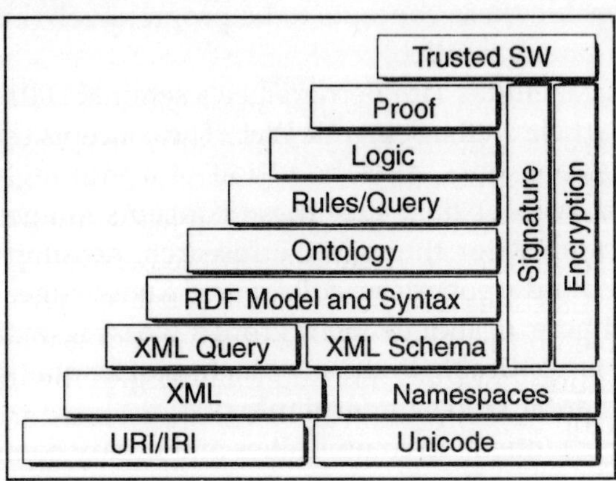

Fig 2.1. W3C Semantic Web Stack Taken from W3C Web Site, Licenced Under CC Attribution 2.5 Licence

As the technologies represented by the Semantic Web Stack continue to mature, there is a tremendous potential for the library community to play a significant role in realising Berners-Lee's vision. In a presentation at Dublin Core 2004, as well as in a number of other presentations over the years, Eric Miller implored the library community to become active in Semantic Web development.

Miller outlines the role of libraries in the Semantic Web as follows:

- "Exposing collections—use Semantic Web technologies to make content available;
- Web'ifying Thesaurus/ Mappings/ Services;
- Sharing lessons learned;
- Persistence".

While all of these roles are significant, the idea of moving thesauri, controlled vocabularies, and related services into formats that are better able to work with other Web services and software applications is particularly significant. Converting these tools and vocabularies to Semantic Web standards, such as the Web Ontology Language (OWL), will provide limitless potential for putting them to use in myriad new ways. This will enable the integration of research functionality—such as searching and browsing diverse resources, verifying the identity of a particular resource's author, or browsing sets of topics related to a particular concept—into all sorts of tools, from online reference sources and library catalogues to authoring tools like those found in Microsoft's Office Suite.

Miller also emphasises the role that libraries can play in helping to realise the trust layer in the Semantic Web Stack, stating, "Libraries have long standing trusted position that is applicable on the Web". The Semantic Web has a lot to gain by recruiting libraries and librarians and involving them in the development process. The W^{3}C's stated mission is "to lead the World Wide Web to its full potential by developing protocols and guidelines that ensure long-term growth for the Web". This focus on protocols and guidelines helps explain why the Semantic Web Stack includes little to no mention of content. For example, it includes an ontology layer, which is primarily represented by OWL—a Web Ontology *Language*—a specification for adding Semantic Web enabling functionality to existing ontologies.

More recently, another Semantic Web technology—Simple Knowledge Organisation System (SKOS) Core—has been designed for the encoding of the contents of thesauri. The W^{3}C's emphasis has been on how to encode ontologies, which fits with their stated mission. The source of ontologies and vocabularies is outside the scope of the W^{3}C's concerns, although the usefulness of such ontologies is certainly dependant on their validity and trustworthiness. This is where Miller's thoughts on the role of libraries seem most relevant.

Libraries have a long-standing history of developing, implementing, and providing tools and services that make use of numerous controlled vocabularies. Presumably, part of the process of 'web'ifying thesaurus, mappings and services' involves converting existing tools into Semantic Web standards, such as OWL and SKOS. Miller, and other vocabulary experts recognise that this would be of tremendous value to Semantic Web initiatives. Taking these steps would reduce the need for Semantic Web development to revisit decisions made over the centuries that libraries have been organising and describing content, which ties into the related idea of 'sharing lessons learned'.

INCREMENTAL PROGRESS —INITIAL DEVELOPMENTS

Progress on bridging the gap between the Semantic Web community and the library community has been underway for some time. A variety of projects are in progress, or completed, that will help to bring more of the tools that libraries develop into the Semantic Web and more general Web Services spheres. Many of these projects are being developed within the Dublin Core Metadata Initiative (DCMI), which draws heavily on both the Semantic Web and library communities, as well as a variety of other information architecture and metadata communities. One example of such collaboration is the expression of a sub-set of MARC Relator Terms in RDF for use as refinements of the DC contributor element.

Relator terms allow a cataloguer to specify the role that an individual played in the creation of a resource, such as illustrator, calligrapher, or editor. Allowing some of these terms to be used as refinements of contributor allows the expression of much more specific relationships between individuals and the resources they create. An example of the use of MARC Relator Terms, both in a MARC record and in Dublin Core, can be seen in figure. Figure depicts a mnemonic MARC record with personal name added entries for correspondents.

The 700 tags at the end of this record each include a subfield e, which contains a MARC Relator term identifying the role of these individuals. The corresponding Dublin Core Record in 2b represents this same information using the 'marcrel' namespace with the Relator code 'CRP', which corresponds to the term 'correspondent.' The concept of author added entry, represented by MARC tag 700 in 2a, is implicit in the Dublin Core example because the Relator terms are all element refinements of dc:contributor.

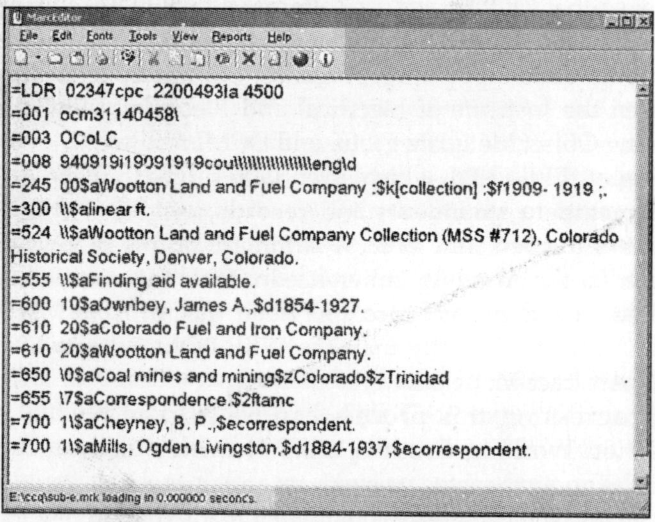

Fig 2.2. Relator Terms in and MARC

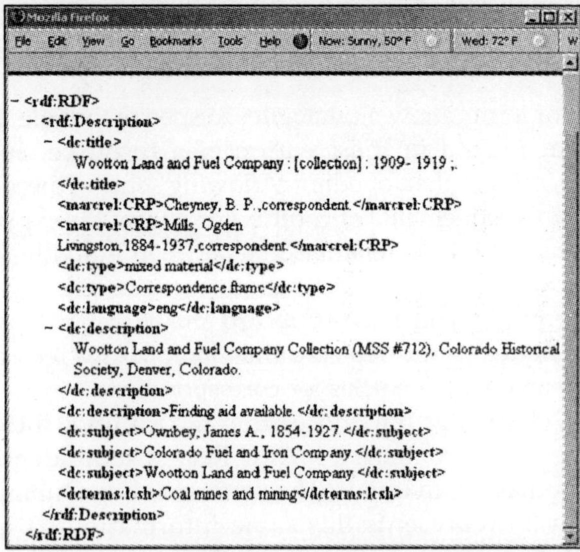

Fig 2.3. MARC Relator Terms in and DC

Another example of collaboration can be seen in the ongoing work to bind the Metadata Object Description Schema (MODS) metadata element set to RDF and to the DC Abstract Model so that MODS terms, or alternately new DC properties derived from or related to these MODS terms, could be available to Dublin Core Application Profiles. Similar collaborations between the Institute of Electrical and Electronics Engineers Learning Object Metadata group and DCMI resulted in an RDF binding of IEEE-LOM, which essentially serves to make IEEE-LOM metadata statements and records useable within the context of the Semantic Web. A summary of this process was reported at the Ariadne Conference in 2003. This presentation resulted in a joint-task force between the IEEE and DCMI communities to formally map the IEEE-LOM Schema to the DCMI Abstract Model as well.

Progress on this process can be tracked on the DC Education Working Group's Wiki. However, both of these examples apply to metadata elements and resource descriptions themselves. The progress that has been made on bringing tools from the library world into the Semantic Web has, thus far, been entirely focussed on the idea of exposing library collections. Incorporating elements used in library resource descriptions into the sets of resource properties that are used to enable the Semantic Web is a large step, and enables library metadata to interoperate with Dublin Core and other RDF encoded metadata. Authority records, library thesauri, and library controlled vocabularies, if converted into formats that support Semantic Web technologies, have an even greater potential for revolutionising the way users—and machines—interact with information on the Internet.

AUTHORITY CONTROL—CORE PRINCIPLES

The benefits and virtues of authority control have been debated and restated for decades. When we apply authority control, we are reminded how it brings precision to searches, how the syndetic structure of references enables navigation and provides explanations for variations and inconsistencies, how the controlled forms of names, titles, and subjects help collocate works in displays, how we can actually link to the authorised forms of names, titles, and subjects that are used in various tools, like directories, biographies, abstracting and indexing services, and so on. We can use the linking capability to include library catalogues in the mix of various tools that are available on the Web. In order to enable these capabilities in a Web-based environment, it will be necessary to move the records that facilitate linking and aggregating in the library into more universal and generalised encoding. The Library of Congress is taking steps in this direction, particularly through work on MARCXML for Authority Records and the Metadata Authority Description Schema (MADS), along with crosswalks to go between them. A next logical step is to begin work on translating this data into the Resource Description Framework (RDF), which is not a trivial task.

SUBJECT AND GENRE VOCABULARIES FOR THE SEMANTIC WEB

There are a vast number of controlled vocabularies for various forms of subject access to library materials. Some of these vocabularies are classification schemes, such as *Dewey Decimal Classification* (DDC) and *Library of Congress Classification* (LCC).

Others are controlled lists of subject headings or terms, which adhere to national and international guidelines for thesaurus construction, like the Library of Congress Subject Headings (LCSH), the two Thesauri for Graphic Materials: Subject Terms (TGM I) and Genre and Physical Characteristic Terms (TGM II), Guidelines on Subject Access to Individual Works of Fiction, Drama, Etc. (GSAFD), and the Ethnographic Thesaurus. Some of the subject thesauri published by The Getty, such as The Getty Thesaurus of Geographic Names (TGN) and The Art and Architecture Thesaurus (AAT) are truly hierarchical thesauri. Many of these controlled vocabularies are registered as DCMI Encoding Schemes in the DCMI Terms namespace.

Registered Encoding Schemes qualifying the DC Subject element include:

- Dewey Decimal Classification (DDC),
- Library of Congress Classification (LCC),
- Library of Congress Subject Headings (LCSH),
- Medical Subject Headings (MeSH),
- National Library of Medicine Classification (NLM),
- The Getty Thesaurus of Geographic Names (TGN),
- Universal Decimal Classification (UDC).

However, when these vocabularies are used as values of DC Subject in metadata records outside of the library context, the syndetic structure of the source vocabulary is all but lost. There is no way for search tools or other applications to make use of information about related terms and variant forms as part of the entry vocabulary. In some cases, item metadata for Dublin Core records is included within a larger system that relies heavily on MARC data, such as OCLC WorldCat. When this is true, many of the Library of Congress controlled vocabularies are indirectly linked to these Dublin Core records by virtue of the availability of MARC authority records for the controlled vocabularies in those systems.

Systems outside of these application environments need to be able to retrieve and translate or otherwise make use of MARC authority record data to make effective use of the hierarchies, equivalency relationships, and structures in the content of controlled vocabularies. These vocabularies present tremendous potential for improving access to web resources and Semantic Web data, as well as enhancing networked applications.

Search engine results could be dramatically improved, both in terms of precision and recall. Different subject vocabularies covering the same concept space could be merged together or associated, providing an environment where differences in terminology between different communities would provide less of a barrier to effective browsing of resources. Front-end interfaces could be built for a variety of online reference tools that take advantage of the rich structure of relationships between topics that is provided by controlled vocabularies. In some regards, libraries are only now realising the full potential of catalogue records to provide innovative and new browsing interfaces.

An example can be seen in North Carolina State Library's new, Endeca powered, catalogue interface, which is presently built entirely on the structure of bibliographic records. This new catalogue interface allows users to refine a search by navigating through record clusters that share a particular property. Drawing on the idea of faceted classification, clusters can be grouped by subtopic, genre, language, time-period, geographic region, and in a variety of other ways. These facets are derived from information in various access points, subject headings and subdivisions in a particular bibliographic result set.

It is easy to envision a similar technique being used to broaden searches and even to present initial browse interfaces to specific collections of information resources. When interfaces start to leverage the power of authority control in new and interesting ways, the benefit to users will be immense. Another example of initiatives to leverage authority control is OCLC Research's Terminology Services project to 'offer accessible, modular, Web-based terminology services'.

The Terminologies Pilot Project in October 2005 explored techniques for encoding sample vocabularies, means of mapping between them to help users identify relationships, and methods for incorporating the resulting services into other applications and tools. These services are the beginning of a rich tapestry of semantics that can be delivered within a user's current context, whatever that context is. In some cases, the services may be entirely carried out by server-side applications.

Almost any application that serves content dynamically could include a navigation system that draws on the hierarchies and relationships between terms in LCSH, and could provide search interfaces that draw on term equivalencies to retrieve a broader set of resources when doing keyword searches. Additionally, there could be services that exist within client side applications, pulling vocabulary structures from the network and integrating them into authoring tools.

One such service component prototyped for the OCLC pilot uses the Microsoft Office 2003 Research Services Pane to access genre terms. "... if a college student wishes to categorise a reading list of fiction titles based on genre, he could copy the titles into a Microsoft Excel 2003 workbook, open the Research services pane, send a search to the OCLC Research GSAFD vocabulary service, and then place the results into his document". This provides the user with the ability to browse and search genre categorisations without having to leave the application in which the search results will be used.

Additionally, the more sources of data are made available in this way, the more automated the process can be. If the Research Services Pane had access to bibliographic records, genre or subject categorisation could be fully automated and available at the touch of a button. A cataloguer could use a similar tool to suggest appropriate terms from a controlled vocabulary, which will lead to lots of cost saving opportunities. Similar applications could be developed as browser plug-ins or extensions.

A sidebar application could be built for FireFox that could harness the power of controlled vocabularies when browsing Web resource that provide some degree of keyword tagging or folksonomy support. Imagine browsing a resource like Flickr and being able to query LCSH for relationships that may be defined between subject terms through the tags labelling the subject of a particular photographic image and tags for various related concepts.

The sidebar could include hyper-linked broader, narrower, equivalent, and associative terms that would pull together additional photographs tagged with those related terms. In a different context, such an application could attempt to scan html source code for word frequency and try to guess the primary topics, returning related terms from a controlled vocabulary, and perhaps linking to search engine results for the concepts represented. Additionally, a similar service could be provided using a word highlighted by the user. The possibilities are endless.

NAME AUTHORITY FOR THE SEMANTIC WEB

The benefits of authority control—search precision, more powerful navigation, collocation, and linking between various tools and resources—apply to metadata about the creators of resources as well as to subject access. The library community is well positioned to play a significant role in these developments. Libraries have been dealing with identification, disambiguation, and collocation of names of content creators since, the beginning of cataloguing. The different forms of name used by the same creator in various print publications and other types of resources have always led to some degree of difficulty in grouping works together.

The syndetic structure of name authority files has proven itself a very useful tool to help collocate works by an author regardless of the form of name on a particular item. The proliferation of resources on the Web extends the scope of the collocation problem. Initiatives are appearing in the Web community to help provide better mechanisms for identifying persons, families, and corporate entities that have a role with respect to information resources.

InterParty is a European Commission funded project exploring the interoperation of 'party identifiers,' which would provide standard identification numbers to serve the same purpose that authorised forms of names serve in library applications: to help collocate and disambiguate individual content creators. More recently, some of the InterParty members and others submitted a similar proposal for International Standard Party Identifiers (ISPI) as an ISO standard.

More directly related to Semantic Web Development is the Friend Of A Friend (FOAF) project. FOAF is about "creating a Web of machine-readable homepages describing people, the links between them and the things they create and do". Finding ways to integrate these initiatives with existing mechanisms for name authority control in libraries can help to bring library catalogues into the mix of tools available on the Web.

Additionally, the availability of library authority data in a more Web-friendly format has the potential to positively influence the organisation of the broad spectrum of Web content already available. The development of a Virtual International Authority File (VIAF) has been a key idea moving forward this initiative.

Virtual International Authority File (VIAF)

Presently, authority files are maintained and developed by a large range of national bibliographic agencies. To make the most of this potential, it is useful to first integrate the somewhat disparate sources of authority data that exist even within the library community. These agencies develop files that are generally focused on the creators of content relevant to a particular national and cultural identity. As geographic boundaries become more and more porous, and culture becomes much more international, there is increasingly overlap between the authority files maintained by these agencies.

The concept of a Virtual International Authority File (VIAF) has been discussed since, the 1970's within the

International Federation of Library Associations and Institutions (IFLA). Initially, IFLA envisioned a single shared file; more recently the concept has evolved into one of linking existing national and regional authority files. The primary objective of this vision is to facilitate sharing the workload and reducing cataloguing costs within the library community. The community is expanding, especially in Europe, where libraries are viewed as one of many 'memory institutions', along with archives, museums, and rights management agencies.

Ideally, authority files can be freely shared among all of these communities. A shared file would reduce the cost of doing authority work by avoiding repetition of effort while combining various forms of names that are particular to resource published within the context of a particular region, culture, or nation. Combining or clustering the forms of name will result in a much richer set of authority information, enabling users to access information in the language, scripts, and form they prefer.

Additionally, a single international authority file system will be far more useful when integrated into various Web retrieval tools and Web content descriptions. Such a tool could be used by a wide range of Web systems to improve the precision of user's searches and to provide the user's preferred display of the language and script of names. Authority records are used to collocate resources that utilise varying forms of name, but collocation does not need to dictate the script or language used by the end user display.

Figure shows how a single entity—whether it is a concept, person, place, or thing—has a variety of labels that identify it in different languages and scripts. Traditionally, library systems have relied on a preferred label for all entities, although the preference would vary depending on the geographic context of the system.

Merging or linking records that utilise different languages and scripts allows the end-user to select the language and script used to display information about entities irrespective of system's default preference. This is appropriate in a truly global Web, where geographic and national boundaries are considerably less significant.

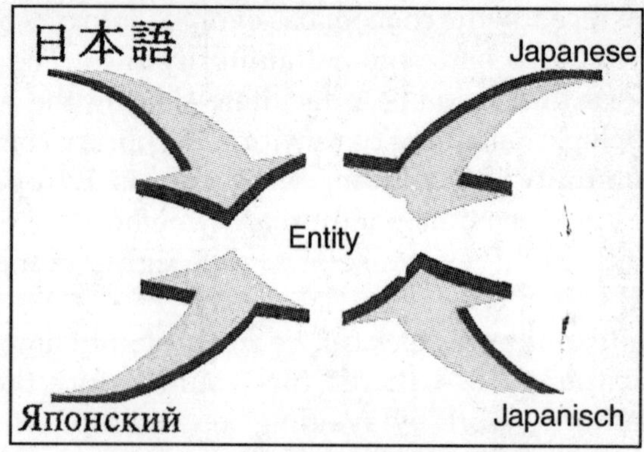

Fig 2.4. One Entity—Many Labels

A variety of projects have sought to address this language challenge in recent years, exploring mechanisms to combine individual authority files. One such project, the European Commission funded Author project converted a sample of authority records from five European bibliographic agencies in France, England, Belgium, Spain, and Portugal into the UNIMARC format and made them available as a searchable file. "The challenge was that each library has its own language, cataloguing rules, bibliographic record format and local system for its online authority file". Combining these records into a single UNIMARC file required a large amount of record normalisation. No attempt was made to link the records for the same entity.

More recently, OCLC Online Computer Library Center Inc., the Library of Congress, and Die Deutsche Biblioteck (DDB) began a joint project to test the idea of a VIAF. OCLC used matching algorithms to link name authority records of these two national bibliographic agencies and built a server to store the combined records. Additional phases of the project will involve ongoing maintenance to update the central file when either source is updated and possibly the development of a multilingual end user interface. Following the evaluation of the project, the addition of new partners will be explored, particularly those potential partners with non-roman authority records.

LEVERAGING A VIAF ON THE SEMANTIC WEB

When combined with developments in the broader metadata, Web-design, and Semantic Web communities, the power and utility of VIAF outside of libraries becomes clear. Authority record data can be associated more easily with a variety of Web resources, allowing users and potentially machines to immediately start to evaluate the information they are looking at. A quick search of bibliographic data related to a given resource author allows the retrieval of her dissertation, which could be mined for data about the degree granting institution.

Other bibliographic records could be retrieved to help evaluate the original Web resource and related works could offer pathways to additional relevant resources. As other resources start including metadata that uses identifiers or headings to link to a VIAF, the opportunity to connect more interesting bits of information can add significant value to any Web-based information resource. Wikipedia entries, journal articles, Who's Who biographical info, an individual's blog, their homepage, or the homepage of their place of work can all be interconnected, as well as linked to journal articles, bibliographic records in catalogues and in e-commerce sites, and a variety of other scholarly resources. These interconnections have extensive implications for research.

Once there is a corpus of biographical information combined into a data store that is connected to authority data, the information can be used to make inferences about any document, article, Web page, or blog entry that turns up when searching for information. For example, imagine a blog post that includes information about its author's identity. This information could be referenced against available biographical data and used to make inferences about the veracity and objectivity of the post's content.

If the author were affiliated with the Recording Industry Association of America (RIAA) a trade group representing the U.S recording industry, or the Electronic Frontier Foundation (EFF), a non-profit legal organisation focused on defending 'digital rights', heavily involved in fighting bad uses of Digital Rights Management technology, and opposing limitations on fair use, the statement is likely to be much less objective than content posted by a Harvard law professor. While an agent or search tool couldn't necessarily flag such resources as potentially biased without additional information about the affiliate organisation, it would still be very useful to present these additional facts to the user when returning search results.

The metadata community has a number of initiatives underway for describing people, both as agents of resource creation and for the utility of describing relationships between people, describing connections between people and organisations, and for capturing other contact information and other descriptive information about individuals and groups. Examples of such initiatives include the Dublin Core Agents Working Group's work on defining a metadata standard for agent description and identification. Ultimately, this work should result in the development of an Application Profile for agent description.

Also, work has been completed on 'Reference Models for Digital Libraries: Actors and Roles' within the DELOS/NSF Working Group. This work culminated in Final Report, issued in July 2003. Interestingly, this work goes well beyond the scope of authors and content creators; instead the DELOS/NSF model categorises Actors as Users, Professionals, and Agents. In this context, agents are the traditional content creators that help populate a digital library and professionals are the developers of the digital library itself and the providers of digital library services.

The scope of their work may be much deeper than is necessarily relevant to discussions of authority control on the Semantic Web, although the models used and conclusions drawn may prove to play an important role in future discussions about authority control for names. Another initiative, the Friend Of A Friend (FOAF) project described earlier, is of particular use to the Semantic Web community, because it was conceived with the Semantic Web in mind and is built upon the RDF data model.

FOAF expresses identity through any property value pair, allowing you to aggregate data about individuals using any unique property, such as an e-mail address or the URL for a home page. FOAF is primarily designed for community building, but when the possible privacy issues of sharing personal data are resolved there is much potential for FOAF to help aggregate public information about individuals. FOAF could be used to aggregate all sorts of resources, both by and about individuals—Again, resources such as, Wikipedia entries, journal articles, Who's Who biographical info, the individual's homepage, their blog, or their place of work.

This information could be glommed into a program like Piggy Bank—a FireFox extension for viewing, collecting and merging RDF encoded data, developed by the Simile project —or any other Semantic Web enabled tool, and processed along with other local or remote data stores. For example, a local data store of vcards and/or FOAF data might include private data, such as phone number, calendaring system, and e-mail address. The very presence of that particular identifier in a local store of RDF data about people might change the context of any information interaction with a Wikipedia or Who's Who entry.

Using any 'unique' property to identify entities will certainly help to aggregate most of them, but it would miss entities that are not described using a particular piece of identifying information. Inferences about which descriptions represent the same entity will only go so far in establishing a positive match. The ability to completely aggregate such data becomes even more powerful when the identifying properties can be referenced against the VIAF to determine alternate forms of name and representations in alternate scripts. This allows a query of available RDF data to be much more comprehensive when deciding what pieces of data should be aggregated.

MARKUP AND ENCODING OF AUTHORITY DATA

One of the most valuable activities that libraries and librarians can engage in, both to help realise the Semantic Web and to generally increase the findability of electronic resources in general, is the process of creating versions of vocabularies in machine-readable format. Thesauri, authority files, classifications schemes, and subject heading lists—collectively referred to as Knowledge Organisation Systems—have enormous potential for enhancing the discoverability and organisation of resources in a networked environment.

The potential only increases when such systems are provided in formats designed for emerging Web technology, such as OWL and SKOS—two of the ontology schema of the Semantic Web.

- Knowledge organisation systems can enhance the digital library in a number of ways. They can be used to connect a digital library resource to a related resource. The related information may reside within the KOS itself or the KOS may be used as an intermediary file to retrieve the key needed to access it in another resource. A KOS can make digital library materials accessible to disparate communities. This may be done by providing alternate subject access, by adding access by different modes, by providing multilingual access, and by using the KOS to support free text searching.

The perceived benefits of knowledge organisation systems are of particular importance, and apply to networked resources beyond the scope of digital library materials. The availability of machine-readable representations of various thesauri and other controlled vocabulary enables more effective search and retrieval, better browse functionality and general organisation of materials online, and the automatic creation of context sensitive linkages between available resources and data sets.

Additionally, and most importantly for Semantic Web development, providing controlled vocabularies outside of traditional library systems enables a variety of applications to more effectively merge and manipulate data and information from disparate sources. There are many steps that need to be taken to realise this set of goals. Firstly, the library and

Semantic Web communities must agree on how best to encode these vocabularies.

Many of the subject schemes already exist in one or more machine-readable representations. Much of LCSH exists in MARC records in library catalogues and the databases of cataloging services such as OCLC's WorldCat and RLIN 21. All of the LC controlled vocabularies are available as complete files of MARC 21 or MARCXML formatted authority records through the Cataloguing Distribution Service of the Library of Congress.

The Getty provides licenced access to its vocabularies in three formats: XML, relational tables and MARC, and provides sample data from each vocabulary for free. At first glance, these formats do not appear to be of much use in the context of RDF, but the standardisation and global use of MARC makes it possible to convert these into RDF-friendly data. One approach is the creation of URIs to identify each terminal node on the source XML structure as a unique concept that can be used as a property in the RDF and DC Abstract Model sense. This prospect has the potential to retain as much of the detail available in the source format as possible, but may prove unnecessary and undesirable due to the complexity of the resultant sets of properties.

On the other hand, the information from MARC records may in fact be useful for automatic processes and machine activities. The richness of MARC authority data, and the time and effort invested in developing, encoding, and sharing this data, provides a unique and powerful set of vocabularies. However, it remains to be seen whether the complexity of the resulting XML records would be an impediment to interoperability. An alternative approach involves simply cross-walking the XML data into an already defined RDF-friendly form.

Along the way, detail about relationships between terms will likely be lost, but the end product will probably be much simpler to work with. One possible target RDF vocabulary, the Simple Knowledge Organisation System (SKOS) Core has much potential in this context. SKOS Core provides a model for expressing the structure of what they refer to as a 'Concept Scheme'. "Thesauri, classification schemes, subject heading lists, taxonomies, terminologies, glossaries and other types of controlled vocabulary are all examples of concept schemes".

SKOS Core provides a means of expressing most of the semantic relationships included in most library subject vocabularies. For example, 'prefLabel' and 'altLabel' represent 'use' and 'use for' references, while 'broader' and 'narrower' are used to identify hierarchical relationships. SKOS allows for the creation of new labels and the encoding of more specific types of relationships as well. Additionally, SKOS provides mechanisms for various types of notes—scopeNote, definition, example and note.

The SKOS Core community has drafted documentation on 'Publishing a Thesaurus on the Semantic Web," which provides a guide for using SKOS to both describe and encode vocabularies in RDF. Converting large controlled vocabularies into RDF data is certainly a good way to get sample data sets to use to build prototype services. However, the long-term maintenance of such data stores may be problematic. As changes are made to the source vocabulary, those changes need to be propagated through to all the various formats that the vocabulary is made available in.

In the context of SKOS, this is a manageable task. SKOS extensions have been proposed to allow for versioning and the tracking of changes made to controlled vocabularies over time.

However, in cases where vocabularies are likely to be managed in a variety of different formats, the SKOS extensions are less helpful. Another approach is to harvest the source data in its native format and translate it into a variety of output formats either as nightly batch processes or on-the-fly as data is requested.

Progress is being made in this area, such as OCLC's work on exposing vocabularies in a variety of delivery formats, including MARCXML and SKOS. It doesn't matter whether the data store is MADS, MARC, RDF, or some arbitrary flavour of XML, it can be transformed into another format either on-the-fly or as a batch process. A centralised name authority database could be created from the national authority files available in various library communities and stored as normalised MARC 21.

If this data store is deemed useful to the Friend of a Friend (FOAF) community, the data can be turned into RDF. Similarly, Web services like Flickr could convert and makes use of Library of Congress Subject headings to augment both the searching and development of their folksonomies.

3

The Art of Indexing

PRINCIPLES AND PROCEDURES

The Producer Price Index (PPI) has one of the longest histories of any economic statistic. The first PPI under its previous title of Wholesale Price Index (WPI) was published by the Board of Trade in 1903 in a parliamentary paper on Wholesale and Retail Prices. The series ran from 1871, and represented the weighted arithmetic mean of price relatives of 45 commodities, mainly basic materials and foodstuffs. Prices were largely derived from the average values recorded at the time of import or export.

In 1935, indices were rebased on 1930=100 and continued to be published until 1955. These earlier indices were rather crude and did not attempt to measure prices of finished goods at all. A description of these early statistics is contained in *Stafford,* while the indices are shown in *Mitchell.* The present structure of the PPI largely derives from the mid 1950s. An article published in 1956 effectively sets out the concepts underlying the present set of indices. Since, that time, there have been seven rebasings but the basic concepts have remained unchanged.

BASIC CONCEPTS

The two main sets of indices which are published for the home PPI are: *Output indices*—the prices of goods produced by manufacturers in the United Kingdom for sale in this country, and *Input indices*—the materials and fuel purchased by UK manufacturing industry as part of their current expenditure. These include imports of raw materials and semi-manufactured goods as well as home-produced inputs of materials, fuel and semi-manufactured goods. The latter are generally represented by the output price indices of the appropriate industry.

Output PPIs are commonly known as 'factory gate' prices to reflect the fact that they measure prices of goods before they are transferred to the distribution or retail sectors. This is a crucial difference between the PPI and the Retail Price Index (RPI), also produced by ONS, which measures prices of goods and services paid by households. Other important points are that PPIs reflect prices at the time of order rather than delivery and should reflect actual prices achieved rather than any notional list price. An article comparing movements in the RPI and PPI over the period 1990 to 1994 was published in Economic Trends in August 1998.

USES OF PPI

The PPI has three main categories of customers:

- Other parts of the Office for National Statistics, which use the data for deflating the national accounts, particularly the index of production, capital expenditure and stockbuilding;
- Economists at the Treasury, the Bank of England, and City institutions, who regard the PPI as a measure of current inflationary processes in the overall economy. The DTI, MAFF and industrial economists also use PPIs for monitoring price pressures on sub-sectors of UK industry; and
- Commercial customers, including MOD and its suppliers, who use the indices as an impartial measure of prices for contractual purposes, and for comparing with their own patterns of purchases and sales.

EXPORT PRICES

Export price indices (EPIs) have been collected since, 1993. These are collected in a broadly similar way to PPIs but prices for export rather than the UK market are requested. EPIs have been used to deflate the export component of the Index of Production, as well as the value of exports of manufactured goods recorded in the Balance of Payments, since, the publication of the 1996 National Accounts. The rationale for developing EPIs to deflate these flows within the national accounts is set out in *Williamson and Ruffles.* At present, EPIs cover around half of manufactured goods, and it is planned to steadily increase their coverage over the next few years.

IMPORT PRICES

Import prices covering raw materials and semi-manufactured products have always been collected as part of the material and fuel input indices. The categories covered are divisions 00 to 68 of the Standard International Trade Classification (SITC). A recruitment exercise is currently under way to develop import price indices (IPIs) covering capital goods as well as finished intermediate products.

RESOURCES USED

The present numbers of suppliers and items for the main PPI enquiries are:

	Suppliers	Items
PPI (home sales)	4,000	9,000
Import Prices	400	900
Export Prices	1,000	2,500

The number of export price items is presently being extended and may increase to a maximum of 5,000. The estimated total government costs of conducting the PPI, including export, import and service sector prices were £2.0 million in 1997/98, and involved 52.2 staff years. Compliance costs for industry—that is the estimated cost of the time spent by contributors in providing the data—were £200,000 in 1996/97.

STANDARD INDUSTRIAL CLASSIFICATION

Since, 1995, the Standard Industrial Classification (SIC) used in the PPI system has been the 1992 version. More detailed information was published in the Official Journal of the European Community *OJEC*, which also allows comparison with the Combined Nomenclature used by Customs and Excise. SIC(92) is consistent with EUROSTAT and United Nations recommendations and allows consistent comparisons between European countries.

Earlier classifications have been

- 1980 SIC from 1983 to 1995.
- 1968 SIC from 1973 to 1983.

In terms of all manufacturing industry, the main differences between the most recent SICs have been:

- 1968 SIC to 1980 SIC Petroleum refining was excluded from all manufacturing, while output of slaughterhouses was included in all manufacturing.
- 1980 SIC to 1992 SIC Petroleum refining was included in all manufacturing.

A reasonable length of time-series is shown at the time of reclassification.

PUBLICATION

High-level PPIs are published first in a monthly PPI First Release. More detailed figures are published in Business Monitor MM22—around 900 PPIs are produced each month. Results are also published in the Current Cost Accounting Monitor and in the Aerospace and Electronics Cost Indices Monitor.

PRICE COLLECTION

STATUTORY BASIS

The collection of producer price indices, which had previously been voluntary, was moved to a statutory basis in 1991. The move was to improve the quality of the overall and component indices and ensured a greater response to recruitment forms, particularly in areas such as aerospace and shipbuilding, where companies were previously reluctant to provide data because of the complicated nature of their industries. Price collection in Great Britain is statutory under the Statistics of Trade Act 1947; and since, 1993 has also been statutory in Northern Ireland under Article 5 of the Statistics of Trade and Employment Order 1988.

PRICES REQUESTED

At the time of recruitment to the home PPI, ONS request that companies supply price quotations for items which have the following attributes:

- Are representative of the company's production in the relevant heading which is a six-digit code within the 1992 Standard Industrial Classification.
- Are manufactured and sold within the UK. The definition of UK manufacture is that the nature of the good must be changed within the UK. As examples, assembly of imported parts within this country would be included, but not a simple repackaging of an imported good.

Prices are then requested on a monthly basis:

- The prices quoted should represent a price which would be achieved in a significant proportion of UK sales, after discounts and excluding VAT.
- The product must be quoted on the same basis each month - *i.e.,* the same product and same terms of sale.
- The product and terms of sale must be described in enough detail to ensure consistency each month.
- The price must be recorded at the time at which the product is ordered. PPIs are published on this basis but for such purposes as deflating turnover in certain industries, PPIs are lagged so that they relate to time of delivery.
- Prices are ex-works price, *i.e.,* excluding any delivery charge outside the factory.

The most recent price history is returned to the contributor. Prices should be recorded as well as the date of any change. A contributor may choose to supply data in the form of a price index. Prices may be supplied up to three months ahead. The price averaged over the month as a whole is then calculated by the ONS.

Excise Duties

The headline PPI includes excise duties on such items as tobacco, petroleum products and alcoholic drinks. For analytical purposes, an additional all manufacturing PPI excluding excise duties is published in the PPI First Release, so manufacturers in these industries are asked to provide prices both including and excluding excise duties, and indices are published on both bases. Since, 1998, the series excluding duty have been used for deflation in the national accounts, in line with international guidelines.

Average Prices

Generally, contributors are discouraged from simply providing average prices covering all transactions in a particular month. Experience has indicated that such average prices tend to be very volatile and can be affected by an occasional very large order. Such fluctuations reflect changes in customer mix rather than genuine changes in prices. For this reason, contributors are asked to quote prices for a similar transaction each month, though there are industries such as the manufacture of construction materials, *e.g.*, bricks or cement, where average prices are accepted as a preferable alternative to unrealistic list prices.

Charge-out Rates

It is difficult for contributors in particular industries such as ship-building and repair, to provide quotes as so much of their work is one-off in nature which means it is difficult to quote for the same product over a period of time. In such cases, hourly charge-out rates give an approximation to the trends for the product or service itself, whilst keeping the compliance costs to a minimum.

However, they can lead to distortions in not allowing for productivity increases over time and excluding any price movements in the raw materials involved. There are exceptions but this method of pricing is generally best avoided if possible.

Where labour charge-out rates are used, ONS staff are advised to:

- Ensure they cover one specific type of a constant mix of labour.
- Avoid industries where productivity gains or development are likely to be rapid.
- Avoid industries where the materials element in prices is high.
- Ensure the quoted rate reflects what the customer actually pays.

Rates per tonne of material are more likely to be satisfactory than labour charge-out rates, but ONS staff are asked to:

- Ensure the rate is what the customer pays after discount.
- Include the cost of the material and ensure this is specified precisely.
- Ensure quotes cover specific products or product types.
- Ensure the working of the material is the predominant element in the product being quoted for. Design charges should be excluded.

Import Price Collection

Prices of imported raw materials and semi-manufactured goods are also collected as part of the PPI system. Contributors are selected from a list of importers supplied by Customs and Excise. They can either be manufacturers in their own right or may operate as importers who then sell on to manufacturers; in the former case they should represent the price they typically pay for the product quoted, in the latter case they should record the price they would charge to a UK manufacturing company. They can either be manufacturers in their own right or may operate as importers who then sell on to manufacturers; in the former case they should represent the price they typically pay for the product quoted, in the latter case they should record the price they would charge to a UK manufacturing company.

Export Price Collection

Export prices are collected on a separate form from the home PPI.

The crucial differences are:

- Goods must be manufactured in the UK and destined for export.
- Quotes are requested for both EC and non-EC destinations
- Prices should be supplied in the currency which their overseas customer pays.
- The ideal definition is FOB but other terms are acceptable, on the grounds that trends on the various definitions should be similar. Prices should be provided on a consistent basis—*i.e.,* the same good to the same destination. Prices to another part of the same company are generally avoided, but will be accepted if necessary. In such a case, export prices as quoted on the company's INTRASTAT form or Customs documentation are acceptable.

Field Officers

A recent innovation is the use of a field officer to liase with contributors to ensure that the prices they provide meet the specified criteria. Such field officers have been used successfully in other countries, particularly the USA and France, and it is planned to increase their use in this country as resources permit over the next few years.

Published Sources

A few price quotations are obtained from published sources rather than direct from companies. Examples are prices for imported metals, which are obtained from the London Metal Exchange and for meat which come from the Meat and Livestock Commission.

CALCULATION OF INDICES

Price Relatives

The next stage after collecting prices for a specific good from companies is to derive a price relative, which is the pure price for an item divided by its price in a base year, currently 1995. Algebraically, the price relative at time t is equivalent to $\frac{P_i * 100}{P_b}$. The price relative in general follows the same movements as the price of the item but allowance is made for changes in specification. Around 2,400 specification changes were undertaken in the home PPI during 1996.

Laspeyres Indices

Producer price indices are base-weighted indices—that is to say they are weighted according to the sales or purchases in the base year, currently 1995.

The simplest form of a Laspeyres index is:

$$\frac{100 * \sum Q_b P_t}{\sum Q_b P_b}$$

where Q and P are the quantities and prices respectively of products—the subscript b denotes 'in the base period' and the subscript *t* denotes 'in the current period'. The base year is updated every five years, so that 1995 = 100 PPIs were published for the first time in October 1998. Until recently, the base year underlying the PPI was actually one year earlier than the reference year, *e.g.*, the PPI for 1985=100 was based on weights relating to 1984. However, the base year and reference year have coincided from 1995 when the indices based on 1990=100 were reclassified from the 1980 SIC onto the 1992 SIC.

Gross and Net Sector

PPIs are measured on two different bases—gross and net of inter-sector sales. As an example of the concepts, the motor industry is comprised of many companies supplying parts to a few car manufacturers who then produce the final product for sale to the customer. The gross sector output of Division 34 would include both the sales of the parts and the sale of the finished cars. The net sector output of Division 34 would measure only the finished product and exclude the intervening stages.

All sales of capital goods are regarded as final products, and so are not netted out. Most countries calculate PPIs on a gross basis, and the UK supplies PPIs on this basis to EUROSTAT. However, the high-level output price indices given prominence in the First Release are on a net basis. The argument for the latter presentation is that this is the measure which best reflects manufacturing inflation on the rest of the economy.

Since, inflation affecting the output prices of intermediate goods will implicitly be factored into the output prices of finished products, the gross sector approach can be seen as duplicating the contribution of the manufacture of intermediate goods. Gross sector indices, however, also contain valuable information, and are used to deflate the total turnover of industries, which by definition are on a gross basis. Apart from the highest-level indices in the First Release and tables of Business Monitor MM22, the rest of the indices published since, October 1998 have been on a gross sector basis.

Level of Detail Collected

Contributors are initially asked to select a representative quote at the 6-digit SIC(92) level. PPIs are calculated at the 6-digit SIC (92) level and are grossed to the 4-digit class and higher levels. Items are numbered within the 6-digit heading they are recorded, so that for example a washing machine would come within SIC (92) code 297113 with the ten-digit code of the form 2971130001.

Export Price Indices

EPIs are collected at the 6-digit Combined Nomenclature (CN) level published annually by HM Customs and Excise. This is also known as the Harmonised System (HS). For publication purposes and for deflation in the national accounts, the indices are aggregated to a three-digit CN level. For the purposes of deflating turnover for export, EPIs are converted to SIC(92) by the Balance of Payments branch of ONS, who forward them on for deflation of the export component of the Index of Production.

Import Price Indices

IPIs are collected using the 6-digit CN, but published according to the Standard International Trade Classification (SITC). The detailed relationship between CN and SITC is shown in *Guide to the classification for Overseas trade Statistics* published annually by HM Customs and Excise.

Reconstitution of Indices

A reconstitution of an index occurs when an item is to be deleted or added to an index. This is distinct from a specification change, where a contributor changes the specification of an item for which prices are supplied, but the weights of the item are unchanged. In a 'recon', the weights of an item are changed, together with other changes to ensure weights continue to add up to 100 per cent. A multiplication factor is applied to ensure that the value of the reconstituted index four months prior to the most recent calculated month are unchanged.

Derivation of Weights

The PPI is at present re-weighted every five years. The most recent results were first published in October 1998 with 1995=100. The weights used in the PPI system have two main sources:

PRODCOM

The value of sales in the base year is extracted from the PRODCOM enquiry. PRODCOM, an acronym for Products of the European Community, collects data on sales from some 25,000 contributors annually under a EUROSTAT directive. An attempt is made to exclude the value of exports from the weight at index level. However, due to the lack of data, total sales including exports are used to calculate each contributor's weight at item level.

To reduce variability at index level, sales from two years are used to derive weights. It is important to note that the weights within the PPI are product-based, while the turnover figures underlying the Index of Production (IOP) are based on the main industrial products of particular companies. For IOP purposes, adjustments are made to the PPIs to allow for this difference in coverage and also the fact that PPIs relate to time of order while IOP relate to time of delivery.

Purchasing Data

Data on manufacturing companies' purchases of materials and fuel were obtained from quinquennial Purchases Enquiries, until recently. The last of these was collected in respect of 1989. To minimise contributors' costs, information on purchases is now collected as part of the Annual Business Enquiry (ABI). Particular industries are targeted on a rotating basis so that all industries are covered in a five-year period.

Input-Output Tables

Input indices are calculated from ONS's Input-Output Tables, which use ABI and PRODCOM data as sources. As a result, input indices shown in table of Business Monitor MM22 are calculated no lower than Input-Output Group level. To derive weights for the high-level net sector indices, it is necessary to exclude transactions between industrial groupings. These are also derived from the Input-Output tables. A methodological manual explaining these tables was published in 1997.

Import Price Indices

A contributor's weight in the import price index system is derived from the value of a company's imports in particular 6-digit CN tariff headings as obtained directly from the company. Weights at tariff code heading and above are derived from the total imports recorded in the Customs and Excise Returns in the base year.

Export Price Indices

A contributor's weight in the export price index system is derived from the value of the company's exports at a six-digit CN heading for EU and non-EU destinations separately.

This is in general taken from the Customs and Excise returns in the base year confirmed by the company if necessary. Weights for EPIs above 6-digit headings are taken from the Overseas Trade Statistics for the base year.

Seasonal Adjustment

To assist economic analysis, four high-level PPIs are published in seasonally adjusted form. On the output side, these are the indices for all manufacturing excluding excise duties, and manufacturing excluding the food, beverages, tobacco and petroleum industries. On the input side, the indices for all manufacturing and manufacturing excluding food, beverages, tobacco and petroleum industries are seasonally adjusted to take account of volatile seasonal movements, especially in electricity and food input prices. The US Bureau of the Census seasonal adjustment package is used. Once a year, full results are taken on board for the most recent three months, but otherwise only the most recent two months figures and the month a year before the current month are revised.

SAMPLE RECRUITMENT

Home PPIs

The sampling frame of companies for domestic PPIs is the production survey in the base year at the time at which recruitment takes place. For 1990, it was the Quarterly and Annual Sales Enquiries (QSI/ASI) while it has been the PRODCOM enquiry for 1995, which will continue in future base years. Until recently, sampling has been on a cut-off basis—so that only the largest firms in each industry are selected for new recruitment, though in the past, when recruitment was on a voluntary basis some small firms were selected, some of whom are still in the sample. The contributor coverage at the all manufacturing level amounts to some 44 per cent of production.

Import Price Indices

Importers of raw materials and semi-manufactures are recruited to the IPI panel by selection of the largest importers in specific headings recorded on Customs and Excise returns.

Export Price Indices

Exporters are recruited to EPIs by selection of the largest exporters in specific 6-digit CN. So whilst agents can be recruited for the IPIs, they are not recruited for the EPIs; only exporters who are also manufacturers are included in the panel.

Prices Supplied by other Government Departments

Other government departments provide indices for a few industries, as follows:

- *Department of Trade and Industry (DTI)* provides indices for energy industries, including electricity, gas and petroleum, based on DTI's monthly surveys to companies in those industries.
- *The Ministry of Agriculture, Fisheries and Food (MAFF)* provides monthly prices on many of the outputs from UK agriculture purchased by UK manufacturing industry. These prices are either taken from MAFF surveys or from the Meat and Livestock Commission, the Home-Grown Cereals Authority or the National Farmers Union.
- *The Department of the Environment, Transport and the Regions* calculates price indices for output of construction.

Trade Associations

In the past, when the PPI was a voluntary survey, data for certain industries, such as brewing, were provided by trade associations. In recent years, the trend has been to move away from such quotes and to recruit data directly from companies. Very few quotes are now collected from trade associations.

New Price Quotes

The base price for an item is the price in the base year, currently 1995. If a new item is recruited after the base year, a notional base price is set so that the initial price relative for the item is calculated to be the same as its parent index. For instance, suppose a new manufacturer of washing machine is recruited in January 1999. If the value of the item's first stage parent index 'cloth washing and drying machines' - 2971130000 under SIC (92) -stands at 120.0 at that time, and the price of the washing machine is £300, then the base price will be assumed to have been £250 in 1995, so that a price relative of (300/250)*100 =120.0 in January 1999 is calculated—the same as its parent index. From that point on the price relatives for the new item will be calculated relative to a notional base price for that item of £250 in 1995.

NEW SAMPLING SCHEME FOR HOME PPIS

The methodology used to calculate the PPI has been reviewed and between 1999 and 2000 a new sample design is being introduced. Once this design has been fully phased in a new estimator will be introduced. This will require an extended parallel run and is not likely to be introduced until late 2001.

The main elements of the new sampling scheme are:

- Sampling from Prodcom;
- Using an optimal allocation; and
- Sample rotation.

Sampling from Prodcom

The new PPI sample will be chosen from those companies selected for Prodcom. This will ensure that the most up-to-date information for products and sales will be available for the sample. The sampling units for the PPI sample are contributor product pairs, which are created by matching contributors to the products they produce. For instance if a Prodcom contributor made five products then five contributor-product-pairs would be created.

Optimal Allocation

To ensure that the PPI sample gives the best results possible within its limit of 9,000 price quotes a month an optimal allocation has been calculated using data from 1996 Prodcom.

The objectives in calculating the allocation of price quotes between six digits were:

- Minimising the sampling error of the all manufacturing index;
- A maximum of 9,000 price quotes in total;
- Providing the highest quality four digit indices possible;
- Each six digit index to have at least three contributor product pairs;
- Each four digit index to have at least five contributor product pairs;
- Broadly the same resources should be needed for monthly calculation of the PPI.

The allocation calculations were statistically complex. In very simple terms the allocation of price quotes for a stratum within a six digit was related to:

- The squared value of sales;
- The number of contributor product pairs; and
- The variance of the prices for the product.

The higher the relative value of any of these, then the higher the allocation. To minimise the sampling error for the overall index, each contributor provides only one price quote per product. The only exception to this is where the optimal allocation was greater than the number of contributor product pairs available from the Prodcom sample. In these instances contributors were asked to provide two or three price quotes for a product.

Effect of New Sample

Using the optimal allocation to select a sample from the contributors to the 1996 Prodcom survey showed two main effects on the sample. The first was that it increased the number of contributors from 3,700 to just under 7,000 but with the same total of 9,000 price quotes. As a consequence, more of the contributors were providing fewer price quotes. 70 per cent of the new sample provide just one price quote in total compared to 38 per cent of the present sample. The sample has also been re-balanced to better reflect current production.

The total number of price quotes for most products has remained fairly stable, but there are a few indices that have gained or lost a large number of price quotes. These include a large decrease in price quotes for navigation instruments and large gains for computers, motor vehicles and aircraft. Comparing the sample selected from 1996 Prodcom with the current panel showed that out of the present 9,000 price quotes from around 3,700 contributors, 2,000 price quotes were retained.

Phasing in the New Sample

The 7,000 new price quotes to be recruited to the PPI sample are too many to obtain in one exercise.

Recruitment of new price quotes will therefore be done in three 'waves', each comprising of a set of four digits:

- The first wave requires about 3,000 new price quotes to be recruited between June and December 1998. The new quotes will be run in parallel with the current sample from February 1999 for a few months during which time the PPI will be published using the current sample. Once the impact of the new sample has been assessed it will be linked into the PPI. The length of time the parallel run can be carried out may be limited by the resources available;
- The second wave of 1,000 new price quotes will be recruited between January and June 1999, and will be linked into the PPI indices after July 1999, depending on the results of the parallel run in the first wave. This wave will be selected from 1997 Prodcom;
- The third wave of 3,000 new price quotes will be recruited between June and December 1999, and will be linked into the PPI indices after February 2000, depending on the results of the parallel run in the first wave.

This wave will probably be selected from 1997 Prodcom, although there is a chance that 1998 Prodcom might be used if the timing of Prodcom results and PPI selection can be brought closer together. It is important to note that the updating of the sample will have no impact on back data.

Sample Rotation

The proposed method of rotation for the PPI is to select the sample afresh from each year's Prodcom sample. Contributors who have been dropped from the Prodcom sample will no longer be available for the PPI, but their replacements will be available. Selecting a new sample each year will retain a large proportion of the contributor product pairs in the PPI sample, but will allow rotation for the smaller contributors. It is proposed to introduce rotation for the PPI once the new sample has been fully introduced.

The main benefits of rotation for the PPI are that it will:

- Pick up new products and new contributors;
- Pick up existing companies making a product for the first time;
- Update company structures once a year only, and provide sales figures if structures have changed;
- Fill in gaps in the sample caused by contributors dropping out; and spread the burden of completing forms between smaller contributors.

PROCESSING AND DATA VALIDATION

Contributors return price movements by means of a preprinted form containing the most recent details provided to the ONS. These are sent to contributors at the beginning of each month. They return their latest prices, and may provide future prices if they know the position for the three months ahead. The form asks contributors to check if the specifications are still up-todate and representative and to amend accordingly. Forms for companies in Northern Ireland are despatched via the Department of Economic Development in Belfast.

Data Validation

There are two tests which staff use to check price movements on the home PPI with contributors:

- *Monthly Movements Outside the Range -2.5 to +5 per cent*: These are known as 'dubious' price movements and are only input after checking with the contributors. Any information given by the contributor is included on the computer system. For the more volatile export and import price indices wider gates of -7.5 to +7.5 per cent are used.

- *Monthly Movements Outside the Range -25 to +25 per cent*: These are known as 'incredible' price movements. These are also queried with contributors. Unlike 'dubious' price movements, these must be specifically confirmed on the computer system with an explanation—otherwise they will be rejected.

As well as these checks before returns are input, there are also the following checks at later stages. Indices which move by more than 5 per cent are highlighted in prints following the two monthly calculation runs. Reasons for such movements must be shown on the printouts and circulated to internal users of the data. 'Too stable' letters are sent to contributors whose prices are recorded as not having moved for a set period, currently around eighteen months.

Data Collection by Telephone

Telephone Data Entry (TDE) is a means by which contributors return prices by inputting prices via their telephones. This was pilot tested largely successfully with service sector prices and was extended to the main PPI during 1997 and 1998.

Imputation

The PPI computer programmes impute for non-response in the most recent few months.

The rules for the home PPI are:

- If response in the lowest level index is over 50 per cent, the computer imputes based on a simple average of the observed movements in the received returns within the relevant sub-category.
- If response in the class is under 50 per cent, the computer imputes based on the simple average of movements at division level.

Imputation for EPI and IPI are similar, though if response at the first stage is below 50 per cent, imputation is based on movements for EC exports, non-EC exports or total imports as appropriate.

Treasury Targets

Targets are agreed with HM Treasury for response rates and revisions to ONS's key economic statistics.

The PPI is subject to two Treasury targets:

- Response in the all manufacturing output index at the first time of publication should exceed 82 per cent, with response weighted according to sales, and
- The revision in the estimate of the year to year all manufacturing output price index should not exceed 0.125 per cent between time of first publication and the first 'firm' estimate published two months later.

Allowances for Quality Changes

Care must be taken when a the specification of an item changes to ensure that only the 'pure' price change is recorded as such for PPI purposes. As well as changes of good, specification changes take place for alterations in terms of terms or units of sale. There are three types of specification changes in the PPI system:

Revisions Policy

The policy is to show significant revisions, but to suppress minor changes to avoid unnecessary inconvenience to users of the PPI. Indices for the most recent two months are shown as provisional and can be changed as later data are received the following month. Indices published for the third month are made firm as long as response is 95 per cent or more. Indices are always made firm after five months. Once an index is made firm it is only changed if there is a revision of 0.2 or more. Only the most recent five months indices are recalculated normally but earlier data will be revised if the revision in the first stage index is over 1 per cent or 5 per cent. Higher level indices are only changed if the revision is 0.2 per cent or more.

Linking between Base Years

The general policy for linking PPIs between different base years is as follows:

- To link earlier data onto the present base year, users may either link onto the earliest month published on the present base year—which is January 1991 for the 1995=100 database, or follow the national accounts practice of linking on at January 1994.
- To link later data onto an earlier base year—link later data onto the latest month published as firm—say July 1998 for the 1990 = 100 database.

Confidentiality

Under the Statistics of Trade Act 1947, criminal sanctions are in place to prevent the unauthorised release of company data by ONS staff. Depending on the circumstances either the Office or individual members of staff would be liable for fines and/or imprisonment for unauthorised release. In addition, because of the confidentiality of the data, company price information is not released outside the division responsible, apart from direct line managers.

An index is only published if it is felt it would not disclose company information either to a member of the public or another company in the industry, though confidential indices can be used by other parts of the Government Statistical Service for national accounts purposes or for the calculation of other inflation measures as long as the publication of these other outputs is at a sufficiently aggregated level not to disclose the levels of these confidential indices.

Ad hoc Indices

ONS offers the facility to produce *ad hoc* indices to customers specification. For instance, an oil company may supply the weighting details of the various components that go into making an oil rig. For a fee, the ONS will calculate an index with monthly updates.

SUBJECT ANALYSIS

This review updates the 1986 *ARIST* chapter on subject analysis by SCHWARTZ and EISENMANN. The aim is a global approach. Thus, efforts were made to locate and include studies beyond those performed or published in the United States. Although the items reviewed come mainly from the period 1986-1988, earlier works not covered by the previous *ARIST* chapter have occasionally been included. Some much earlier items are referred to when necessary for purposes of comparison or context.

Subject analysis here means the presence, identification, and expression of subject matter in document texts, databases, controlled and natural languages, information requests, and search strategies. From the user's viewpoint, subject analysis is tightly bound to subject access. Therefore, the means by which information on a subject can be retrieved from various sources is also pertinent.

The literature reviewed is grouped into six broad categories:

- Indexing theory and practice;
- Controlled vocabularies;
- Search strategies and searching methods;
- Natural-language searching;
- Automatic indexing and related procedures; and
- The use of citation relationships in information retrieval.

Clearly these categories are not mutually exclusive, and some of the items reviewed could legitimately belong to more than one category.

INDEXING THEORY AND PRACTICE

General Discussions

Much has been written on various aspects of indexing over the years, but no really comprehensive book on the subject seems to have been produced, and those texts that do exist are now somewhat out of date. WEINBERG has compiled a volume of papers that, she claims, covers the 'state of our knowledge and the state of our ignorance' on the subject of indexing. Because her book is based solely on papers presented at a 1988 conference of the American Society of Indexers, the individual chapters vary in quality.

Topics covered include book indexing, automatic indexing, indexing software, database design, and the literature of indexing. Ironically, the outstanding chapter is about searching rather than indexing and is authored by SARACEVIC, who summarises the results of the comprehensive study described elsewhere in this review. He correctly points out that 'people who do research on searching rarely, if ever, cite literature on indexing research and *vice versa*. Yet there is an obvious connection, and perhaps more bridges need to be built between the research and practice of indexing and that of searching."

This observation coincides closely with one of the conclusions made by LANCASTER 20 years ago as a result of the evaluation of MEDLARS—namely, it is highly desirable that the indexers also be the searchers. Elsewhere, WEINBERG hypothesises that indexing fails the researcher because it deals only in a general way with what a document is 'about' and does not focus on what the document offers that is 'new' concerning a topic. She suggests that this distinction is reflected in the difference between 'aboutness' and 'aspect,' between 'topic' and 'comment,' or between 'theme' and 'rheme' but she fails to convince that these distinctions are really useful in the context of indexing or that it might be possible for indexers to maintain them.

A related study is the doctoral dissertation by CROWE, who discusses the feasibility of indexing the 'subjective viewpoint' of an author. She suggests that the indexer focus on the "problem situation' addressed by the author, including the questions addressed in the author's work. Aboutness is a slippery concept. The subject content of a document is sometimes referred to as intrinsic aboutness. What the document may be used for, why it was acquired, and other variable external' considerations are referred' to as extrinsic aboutness.

GORDON looks at indexing not in the context of aboutness as used by BEGHTOL and KHANZHIN but in relation to the interdependencies of the document descriptions, queries, and matching algorithms of the information retrieval system in use. He argues that a change in any of the three parts of the system mandates alterations in the other two if the system is to operate effectively. COCHRANE also reflects this holistic point of view. GRUNBERGER tested the assumptions that the frequency of a term on a page and the location of that term within a paragraph are good indicators that such a term would be selected in indexing. Neither of the hypotheses was supported.

AZUBUIKE and UMOH advocate maximum indexing, a concept that calls for exhaustively indexing a document using a variety of indexing strategies. While some would maintain that exhaustively indexing a document from both general and specific aspects leads to low precision in retrieval, the authors argue against this view. CHANG refers to the limitations associated with permuted title indexing and citation indexing and concludes that intellectual effort in indexing is still necessary. Based on the idea that knowledge is symbolic, VICKERY provides a review of methods whereby knowledge can be represented.

The review includes discussion of the use of symbols and symbol structures, semantics, and roles, categories, and relations present in subject statements. The arrangement and representation of knowledge as reflected in classification schemes and thesauri are also touched on. In addition, work in the area of 'semantic primitives' or 'semantic factoring' is reviewed and leads to a brief discussion of several means of representing knowledge for reasoning, including symbolic equations, frames, and semantic nets.

The review closes with a short description of a prototype reference and referral expert system developed by the author and his colleagues that uses many of the knowledge representation techniques reviewed. The continual problem of the interaction of the subjective and objective in the organisation and retrieval of information is addressed by

NEILL through a review of the works of Brenda Dervin and Karl Popper as well as other writers whose works were influenced by or amplify Dervin and/or Popper.

The effect of the subjective in classificati6h and in indexing is discussed along with its impact on information retrieval, leading to a description of an information system called Projekt INSTRAT, which utilises some of Popper's concepts. The review concludes that although subjective and objective viewpoints follow different paths, their final solutions are similar. BLAIR looks at indeterminacy in indexing — *i.e.,* the probability that a term the user chooses will be in the set of potential terms available to the indexer *and* in the set of terms used by the indexer.

Increasing the number of terms assigned to a document increases the chances of a hit, but success is not guaranteed. Blair suggests that the user should always identify a highly relevant document as a model for further searching. CROFT outlines some areas of research in artificial intelligence, such as the development of expert systems, that should be fruitful in solving the problems of indeterminacy in both indexing and term selection for retrieval. Expert systems are designed to assist the user in query formulation and selection of relevant documents.

Predominantly non-verbal fields of knowledge present special difficulties in indexing. Geographical and geological mapping are two primarily visual fields that are not served well by verbal systems. GRANDE explores the ideograph as a model for database design, indexing, and retrieval of geological information, while MARKEY discusses consistency aspects in the indexing of visual materials.

The requirements for indexing in videotex and related systems are addressed by YEATES, with special reference to the British Prestel system. Prestel's indexing approaches include: menu-controlled reference frames, alphabetical name and subject indexes, keyword indexes, gateway indexing to other systems, online and print indexes, user-controlled indexes, mnemonic page numbers, and Pagemarker—a 'bookmark' feature that allows users to tag specific pages for later rapid recall. ASRIBEKOV deals with the broad subject of textual compression in information systems. Conversion of primary text to alternative forms and to secondary representations are both covered.

Precoordinate Indexes

It is a curious anomaly that in an age in which the online searching of databases is commonplace, greater interest exists than ever before in the characteristics of precoordinate indexes in printed form. Moreover, literature on this subject continues to pour out. The reason, of course, is that computer processing provides an efficient means for generating multiple entries systematically from a single input supplied by an indexer. A book by CRAVEN gives a useful overview of the subject, although its value is reduced by the fact that some of the approaches included are not described clearly or illustrated with sufficient examples.

Elsewhere CRAVEN describes a coding scheme for expressing relationships among terms within a string used as input to index-generation programmes. He also examines the possibility of extending the concept of string indexing from index display to the provision of descriptor phrases for proximity searching. One of the most sophisticated approaches to precoordinate indexing was developed by Jason Farradane more than 30 years ago. Termed 'relational indexing,' the method involves the use of role indicators to express precise relationships among terms.

Farradane's work is described by BROOKES. SCHNELLING points out the limitations of alphabetical subject catalogues based on a controlled vocabulary of subject headings. He proposes a method combining standardised and free terms. For each broad area covered by a catalogue it is necessary to derive a 'pattern'—a set of categories into which the literature seems to fall naturally. These categories can then be adapted as standardised subject headings or subheadings.

However, within the general framework provided by this pattern, it will be necessary to index in more detail by the use of free terms. He illustrates the approach advocated by a discussion of indexing requirements in the field of literary scholarship in general and Shakespeare in particular. The somewhat grandiose title applied to this approach—'pattern indexing'—suggests something quite new.

In fact, the only thing claimed is that while a broad terminological structure can be pre-established for any field, the fine details of indexing will always require the use of free terms. While this is eminently sensible, it is hardly original. This fact is recognised by HARRIS, who refers to the process of indexing with a combination of controlled and uncontrolled terms as use of a 'part-controlled vocabulary.' He suggests that this technique is "probably widely used in various kinds of information service, but has not been formally recognised as a design option for librarians". The string indexing system that has generated the most literature, of course, is PRECIS and it continues to do so.

DYKSTRA contributes a primer on the subject. MAHAPATRA and BISWAS study the interrelationships of the role operators used in PRECIS indexing, and DYKSTRA suggests that PRECIS'S clear rules lend themselves to use in automatic indexing. Somewhat related to PRECIS is POPSI. BISWAS and SMITH describe a variation of POPSI that they refer to as a computerised deep structure indexing system. One of the oldest and most respected of the printed indexes is that produced by Chemical Abstracts Service (CAS). The indexing policies of CAS are discussed by ROWLETT, and the history of subject indexing at CAS is covered by ZAYE *ET AL.* On the international front, BIELICKA and SCIBOR review indexing trends in Poland and compare them with international trends. GHANI explores the potentialities and problems of using uniterm indexing in the Arabic language. Many of the problems outlined center around problems of standardisation in the language itself.

Quality of Indexing

It is difficult to look at the quality of indexing in isolation—*i.e.,* without evaluating some information retrieval 'system' in which the indexing is only one of several factors affecting overall performance. Indeed, more work may have been done on consistency of indexing than on quality. Recently, however, some interesting approaches to the evaluation of indexing have been introduced. WHITE and GRIFFITH use methods external to the indexing system being studied to establish a set of documents judged to be 'similar in content.'

Using sets of this kind as the basis for evaluation, they look at three characteristics of the index terms assigned to items in the set within a particular database:

- The extent to which terms link related items. The obvious measure of this is the number of terms that have been applied to all or most items in the set. The items can be considered closely linked if several subject terms apply to all of them.
- The extent to which terms discriminate among these sets within the database. The most obvious measure of this is the frequency with which terms that apply to most documents in the set occur in the database as a whole. Very common terms are not good discriminators. For example, in MEDLINE the term 'human' may apply to every item in a set but is of little value in separating this set from others since, it applies to so many items in the database. On the other hand, terms that occur rarely in the database will be useful in highly specific searches but of little use in identifying somewhat larger sets.
- The extent to which terms discriminate finely among individual documents. Rarity is an applicable measure here also. So is the exhaustivity of the indexing: a term may apply to all items in a set, but cannot discriminate among its members; the more additional terms that are assigned to each member, the more individual differences can be identified.

To look at quality in this way, one must first establish the test sets, retrieve records from a database for the members of each set, and study the characteristics of the terms assigned. White and Griffith used the technique to compare the indexing of their test sets in different databases: MEDLINE was compared with PsycINFO, BIOSIS Previews, and Excerpta Medica. A comparison of databases in this way is a check on the assumption that test-set items are in fact similar in content. White and Griffith used co-citation as the basis for establishing their test sets, although other methods, including bibliographic coupling, could be used.

The value of this work is limited by the fact that only very small clusters were used. Moreover, the validity of the method as a test of human indexing depends entirely on one's willingness to accept a co-citation cluster as being a legitimate standard. One could make a persuasive argument that it makes more sense to use expert indexers as a standard for judging the legitimacy of the co-citation cluster. WHITE and GRIFFITH claim that the method is useful to a database producer as a check on the quality of indexing, and they present examples of terms that should perhaps have been used by MEDLINE indexers or added to the controlled vocabulary.

However, such 'quality' checks can be done more simply. Sets of items defined by a particular term or terms can be retrieved from several databases and their indexing compared without the use of co-citation as a standard. In fact, this type of study has also been done by the same group of investigators. For 11 requests posed by specialists in the medical behavioural sciences, comparative searches were performed in MEDLINE, Excerpta Medica, PsycINFO, SciSearch, and Social SciSearch.

In the first three databases the searches were performed on:

- Controlled terms; and
- Natural language.

In the citation databases, searches were performed:

- Using the natural language of titles; and
- Using citations to known relevant items as entry points.

While the purpose of the investigation was to study the quality of MEDLINE indexing, little was discovered that could be posed as recommendations to the National Library of Medicine (NLM) on indexing practice, although some recommendations on indexing coverage could be made.

The most important findings of the study were that:

- The incorporation of natural-language approaches into search strategies resulted in significant improvements in recall compared with the use of controlled terms only;
- Citation retrieval should be considered an important adjunct to term-based retrieval because additional relevant items can be found using the citation approach; and
- No single database is likely to provide complete coverage of a complex multidisciplinary literature.

The work reported by White and Griffith and by McCain *et al.* forms part of a series of investigations done at the College of Information Studies, Drexel University, to evaluate various aspects of NLM's coverage and handling of the literature of the medical behavioural sciences. GRIFFITH *ET AL.* present an overview of all the studies, including the coverage of the databases, the quality of the indexing, and the results of searches in the medical behavioural sciences.

AJIFERUKE and CHU are critical of the 'discriminating index' for terms used by White and Griffith, which takes into account how many times a term is used within a database but not the size of the database. They propose a new measure that does. HRAŠOVA and JANÁKOVÁ conclude that consistency in keyword indexing is greatest when very few or very many keywords are chosen. This makes sense. It is relatively easy to agree on the two or three most important terms. Consistency will begin to decline after this but is likely to increase again when virtually all terms that could possibly be assigned to a document have been assigned.

One factor that might have some influence on the quality of indexing is the availability to the indexer of appropriate reference tools. BAKEWELL gives details on almost 200 books of possible value to indexers. To improve indexing and classification procedures, to make them more responsive to user needs, it is necessary to understand the bases on which people categorise or group documents in everyday life. KWASNIK, for example, is looking at the categories into which people sort their mail. She presents some preliminary results based on her observations of eight members of a university faculty.

The average number of terms assigned to a document in indexing tends to have a significant effect on the performance of a retrieval system. CLEVELAND and CLEVELAND studied the effect of indexing depth on retrieval performance for conventional Boolean searching methods and for the 'indirect method' of retrieval devised by GOFFMAN. They concluded that the latter, unlike the former, is relatively insensitive to indexing depth.

The indirect method involves the matching of a query against document clusters, which are established on the basis of term co-occurrence, the identification of the cluster that best matches the query, and the identification of the cluster member closest to the query. This document can then be used to locate other related items. CLEVELAND *ET AL.* also tested the hypothesis that when the indirect method is used for searching, indexing from full text is not essential to optimum retrieval. They conclude that optimum retrieval results can be achieved with less than full text when the indirect method is used.

CONTROLLED VOCABULARIES

General Discussions

The term 'index language devices,' which can be traced back more than 20 years, is somewhat misleading in that some of the 'devices' referred to are legitimate components of index languages while others, such as term weighting, are outside the index language *per se* and are more correctly referred to as 'indexing devices.' A detailed analysis of two important devices—weighting and relational indicators—is provided by KÖRNER. Role and relational indicators, various approaches to the linking of terms, facets, human and automatic weighting are all included in his review. KRISTALÑYI *et al.* suggest the use of the universal facets of time and space as a way to increase compatibility in various automated systems in the Soviet Union.

CHANDRASEKHARAN *et al.* apply graph-theoretic techniques to solve the 'minimum vocabulary problem' for a dictionary—*i.e.*, to identify the smallest set of words needed to define all the words in the dictionary. They claim that the minimum vocabulary principle can be applied to reduce the size of a controlled index language but fail to elaborate on this application. EASTMAN reports on a preliminary study of the extent to which overlap in postings occurs among hierarchically related terms in a controlled vocabulary, using data from MEDLINE and Medical Subject Headings, and she considers the implications of the overlap phenomenon for searches involving negations.

NELSON and TAGUE discuss the distribution of index terms over a collection of documents. They point out that a rank-frequency distribution well describes the distribution of terms of high frequency, while a frequency-size distribution provides a better picture of the distribution pattern for low frequency terms. They describe a 'split model,' using a rank function for the high frequency terms and a size function for the low frequency terms, the point of transition between the two being determined empirically or by rule.

On a more practical level, NELSON found that users of an online public access catalogue (OPAC) at the University of Western Ontario tend to employ terms that occur very frequently in the catalogue. The construction of controlled vocabularies involves the establishment of relationships among 'subjects.' JOHANSEN makes a distinction between relationships established on 'linguistic' and 'non-linguistic' levels and attempts to present a 'method of disclosing the structure of a subject by examining its constituent elements and their mutual relationships.'

SUOMINEN deals with the subject of syntactic relations in index languages. STIEG and ATKINSON compare indexing and indexing languages in the ERIC, LISA, and Library Literature databases as one aspect of a broader comparison of these three sources. Bibliographic classification schemes, lists of subject headings, and thesauri are all examples of index languages—*i.e.*, vocabularies that can be used to represent the subject matter of documents and of information needs. BIELICKA *et al.* and JABRZEMSKA and SCIBOR review the types of index languages in use in Poland, and STANCIKOVA presents a similar review for Czechoslovakia.

Information retrieval in the humanities is generally considered to be more difficult than it is in the sciences because the terminology used by humanists is less precise. WIBERLEY explores this situation by studying the entry terms used in leading encyclopaedias and dictionaries in the humanities. He concludes that although some of the terms are imprecise, most of them are quite precise and consist of names of individuals or of creative works; this finding suggests that subject access in the humanities may be less of a problem than previously supposed.

SANTAVICCA points out the crucial role that a knowledge of languages plays in the selection of terms for indexing, thesaurus control, cross-references, and access points. He suggests that the manipulation of text in international databases requires a kind of trilingualism: a knowledge of the user's native language, a knowledge of the foreign language in question, and a knowledge of the system's operating language. An inability to exploit any of these will result in diminished system performance. He concludes that the importance of studying foreign languages must be recognised if users are to be well served.

Classification Schemes

In a brief overview, ROMAN provides an introduction to classification, which is seen as the adaptation of prevalent philosophical views to library materials. She examines recent changes in thinking that have influenced current views of classification. BEGHTOL discusses classification in terms of the underlying justification of the system.

In the past, classification systems have been based on literary, scientific, philosophical, or educational warrant. She suggests that more investigations will occur in the future in the area of 'enquiry warrant' systems built as direct responses to user demands. While she seems to trace the idea back only to 1984, it was discussed as 'user warrant' by LANCASTER in 1972. In a comparison of five classification schemes for physics and chemistry, SNOER considers the impact of online catalogues on classification systems.

The schemes examined are the Library of Congress Classification system (LCC), the Dewey Decimal Classification system (DDC), the Universal Decimal Classification system (UDC), and the former and present systems of the University of Copenhagen. The author stresses the value of using UDC's Common Auxiliary for Place in existing call numbers to enhance retrieval. She concludes that radical revision of classification to suit the online environment is not necessary but that improvements can be made to existing schemes.

In a more global view than is often encountered, HOLLEY examines the impact of electronic technology on classification and subject cataloging and speculates on how this might affect third world countries. He fears that changes occurring in approaches to subject access and subject analysis in the developed countries will not take the needs of the third world into consideration. The International Federation of Library Associations (IFLA) is encouraged to provide a forum for the third world to cope with this situation.

The value to users of an index to a classification scheme is observed by NAKAMURA, who points out that even though such indexes are often rejected on the grounds of inflexibility, the very nature of such a fixed system is helpful for the user who is unfamiliar with a particular scheme. However helpful an index may be, it cannot fully compensate for the difficulty in using classification as a search tool. The author suggests a number of approaches to concept classification as possible remedies.

Since, its controversial entrance into American public libraries over a century ago, fiction has remained something of a stepchild in terms of access. BAKER, BAKER and SHEPHERD, and SHEPHERD and BAKER examine the application of classification to fiction in American public libraries. Their survey of the literature indicates that patrons find classification a useful tool in locating the types of books they want. Suggestions for further study are included. On the same topic, SAPP describes four classification schemes for fiction: LCC system, DDC system, Frank Haigh's fiction classification scheme of 1933 (HAIGH), and L. A. Burgess's scheme of 1936 (BURGESS). These are evaluated along with discussions of shelving schemes, subject headings, and topical access to fiction through standard print indexes.

Mention is also made of experiments by the Danish librarian Annelise Mark Pejtersen in online subject indexing for fiction. SAPP recognises the difficulties in classifying fiction and recommends further study to determine if the need for classification here justifies the effort. New systems, and modifications to older ones, are evolving in response to demands for more effective subject retrieval. LIU-LENGYEL describes the development of the Chinese Classification System over 2,000 years and notes the problems that lack of standardisation has caused in Chinese libraries. This may have been somewhat remedied by the adoption of the new Chinese Book Classification system as a standard in 1981.

SUKIASYAN examines trends in classification in the Soviet Union. Several projects have explored the value of classification schemes for retrieval in OPACs. Some researchers are looking at the LCC system and the DDC system for this purpose. Using OCLC MARC records as a research base, MARKEY and MARKEY and DEMEYER have tested the potential of the DDC system for retrieval. They demonstrate that, used in combination with Library of Congress Subject Headings (LCSH) and keywords in title, DDC can increase recall and retrieve relevant items not retrievable by any of the other fields on the record.

CHAN has examined theoretical issues related to whether or not the LCC can be used to enhance subject retrieval in an online catalogue, while WILLIAMSON is also working on a project to test the potential of using LCC for subject retrieval. HUESTIS reviews strategies for overcoming the major problems involved in the use of LCC in OPACs. KHOSH-KHUI has looked at the relationship between length of class numbers in LCC and DDC and subject specificity.

Although the length of number in both schemes does increase with specificity, it is not in itself a good indicator of specificity of subject headings assigned to items or of the number of headings assigned. GOPINATH discusses the use of classification schemes and thesauri in a symbiotic relationship that can improve information retrieval. The concept of a 'thesaurofacet' or 'classaurus'—a device that incorporates features of a faceted hierarchical scheme with those of a thesaurus—is a practical application of this symbiotic relationship.

AITCHISON looks at two thesauri that have used the H. E. Bliss classification as a source for construction and considers the merits of using the second edition of Bliss for this purpose. O'NEILL *et al.* look at the problems involved in mapping from one classification scheme to another, with particular reference to the LCC and the DDC systems. They introduce the notion of 'class dispersion' as a measure of the ease with which a class in one scheme can be mapped to another scheme. DUNAYEV and POLYAKOV describe the problems involved in deriving a mathematical description of classification schemes.

Subject Headings

The emergence of OPACs has also caused a revival of interest in subject headings, as they are traditionally used in libraries, and the limitations of these vocabularies for effective subject access in the online environment. WYKOFF provides a brief overview of the history of the use of subject headings in online access. MASSICOTTE describes how displays of subject headings in OPACs can be made more browsable, while MARKEY discusses the integration of Library of Congress Subject Headings (LCSH) in machine-readable form into online catalogues. Over the years LCSH has been the subject of much criticism.

COCHRANE groups the criticisms into four categories of needs:

- The need to improve the form of headings and to add more scope notes;
- The need to improve the cross-reference structure;

- The need to improve subdivision access; and
- The need to improve the syndetic structure of the system by use of classification.

She examines suggestions for improvements and discusses how these fit into the online environment. In an article that begins by reiterating the criticisms of Anglo/Western bias in LCSH and the inability of the Library of Congress (LC) to keep the vocabulary up to date, HENIGE presents a further concern that headings are not being changed to reflect current scholarly consensus. To be effective in reference work, he says that headings must be accurate and in step with current scholarly thought. LC, however, has always taken the position that LCSH should reflect the content of published literature rather than the cutting edge of scholarly research.

DYKSTRA points out that the 11th edition of LCSH adopts the very precisely defined terminology of thesaurus construction, but she argues that its use of 'broader term,' 'narrower term,' and 'related term' is misleading because LCSH does not maintain the precise logical relationships implied by these terms in a carefully constructed thesaurus. LCSH can only be considered as a list of accepted subject terms used in LC; it is not a true thesaurus. It has always been difficult to determine the policies and practices that LC adopts *vis- à-vis* LCSH.

With the exception of Haykin's guide published in 1951, there has been very little explanation available. The revised edition of LC's *Subject Headings Manual* and the second edition of *Library of Congress Subject Headings: Principles and Application* provide two excellent sources to guide the librarian in using the subject headings for items in a collection. Knowing how headings are interpreted and used by LC will help promote consistency among libraries in their application. FROST and DEDE have studied the compatibility between LCSH and the use of subject headings by one large research library.

Methods by which a controlled vocabulary is updated are another matter of general interest. A study by BACKUS *et al.* tested two hypotheses concerning the annual revision of the National Library of Medicine's (NLM) MeSH vocabulary. It was hypothesised that new terms are added to the vocabulary when their broader terms have increased in number of postings and that the distribution of terms in the hierarchical 'trees' of the vocabulary would reflect the distribution of terms in search requests made to the system.

Neither hypothesis was supported. MCCARTHY discusses the extent to which consistency occurs in the assignment of headings in order to bring like works together. She concludes that consistency is not as high as it should be and proposes an increase in the number both of headings assigned to an item, as well as cross-references, as possible remedies. She also recommends that cataloguers examine the literature on the subject in question to see what headings have been applied in the past. She believes that the use of online catalogues increases the importance of consistency in assigning subject headings and also simplifies its achievement.

MILLER presents a very brief outline of the application of automation to the production of LCSH and points out the advantages and disadvantages of the program. Many libraries have made it a standard policy to review and revise the subject headings assigned to catalogue records by member libraries of OCLC, Inc. SALAS-TULL and HALVERSON evaluate this practice in light of the time and expense involved in comparison with the number of changes libraries actually make to the OCLC records.

They examined revisions made by research, academic, and public libraries and found that there was little difference in the number of revisions among the three types of libraries and that the total number of revisions was lower than expected. They conclude with several suggestions for cataloging departments that use subject heading review policies. Since, the 1940s there has been interest in a uniform code for subject headings. With the general adoption of the *Anglo-American Cataloguing Rules,* 2nd edition *(AACR2),* interest in a similarly uniform guide for subject access has been renewed.

STUDWELL and ROLLAND-THOMAS suggest a form for such a code and urge an international effort to develop a standard code. In the same spirit, STREBI offers examples of revision and retrospective conversion of subject headings performed by the Austrian National Library as models for other libraries to consider. The use and effectiveness of subject headings for biomedical materials have also been the subject of recent research.

MASARIE and MILLER compare terms used by health professionals with the standardised vocabulary found in MeSH. Fifty hospital charts were randomly selected and subjected to a computer analysis that matched terms with two MeSH-based vocabularies; the first consisted of MeSH terms, and the second consisted of MeSH terms plus cross-references. Approximately 50 per cent of the words used in the charts matched the MeSH-related vocabularies, with about 40 per cent of these proving to be exact MeSH terms or entry terms. Also working with MeSH, RADA *et al.* evaluated entry terms and tested a method for producing new entry terms.

Documents indexed by MeSH terms were compared with documents indexed automatically to see if the automatic indexer could map from title words to controlled terms through the use of entry terms better than it could without using entry terms. Some entry terms were found to be ambiguous. In a method for producing new entry terms, the authors present an algorithm to map terms from the *Systematised Nomenclature of Medicine* to MeSH. While the new *SNOMED* terms were not helpful in indexing, they did suggest how MeSH might be improved. A new algorithm was formulated to join the two sets of terms, and the combined *SNOMED*/MeSH vocabulary was judged to permit improved indexing over the MeSH terms alone.

Thesauri

WEINBERG and CUNNINGHAM provide a brief comparison of online thesauri with print versions. The interfaces for a number of different vendor systems are evaluated, and the article includes recommendations for improving online thesauri. CHAN and POLLARD provide an annotated directory of thesauri used in online databases. The linking and evaluation of thesauri are necessary tasks in improving retrieval systems. RADA presents a number of considerations in connecting and evaluating thesauri. Experimental linkings of MeSH with the *SNOMED,* CMIT (Current Medical Information and Terminology), and PDQ thesauri are discussed.

In these experiments, similarities are identified and differences are exploited to generate better thesauri. MILI and RADA also report on efforts to merge thesauri to create more powerful vocabularies, and MANDEL reviews the problems involved in integrating thesauri and other forms of controlled vocabulary within an online bibliographic network. SCHONDORF presents a study utilising the Thesaurus Database developed by the Gesellschaft fur Information und Dokumentation in Frankfurt, which examines unconventional relationships among thesaurus terms.

The study presents examples of how these relationships provide orientation support within the thesaurus's vocabulary for indexing and retrieval. ROSTEK and FISCHER describe the computer 'modelling' of a thesaurus within a frame system with a graphical interface. BELLAMY and BICKHAM deal with the development of a thesaurus for the subject cataloging of books in a special library in biomedicine.

SEARCH STRATEGIES AND SEARCHING METHODS

General Discussions

An enormous study of factors affecting the performance of online searches was undertaken over a period of several years at the now defunct Matthew A. Baxter School of Library and Information Science at Case Western Reserve University. The methodology and results for the final phase of this project are presented by SARACEVIC *et al.* The study involved 40 users, each providing one question, and 39 searchers. Interviews with the users were tape recorded. For each question, nine searches were performed, four by project staff and five by outside searchers, for a total of 360 different searches.

A related experiment was also undertaken, involving the classification of user questions by 21 judges. The results of the searches were evaluated by the users in terms of relevance and utility. The bewildering variety of data collected during the project makes effective summarisation virtually impossible. Perhaps the most significant finding was that different searchers were likely to have quite different interpretations of a question and, thus, used different search approaches and retrieved different items.

Moreover, each searcher tended to find some relevant items not found by the others, although the chance that an item would be judged relevant increased with the number of searchers retrieving it. The investigators suggest that these results argue the need for multiple searches for the same question by different searchers, but an alternative conclusion might be that a team approach to the analysis of a question and a consensus approach to an initial search strategy might be the preferred mode of operation.

Earlier FIDEL had also discovered that experienced searchers show little agreement in the selection of terms, and even earlier studies consistently revealed that users of card catalogues also tend not to agree much on what terms to use in searching for items on a particular topic. HARTER looks at problem-solving attitudes and abilities of searchers as factors affecting search success. FAIRHALL categorises the various skills associated with searching performance, while SCHIFFMANN reminds us of the value of 'hedges' in the handling of repeated search requests.

VIGIL contributes a major monograph on the searching of online databases, including psychological factors in searching. Over the past 25 years a number of attempts have been made to measure unobtrusively the quality of reference services offered by libraries. Such studies have focussed on the ability of libraries to answer factual questions. MCCUE has now pioneered the unobtrusive evaluation of online searching in libraries.

Twenty-one public libraries throughout the United States were each asked to perform the same search in two different databases; the searchers did not know that they were being tested. Two 'outside expert database searchers' evaluated the results. Using a point system, each search was scored on strategy, general techniques, and results. General techniques covered such aspects as searcher mistakes in entering terms or use of incorrect procedures. Results were also given numerical scores; a worthless citation earned no points, an excellent one earned.

The library scores ranged from 419 to 155. McCue concludes from her statistical analysis that the only variable that correlated positively with high search scores was the number of items retrieved. This is hardly surprising. In effect the scoring method takes recall into account since, it gives positive scores to 'useful' items but not precision. The entire method of scoring, however, is of dubious quality. In the long run it is the results that matter, so it seems pointless to devise a scoring method that takes not only results but search strategy and search technique as well into account.

HANSEN compares the results of a group of inexperienced subjects who performed manual searches followed by online searches with the results achieved by a matched group of subjects who performed online searches followed by manual ones. The differences in the results were not statistically significant. Nevertheless, she concludes that inexperienced searchers may get the best results when performing a manual search after an online search, at least in the case of 'a large and complex topic with an expanding literature," a conclusion that receives very weak support from her data.

In a doctoral dissertation, DALRYMPLE compares the searching of card catalogues with the searching of online catalogues, looking at the activity as essentially a problem-solving task. Within her experimental setting, users found more relevant items and were more satisfied with their results from the card catalogue. Users spent more time and reformulated their strategies more often when using the online catalogue. The search patterns of users of the CATLINE database of NLM are analysed by TOLLE and HAH and compared with the search patterns of MEDLINE users.

FIDEL discusses how analysis of the search behaviour of human intermediaries can be used to identify rules by which such experts select 'search keys'—descriptors from a controlled vocabulary or free-text terms. She claims that when more research has been performed on expert search behaviour, it should be possible to build a knowledge base for use in an intermediary expert system for online searching. By observing 47 searchers in action, FIDEL concludes that free-text terms and descriptors are selected with about the same frequency.

However, those who prefer the free-text approach and avoid controlled vocabularies are more likely to be searchers on science topics who search several databases for each request. The evaluation of the results of a search involves some criterion for judging the relevance of retrieved items. EISENBERG and SCHAMBER review various approaches to the definition of 'relevance' used by earlier writers and propose a 'user-centric-cognitive model' that views the user as the 'central and active determinant of the dimensions of relevance.'

In a related paper, HALPERN and NILAN discuss the subject of relevance in terms of 'source evaluation,' the weight that a person places on a source of information beyond its substantive content—authority or expertise represented, uniqueness, and so on. After using judges to rate documents on both relevance and utility, REGAZZI claims that no operational difference exists between relevance-theoretic and utility-theoretic models of evaluation.

WAGNER examines the cause of 'false drops' in online searching. They are less prevalent in searches that use only controlled vocabulary terms, but in any case they account for only a small percentage of errors, and that retrieval error is, to some degree, unavoidable, especially in searches seeking high recall. The author stresses awareness of the causes of false drops and advises that the professional be able to explain their occurrence to the user.

BLACKSHAW and FISCHHOFF view online searching as a decision-making process. Volunteer searchers were observed while performing author, title, or subject searches in an online catalogue in a public library. The authors report that searcher performance resembles that revealed in studies of decision making in other contexts.

BELLARDO looked at variables that might affect the performance of online searchers, using two test searches with students from six different library schools. Findings suggest that differences in performance can be attributed to general verbal and quantitative aptitude, artistic creativity, and an inclination towards critical and analytical creative thinking, but the associations are all very weak. High intelligence and other factors often cited as important attributes may not be *necessary* for high performance.

Bellardo claims that searching performance may not be predictable on the basis of cognitive and personality traits. End-user searching has become increasingly common with the growth of home computers, favourable searching rates for the home user and, most particularly, the emergence of more and more databases on CD-ROM. OJALA looks at who end users are, where they are, and why they are searching and makes some projections for the future. SEWELL and TEITELBAUM report the results of investigations of end-user searching of NLM databases over 11 years through transaction logs, interviews, and questionnaires.

SULLIVAN *et al.* compared end-user searching with delegated searching and discovered that the end users were no less satisfied with their results, retrieved fewer items, and achieved a high precision. All aspects of end-user searching are reviewed in a compilation by KESSELMAN and WATSTEIN. End-user searching, in some environments at least, may require a user-friendly interface to make the search process as simple as possible.

POLLITT describes one approach, based on use of a menu, that has been developed at NLM. Called Men USE, it is an improved version of an earlier prototype, CANSEARCH. Pollitt claims that it "provides inexpensive, high-quality, subject-specific browsing and searching of the MEDLINE database for users who have no training or experience in information retrieval". The interface described by BATES is intended to help users develop their own search strategies rather than to be an automatic 'transparent' aid to the user.

WILLIAMS discusses the wider issues involved in the design of transparent systems and describes a number of approaches, which she categorises as gateways, front ends, intermediaries, and interfaces. However, her article is tangential to this chapter because it deals more with interface technology than with interface content. INGWERSEN emphasises the importance of browsing facilities in solving search problems.

Information retrieval studies have increasingly taken the viewpoint that computer-human interfaces can be better designed if they are based on the concept of an adaptive, cognitive model. A review of cognitive models in information retrieval by DANIELS examines recent literature in this area, mainly from the standpoint of the user. A number of natural-language and controlled-vocabulary information retrieval systems that use cognitive models are discussed. The review concludes that cognitive models in the various systems work reasonably well because they function in constrained environments.

Suggestions for further incorporation of cognitive models in future systems designs are offered. VECCIA describes nine online systems that can be used to search the *Washington Post.* She compares the various types of searches the systems permit and notes items excluded from indexing. The downloading of bibliographic records from online searches has become increasingly common. LARGE discusses the subject, including downloading from CD-ROM databases, and looks at the reuse of downloaded records in local databases. JAMESON treats downloading and uploading in greater detail, including legal aspects.

Searching in Online Library Catalogues

Traditionally library catalogues have provided somewhat limited capabilities for searching by subject. The replacement of the card catalogue by online public access catalogues has brought about a great resurgence of interest throughout the library profession in all aspects of subject access. For one thing, it has been found that the proportion of catalogue searches that are subject searches has tended to increase considerably as OPACs fall into place. LIPETZ and PAULSON confirm this trend in a 'before and after' study at the New York State Library.

FROST studied catalogue users at the University of Houston and concluded that students search more often by subject than do faculty. However, on the basis of a study at the City University prior to the automating of their catalogue, HANCOCK suggests that subject searching of manual catalogues may have been more prevalent than previously thought. KASKE has found great variability in the proportion of OPAC searches that are subject searches—by hour of day, day of week, and week of semester. In discussions of online catalogue development in libraries two approaches are particularly evident.

One is to improve the interface between user and system, and the other is to enhance or augment the system itself. An analysis of online subject searches led one group of librarians and information specialists to conclude that an online catalogue must compensate for a user's inability to match his or her subject headings exactly with those of LCSH, must provide more than one searching option, and should permit users to refine large retrieval sets. HILDRETH also argues for a more interactive interface between the user and the system.

One essential feature is to provide the user with information concerning the status of the search as it progresses. The Subject Access Project performed at Syracuse University in the late 1970s determined that augmenting subject headings of traditional bibliographic records with terms from tables of contents and back-of-the-book indexes may be an efficient and relatively inexpensive way to improve subject access in the catalogue. BYRNE and MICCO describe a study in which an average of 21 multiword terms, drawn from indexes or tables of contents, were added to MARC records for 6,000 books.

Results of their studies indicate that searches of these augmented records achieved much improved recall compared with searches on titles or subject headings. DIODATO considers the same issue from a slightly different point of view when he studies readers' descriptions of books to determine if the descriptions match terms from the tables of contents and indexes. He concludes that tables of contents and indexes are two sources of terms that are likely to reflect terms that the user would use in searching for the books.

JAMIESON *et al.* have compared the searching of uncontrolled keywords occurring in bibliographic records with the searching of controlled terms in the records. In recognition of the millions of bibliographic records presently in MARC format in libraries and information centers, CHITTY argues that the issue is not how to improve the information on the record but how best to use the information already present. In actuality, the approaches to improving online catalogues are not a choice between whether the content is enhanced or the interface is improved. The content, the system/user interface, and the user are all integral parts of the system.

DWYER points out that many developments in the bibliographic organisation of libraries over the years have resulted in split files; he proposes that a total retrospective conversion be implemented as one means towards building better catalogues. Quality cataloging is a necessity because the accuracy of a system's content ultimately determines the success of retrieval. Because any transition to an online catalogue involves choices and trade-offs, Dwyer stresses the importance of understanding the true costs involved and of understanding the users' requirements in order to make intelligent choices in questions of design.

LAWRY raises the question, 'Can online catalogues be too easy'? The question indicates a concern that a system that appears to 'think' for the user, by assisting the user in query formulation, search strategy selection, and evaluation of retrieved titles, is unintentionally misleading the user. Lawry stresses the importance of user education to make effective use of all the tools available in the library.

BATES presents a model of subject access in online catalogues based on three design principles:

- Uncertainty;
- Variety; and
- Complexity.

Bates argues that because indexing is characterised by variety, searching should no longer be based on the exact matching of terms but, instead, should help the searcher by displaying and 'making it easier to explore' a variety of terms. Two tools proposed for improving search performance are an end-user thesaurus and a 'front-end system mind'; the former is basically a vast entry vocabulary, and the latter is a semantic network, incorporating the entry terms, that allows a searcher to select from a variety of methods for generating semantic associations.

The design approach proposed is intended to be implemented in existing catalogues based on LCSH without the need for any reindexing. Bates seems optimistic about the future of subject access in online catalogues. Not so BORGMAN, her colleague at UCLA. Based on studies of user behaviour in subject searching—whether in library catalogues or in broader bibliographic databases—she concludes that "we do not yet have sufficient knowledge of user behaviour to make improvements in system design".

Using the OKAPI (Online Keyword Access to Public Information) system, WALKER and WALKER and JONES investigated possible methods for improving subject searches. Automatic word stemming, synonym and cross-reference tables, and techniques for the approximate matching of words were all studied. They concluded that weak stemming is beneficial but that strong stemming is of doubtful utility, that semiautomatic spelling correction should be used in online catalogues, and that cross-reference lists to allow automatic cross-referencing should be compiled using input from cooperating libraries.

The cross-reference lists investigated were extremely simple, incorporating abbreviations, noun-adjective pairs, alternative terminology, alternative spellings, irregular plurals, related terms, numbers, and phrases. The phrases category is a little different from the others in that it consists of word combinations that should not be split up by searching algorithms because the meaning of the individual words is quite different from that of their combination.

A much more comprehensive study was the doctoral research project of LESTER. Her objective was to determine what features would be needed in online catalogues to increase the success of users in matching their search terms with LCSH. Random samples of user subject terms, selected from the transaction logs associated with the NOTIS/LUIS online catalogue at Northwestern University were compared with LCSH. For user terms that failed to match the headings, 22 different strategies for achieving a match were investigated.

Strategies that did *not* improve matching significantly were: use of a spelling checker, singular/plural conflation, phonetic spelling, exact matching in either subject or personal name authority files, and any process involving geographic name authority files. The strategies of right truncation, string searching with adjacency, and searching of keywords with Boolean operators significantly improved the matching whether or not the database were augmented by the inclusion of subject and name authority files and/or the ability to search all fields of a bibliographic record. It is interesting to compare Lester's finding on authority files—that they would have little effect on subject retrieval—with the finding of VAN PULIS and LUDY—that subject authority files are little used even when made available online.

MICCO *et al.* report on a project at Chatham College to develop an expert system capable of searching for and providing access to knowledge at the same level as a skilled reference librarian. The project proposes a system that will develop a user profile and diagnose information need, then connect the user to the information through a network interface that will include the use of CD-ROM technologies. The system is envisioned as using a Macintosh-style interface with windows and a mouse. It would have a three-tiered structure: the first level providing access tools, the second providing access to monographs, and the third providing access to periodicals.

As currently projected, the system will use the same types of heuristics employed by expert human searchers rather than the textual keyword searching approach frequently used in computer-based systems. Several projects that have dealt with the use of classification schemes in OPACs were reviewed in the earlier section on classification schemes.

Information Requests

The effectiveness of a delegated search, of course, very much depends on how well a request made by a user actually reflects the user's information need. Much work has been done on user-intermediary interaction in information retrieval. AUSTER and LAWTON look at various characteristics of the pre-search interview as factors affecting the success of a search. ALLEN claims that the way users understand and express their needs will be affected by the cognitive structures by which they have organised their knowledge of the topic and by the schemata introduced in the questions that intermediaries ask. Differences in personal schemata may mean that the same problem could result in completely different questions as filtered through the minds of different individuals.

One major problem in user-intermediary interaction is that the personal schemata of the user and that of the information specialist may be quite far apart. Moreover, various 'external schemata' may also exert strong influence on the interactions between user and intermediary. Somewhat related to Allen's work is that of DERR, who identifies five types of expressions used by individuals in making demands on information services; he discusses the implications of the differences for practices in information retrieval. PETRUS points out that the imperfect nature of requests makes information retrieval an operation based on probability. The retrieval situation can be described by the theory of statistical solutions.

NATURAL-LANGUAGE SEARCHING

The searching of text by computer can be traced back to the late 1950s, but interest has continued to increase as more and more text becomes accessible online. Based on studies performed with the full text of popular magazines, TENOPIR presents a useful but brief discussion of the relative effectiveness of various types of strategies for full-text searching. COVE and WALSH look at the feasibility of a browsing approach to searching text online. They describe a system that will display text extracts to prompt the user to select words. These can then lead to 'associated words'—*i.e.*, words occurring as the 'nearest neighbours' of the words originally selected—which can generate further displays of text, from which additional 'browse words' can be selected, and so on.

The type of text that is generally accessible online consists of relatively brief items such as journal articles, abstracts, or patents. Because of rapidly declining costs, it is now becoming increasingly feasible to store and exploit the text of much longer items, but how useful would it be to be able to search the complete text of, say, monographs? Based on studies of how library patrons use non-fiction books, PRABHA and RICE conclude that systems that permit the searching of the full text of non-fiction books would be of value to the users of at least the academic libraries. Over the years a number of studies have compared the results of searches in humanly indexed bibliographic databases with results of searches in full-text databases.

The common finding is that full-text databases give greater recall but reduced precision. SIEVERT *et al.* confirm this by comparing results achieved in searching MEDLINE with those achieved through searching two full-text databases in medicine; RO comes to the same conclusion in a different environment.

Unfortunately, this type of result is frequently misinterpreted. The fact that a full-text database gives better recall than a database of humanly indexed bibliographic records has nothing to do with the properties of text *per se*; it is simply due to the fact that text records tend to be longer and thus provide more access points.

A database of records indexed with an average of, say, 50 descriptors may well give better recall than a database of brief abstracts, but one could change these results dramatically by greatly increasing the length of the abstracts or drastically reducing the number of descriptors assigned. It is the length of the record that is the major determinant of what is and is not retrieved, but this fact is sometimes overlooked.

AUSTIN examines some of the implications of natural-language searching, illustrating cases in which natural-language searches have failed. These failures are analysed for possible solutions, leading the author to conclude that computers exacerbate rather than alleviate the need for vocabulary control. HOOD reaches a similar conclusion. Full-text searching tends to uncover details, whereas controlled-vocabulary searching tends to uncover broad concepts. He concludes that a comprehensive search would require more than one method.

Investigators at Syracuse University have undertaken several related studies on what is assumed to be one of the problems of text searching—the implicit reference to topics through anaphora. For example, AIDS can be variously represented by 'the disease,' 'it,' and so on, in a text. In one study the anaphors occurring in abstracts were replaced by their referents. It was then determined what effect this replacement would have on term weighting, based on word frequency counts, and subsequently on retrieval.

The results were inconclusive: in some searches the replacement improved the ranking of documents in search outputs, while in others it actually caused a deterioration of the ranking. It was hypothesised that this anomaly might be caused by the fact that anaphors sometimes refer to topics that are integral to a text, while at other times they refer to topics that are peripheral. This hypothesis was tested. Using abstracts from the PsycINFO database, words or phrases serving as anaphors were judged as being integral in 52 per cent of the cases studied; the comparable value for abstracts from the INSPEC database was 68 per cent.

The authors concluded that the resolution of anaphora may indeed be important if the effectiveness of text searching is to be improved. This is an example of a conclusion that is based on the processing of abstracts but that may not apply to the full-text situation. Presumably, the redundancy of full text will create a situation wherein the frequency with which a topic occurs *explicitly* will generally reflect its importance in the text regardless of how many implicit references may be missed. DOSZKOCS gives a useful general overview of natural-language processing in information retrieval.

The relative merits of natural-language *vs.* controlled-vocabulary approaches to information retrieval are still debated. DUBOIS compares the two approaches, and SVENONIUS looks at the history of the issue and suggests areas for research that "would clarify it in such a way as to contribute to a rational basis for the design of retrieval tools such as thesauri".

BAER and JOHNSON, considering in particular the OP AC situation, conclude that vocabulary control is even more important in the online environment than it is in manual systems. As full-text databases become the norm, there looms a danger that the mere presence of the complete text may be viewed as a labour-saving substitute for subject indexing.

YANCEY points out that the growth of information through full-text services will place even more importance on relevance and warns of the loss of retrieval capability through lack of subject indexing. A combination of full-text and subject-searching techniques to link past and present knowledge is presented as the preferable alternative. TEUFEL describes an approach to text retrieval that he refers to as '*n*-gram indexing.' The texts of abstracts are reduced to significant words through use of a stop list, then reduced further to word stems.

The stems are converted into trigrams; 'high noise' trigrams are replaced by tetragrams or even pentagrams. Natural-language queries are processed in the same way. Retrieval consists of looking for the best matches between *n*-gram representations of documents and of requests. Teufel presents some results of tests using abstracts from the INSPEC database. Problems in the portability of natural-language queries from one database to another are addressed by DAMERAU.

AUTOMATIC INDEXING AND RELATED ACTIVITIES

For more than 30 years investigators have sought ways to replace human intellectual processing by computer processing of text. Methods investigated include automatic indexing by extraction or assignment, automatic extracting, the automatic organisation of terms or documents into classes, automatic approaches to thesaurus construction or the development of networks of semantic relations among terms, and methods for matching natural-language requests against the text of documents or their indexed representations. SGALL and VRBOVA have described work in automatic indexing, automatic extracting, machine translation, and related aspects of text processing under way at Charles University in Prague.

VON KEITZ presents a brief overview of the three types of automatic indexing currently available:

- Inverted-file full-text indexing;
- Dictionary-based indexing; and
- Dictionary/rule-based indexing.

The author asks what roles in automatic indexing should be played by humans and what roles should be played by machines. Although only full-text indexing is fully automatic and is the most frequently encountered, the dictionary and dictionary/rule systems provide higher precision; thus, better dictionaries and rules will yield better indexing. The author concludes that the human role should be one of continuing to develop better dictionaries and rules.

SUZUKI and TOCHINAI compare the keyword density method with a 'mean order' method for extracting sentences in automatic abstracting, and DAS-GUPTA compares the Two-Poisson model of automatic indexing with inverse document frequency and discrimination value models. While the automatic extraction of 'significant' words, phrases, or sentences from documents, based on frequency and/or positional criteria, has been successful for many years, automatic assignment indexing, involving even very small controlled vocabularies, has met with much less success.

However, natural-language processing has progressed to the point at which assignment indexing by computer should now be possible. At least, machine-aided assignment indexing should be practicable. VLEDUTS-STOKOLOV, for example, describes experiments performed at BIOSIS in which terms from a limited vocabulary of 600 biological concept headings are assigned automatically to journal articles. The assignment is achieved by matching article titles against a semantic vocabulary containing about 15,000 biological terms, which, in turn, are mapped to the concept headings.

The automatic aid to indexing developed at BIOSIS is described in detail, and the disambiguation techniques used are illustrated. While, overassignment and underassignment of terms still occur, automatic assignment indexing has certainly made some progress since, the 1960s. Machine-aided assignment indexing is also in place at the National Aeronautics and Space Administration (NASA). This work is described by BUCHAN but in insufficient detail. As might be expected, considerable interest now exists in the possibility of devising 'expert systems' to aid the indexing process. One example is the MedlndEx System being developed at NLM.

Referred to as a 'prototype interactive knowledge-based system,' it uses an experimental frame language and is designed to interact with trained MEDLINE indexers by prompting them to enter MeSH terms as 'slot fillers' in completing document-specific indexing frames derived from the knowledge-base frames. MARTINEZ *et al2.* describe another rule-based system. The American Petroleum Institute's (API) Central Abstracting and Indexing Service (CAIS) incorporates a rule-based, expert system founded on the API Thesaurus, which has been in operation since, 1985.

Terms automatically generated by the system and by API's human indexers are reviewed by a human editor, and the edited terms are added to print indexes and the online index. At present the base contains about 14,000 text rules. SALTON presents suggestions for the automatic indexing of monographs. The method proposed performs a syntactic analysis of the text, selects nominal constructs, weights the terms, and selects terms to act as index terms. Approaches to the machine-aided indexing of patents are discussed by SCHRAMM and BIELA.

ALADESULU studies methods of improving automatic indexing operations to make them more closely approach the intellectual level of human indexing. The approach used involves the recognition of phrases that are semantically equivalent but syntactically different. DYKSTRA observes that the clear rules of the PRECIS system lend themselves to the process of content analysis and automatic indexing. CONGREVE describes a project designed to evaluate the automatic production of PRECIS-based indexes. Among other methods used for automatic indexing are user manipulation of index commands imbedded in the document and system manipulation of keywords in and out of context.

LAMEIN examines the advantages and disadvantages of keyword-out-of-title indexing and describes its use in the law library of the Free University of Amsterdam. The processing of the text of a request against the text of a document collection can be considered as essentially a pattern-matching operation. The objective is to retrieve items in a ranked order, with those that best match the request at the top of the ranking. One way of achieving such a ranking is by weighting the search terms by the frequency with which they are associated with items already known to be relevant, their rate of occurrence in the database as a whole, or other statistical properties.

ROBERTSON describes one weighting formula that he considers an improvement over those previously used. SALTON and BUCKLEY summarise findings of research on automatic term weighting and present models for comparison with more complex techniques of content analysis. CHOROS and DANILOWICZ describe an approach to 'relative indexing,' in which the weights assigned to descriptors associated with documents are modified on the basis of user relevance feedback.

BUELL discusses problems associated with the fuzzy-set approach to weighted retrieval. The calculation of term discrimination values is discussed by WILLETT, EL-

HAMDOUCHI and WILLETT, and CROUCH, while BARTSCHI presents a general mathematical framework for looking at retrieval approaches involving term weighting and the ranking of output, and MURTAGH describes hierarchic clustering methods applicable to information retrieval. CAN and OZKARAHAN also deal with term discrimination values. They introduce a 'cover coefficient' and describe how this can be used in computing the discrimination value for a term.

FAGAN compares two methods for automatically extracting phrases from texts to serve as content indicators. Non-syntactic methods are based on simple text characteristics, such as word frequency and word proximity, while syntactic methods selectively extract phrases from parse trees generated by an automatic syntactic analyser. Retrieval tests were inconsistent but tended to indicate that the non-syntactic methods produced better results. Nevertheless, Fagan suggests that the syntactic approach does have certain advantages and has a greater potential for improvement than does the non-syntactic method. The ranking of documents in 'automatic' information systems is usually based on probabilistic, vector, or fuzzy-logic criteria.

LOSEE building on the work of BOOKSTEIN, presents a probabilistic sequential learning model for ranking. The proposed system will retrieve documents, accept feedback on the retrieved items, and 'learn' from the feedback to enhance future performance, the relevance feedback being an intrinsic element in the sequential learning model itself. An earlier article describes how coordination-level matching can be used for ranking outputs from retrieval systems incorporating sequential learning.

CROFT describes a method for integrating Boolean approaches with probabilistic retrieval methods. He claims that term dependencies derived from queries, when incorporated into a probabilistic retrieval model, can improve performance. The term dependencies can be derived automatically from Boolean queries or from user selection of important phrases from their natural-language queries. RADECKI, MARON, LOSEE and BOOKSTEIN, FOX and

KOLL, S ALTON, and COOPER all deal with the limitations of conventional Boolean searching methods and propose ways in which such approaches can be improved.

Relevance feedback is usually considered an essential element in any probabilistic retrieval method, and this implies the ability of the searcher to locate 'a few relevant items' in a database. One way of achieving this is to match the query against clusters of items rather than against individual items. PANYR considers the place of cluster analysis in information retrieval along with possible search strategies to exploit clusters. GRIFFITHS *et al.* have compared various clustering methods and found that the best retrieval results were achieved by procedures that divide a database into many small clusters. This led them to propose that the optimal cluster will consist of only two items, the ones that are most similar.

However, further tests showed that searches based on nearest-neighbour clusters did not perform any better than conventional 'best-match' searches, although they retrieved a different set of items. Consequently, these authors propose that a retrieval system incorporate both approaches. SALTON *et al.* discuss the use of automatic relevance feedback techniques with Boolean query statements. An extended or 'fuzzy' Boolean logic approach, which relaxes the normally strict interpretation of the Boolean operators, can improve search performance.

ENSER examines clustering techniques using terms from tables of contents, title, and back-of-the-book indexes, and concludes that this technique is viable in a book/text database. SHAW looks at the empirical significance of document clusters as a function of term weight and similarity thresholds. In related work SHAW also looks at the validity of partitions formed on the basis of co-citation. Approaches to the automatic indexing/classification of documents are generally based on data derived from a document/term matrix, showing which index terms or text words are associated with which documents.

Documents may be grouped according to such factors as the frequency with which a term occurs in a document and the frequency with which it occurs in the database as a whole. The relationships between documents and terms need not be considered 'absolute.' For example, words that do not occur in a document may nevertheless be judged 'close' to that document when they tend to co-occur in other contexts with the words that do occur frequently in the document. DEERWESTER *et al.* propose an approach to indexing based on the 'latent' relations among terms and documents, derivable from the document/term matrix. They refer to this as 'latent semantic indexing.'

The model uses a reduced set of about 100 'descriptive parameters' derived by the linear decomposition of a document/term matrix. Each term, document, and query can be represented by values on this small set of orthogonal dimensions, which may be considered as 'artificial concepts.' The investigators claim that results achieved in retrieval tests for the method ranged from considerably better to roughly comparable with performance based on weighted keyword searching. A more abstract, mathematical discussion of the analysis of weighted graphs in the clustering of items is given by GOETSCHEL, while CAN and OZKARAHAN compare two clustering algorithms in terms of stability and similarity factors.

YAKUBOVITZ refers to an associative retrieval system that can overcome some problems of text retrieval without the need for daily updating of a system thesaurus. This system links keyword-bearing documents with adjacent, associated documents having only one keyword in common to form an associative path. An algorithm for the construction of a path that changes keyword three times is presented as an example. THÖNSSEN reports on an interface that connects automatic indexing programmes with automatic thesaurus maintenance programmes. The interface can be used with a personal computer.

STREETER and LOCHBAUM present details on an expert/expert locator (EEL), which matches requests for information with technical organisations. The technical organisations in EEL are represented by their documents, and these documents provide the system with input. The automatic indexing places terms and organisations in a 100-dimension semantic space and determines similarities among organisations on the basis of their use of terms. When queried, the system computes the degree of similarity between the request and all objects in this structure, retrieving those that are most similar.

The approach is similar to the latent semantic indexing described by DEERWESTER *et al.* Another approach to 'automatic' retrieval consists of the development of natural-language interfaces that allow a user to enter queries as phrases or sentences without the need to deal with controlled vocabularies or to express logical relationships among terms. Various natural-language interfaces have been developed over the years.

BISWAS *et al.* introduce an approach that uses fuzzy-set techniques, and they describe it in considerable detail. CLEMENCIN describes a natural-language interface to the 'yellow pages' of France's online telephone directory, while SPIEGLER and ELATA propose a model for analysing a query at a local workstation to determine whether it is 'answerable' before submitting it to some accessible database. Rather than mapping natural-language expressions to a limited number of controlled terms, words occurring in text can be decomposed into smaller semantic units. This is the basis of 'semantic analysis' and the 'semantic code' that was applied to information retrieval at Western Reserve University more than 25 years ago.

SMETÁÈEK describes the SEMAN system that will decompose text words into 630 distinctive 'semantic features'. He mentions several possible information retrieval applications but does not elaborate on them. BELONOGOV *et al.* compare the performance of a retrieval system based on automatic indexing with the performance of a system based on text searching. They conclude that the system with automatic indexing has significantly better recall/precision characteristics and is faster than the other approach. Also, because low-performance terms can be eliminated, the database can be smaller.

BLAIR and MARON, using IBM's STAIRS for full-text legal retrieval, reported average precision values of around 75 per cent; but recall values of only about 20 per cent. SALTON comments on these results and suggests that they are typical of conventional retrieval operations. He presents results for studies that have compared conventional with automated approaches and emphasises that the future lies with the latter. BLAIR reviews the basic model of a relational document retrieval system and demonstrates how documents can be linked during a search in a relational system. He presents an extended model that includes weighted subjects, associative features such as thesaurus links, citation indexing, and co-occurring terms.

At a more general level, CANISIUS discusses potential uses of knowledge-based systems in information service applications and argues that the information profession could become redundant if it fails to exploit the capabilities of such systems, while WORMELL and BALDACCI deal with artificial intelligence and expert systems applied to information retrieval problems. SPARCK JONES, on the other hand, questions the need for artificial intelligence applications in information retrieval systems.

CITATION RELATIONSHIPS

Related documents can be grouped on the basis of direct citation, co-citation, or bibliographic coupling as well as through the more conventional methods of subject indexing. A number of recent studies deal with various aspects of these citation relationships in information retrieval. PAO and PAO and FU have compared results of searches based on citation relationships with results from conventional subject searches in MEDLINE. Not surprisingly, they find that the two methods are essentially complementary, each retrieving some relevant items not found by the other. One conclusion was that the conventional approach by descriptors could retrieve only about half of the 'quality' papers.

In reviewing their own bibliographic references, however, it is distressing to note that none of the items cited was published before 1979, giving the impression that studies of this kind are relatively new. In fact, comparisons of citation retrieval with conventional descriptor retrieval go back more than 20 years. Moreover, the complementarity of citation and traditional approaches was demonstrated long ago and is now taken pretty much for granted. We really don't need more studies to prove it.

MCCAIN reports a similar study. Results from co-citation searches in SciSearch were compared with results from conventional searches in BIOSIS Previews. The subject was the genetics of fruit flies. One of McCain's conclusions is that co-cited author searching "is capable of capturing a large percentage of relevant documents in a broad subject retrieval." TRIVISON compares items retrieved by subject indexes and citation indexes in the field of information science.

Unfortunately, neither conventional subject indexing nor citation links offer a foolproof way of linking documents or groups of documents that are 'logically' related. SWANSON points to two groups of logically related articles—one on the effects of dietary fish oils on changes in the blood and the other on the possible beneficial effects of similar blood changes for patients with Raynaud's disease—that are not closely related by co-citation, bibliographic coupling, or statistical associations among assigned descriptors. In a similar study SWANSON looks at the problems of linking the literature of magnesium to the literature of migraine.

SHAW raises doubts about the validity of some subject relationships supposedly demonstrated by co-citation. Classes formed by co-citation can be statistically invalid even at a high co-citation level. However, critical thresholds that define the limits of statistical validity can be identified. Within these limits there does exist "a narrow region of statistical validity where the associated structures are not an artifact of the clustering procedure and can be interpreted".

KWOK refers to the fact that reference/citation links can be used in information retrieval to form an 'augmented collection' of retrieved items. That is, when a search strategy is applied to a database in the normal way, using text words or controlled terms, the set of items thus retrieved can be augmented by those items linked to them through bibliographic citations. He suggests that the set of terms associated with the items originally retrieved might be augmented by the addition of terms drawn from the items that they cite.

These new terms could be index terms assigned to the cited items, or they could be text expressions drawn from abstracts or titles. He suggests that augmentation by drawing terms from the titles of cited items is most practicable. This is virtually what Mary Elizabeth Stevens was working on more than 20 years ago. SALTON and ZHANG have tested the value of augmenting the set of terms associated with retrieved items by adding title words drawn from 'bibliographically related' items.

Title words were drawn from:

- Items cited by the retrieved items;
- Items citing the retrieved items; and
- Co-cited items.

The authors conclude that while many 'useful' content words can be extracted in this way, many terms of doubtful value will also be extracted; further, the procedure is not sufficiently reliable to warrant inclusion in operating retrieval systems. KWOK, on the other hand, reinterprets their results and concludes that the enhancement may still be worth further investigation. REES-POTTER looks at the potential for using citation, co-citation analysis, and citation context analysis in the updating of thesauri or other controlled vocabularies. She concludes that the analysis of citation content may be used in the development of indexing vocabularies in specialty areas.

CONCLUSION

This review strongly suggests that subject analysis continues to be an area of great interest and activity. The increasing impact of electronic technology, combined with the ongoing expansion of that technology's capabilities, seem certain to have a profound effect on the progress of subject analysis, an effect that will no doubt be expressed in future

ARIST chapters on this topic. The authors hope that continued technological advances will not only stimulate ever-increasing enquiry and experimentation, but that sharing these advances, enquiries, and experiments with less technologically developed countries will also bring about more efficient and more sophisticated means of subject analysis and access on a global scale.

Readers of this review who have been actively involved in information science for a considerable time will recognise that substantial progress has occurred in the past 25 years in certain areas; automatic indexing, full-text searching, and end-user searching are obvious examples. This progress has been accompanied by the increasing convergence of information science and library science. The advent of the online public access catalogue (OPAC) has promoted greatly increased interest in the library community in improving subject access. Indeed some of the most interesting work in this area is now being performed in the traditional library setting, which was not generally true 20 or more years ago. It is interesting to note how history repeats itself.

In the 1950s and 1960s much of the progress in information retrieval occurred through the efforts of scientists, engineers, lawyers, and others who were not information professionals. These individuals were not familiar with the literature of library science, and some reinvention of the wheel occurred. Today a reverse situation may be occurring, with members of the library community reinventing methods that were developed outside the community many years ago. The field of information science seems to have a short collective memory. We know of work done three or four years ago but are unaware of, or have forgotten, work done much earlier. While much of the early work is outdated, some of it is still highly relevant. *ARIST* is of immense value in providing a review and synthesis of research in broad areas performed during relatively short periods of time, but it does not obviate the need for longitudinal reviews, covering perhaps 20 or 30 years, on more specific topics.

4

Search Techniques for Accessing CD-Rom Databases

INTRODUCTION

Due to the development of information technology, information is increasingly recorded in digital format and electronic databases which are continually becoming more complex, information storage and retrieval As the technology obsolete very fast, CD-Rom is also facing problems due to emergence of the DVD. In today's business, education, and government environments the amount of information, data and software being archived and distributed on CD-Rom and DVD-Rom media is overwhelming. For years the medium of choice for storing, archiving and distributing digital content has been the CD-Rom.

As capacity requirements of data intensive applications and databases grow, DVD-Rom, with a capacity potential over 13 times that of CD-Rom, is fast becoming the most popular medium. Single-sided, single layer DVD-Rom media can store up to 4.7 GB of data. Doublesided, single layer DVD-Rom media store up to 9.4 GB of data. DVD which is used primarily with movie/ video features will not affect the CD-Rom, but DVD-Roms will be, which can carry information on both sides of the disc.

DVD-Rom will replace the CD-Rom, but that it will take a few years. As information is increasingly recorded in digital format and electronic databases are continually becoming more complex, information storage and retrieval processes have profoundly changed. Over the past decades three major migrations have occurred in library academic services: from printed resources to online electronic databases; from online databases to bibliographic and full-text CD-Rom databases; and from CD-Rom databases to online Internet access to bibliographic and full-text/full-image databases.

WHAT ARE CD-ROM DATABASES

CD-ROM is abbreviation for 'Compact Disc-Read-Only Memory' a type of optical disk capable of storing large amounts of data up to 1GB, although the most common size is 650 MB. The term 'database' has been used in the literature in two different connotations. In Computer Science this is referred to as a database management system. In this sense a database has a logically consistent structure in which records are actually linked. In library and Information science, these are referred to as bibliographic or inventory in nature and comprise a collection of related logical records here a database is defined as an organised and generally unlinked set of machine, or it can be said, these databases are the electronic version of published literature traditionally appearing in printed form in various field.

Databases are produced by different agencies in a computer readable form, the contents of which are accessible in various ways according to requirements with the help of suitable software. Various agencies are involved in developing databases by collecting information from varieties of sources and packaging the information in the form of databases. Databases can be stored on CD-Rom, on the Internet, or on commercial sites that are accessible only if user's library has a subscription. CD-Rom in the library contains periodical indexes, abstracts, statistics, directories, and other complete texts. Some databases provide information that is primarily numeric, such as data from a recent government census and some contain information that is primarily textual. Database some time also called data bank.

WHY WE USE CD-ROM DATABASES IN LIBRARIES

Access to Cd-Rom databases is fast, accurate and thorough. A clever search by a users may get them in seconds most of the information they need. In contrast, traditional print services may take months for same task, with still great deal of information left out. As a matter of fact, libraries can not possibly continue with the sluggish manual information service methods and hope to remain in business tomorrow.

Libraries can have economic access to information, space saving and users friendly Libraries and information centres used these databases in providing various library services as mentioned below:

- Literature search services, current and retrospective literature searches.
- Current awareness services in various forms including SDI.
- Full text databases may be utilised for search services
- Document delivery services.
- For producing digest trend reports, etc.
- Compilations of bibliographies.
- Abstracting and Indexing Services.

WHY WE DON'T WANT TO USE CD-ROM DATABASES

It is always beneficial to know about the pros and cons of any information so that one can proceed systematically.

- CD-Rom databases are not updated in time, some web journals or indexing services are available online even before their print editions roll out of the press. For example, Engineering Index on disc is updated quarterly, and Dissertation Abstracts on disc only once in a year.
- Retrieval from CD-Rom databases take seconds, as against online databases, which take only milli-seconds, however complex the command search

statement may be of courses with higher bandwidth telecom pipes provided.

- If not acquired from a single producer, CD/DVD Rom databases require skills in using different search engines. Making menu-driven index searching or single keyword searching at command prompt may be easy to use in each system. But, users must make command, or Boolean searches, to get at exacter or less abstract hits. Sometimes users have been found key boarding DIALOGUE syntax instead of SPIRS one to search into MathSci Disc or PsycLIT from SilverPlatter, and vice versa. Both the search engines are so dissimilar in construct. Again, generally, users keyboard a collection of key words at the command prompt. They are flummoxed to discover that one access engine parses the search statement with 'or' operator between words, and the other with 'and' operator. The former results come in too many hits and the latter in too few. Therefore, all new uses require basic education in the techniques of bibliographic database searching.
- If adequate jukeboxes are not provided for permanent mounting of optical databases, it is a great hassle for users to switch from one disc to another for either a different file or part of the same file. By comparison, on online services, like DIALOGUE's the process is just a click away.

Yet another disadvantage of CD-Rom, they are vulnerable to damage by dust, fingerprints and scratches, etc. Therefore they need very careful handing. Libraries will have to make backup copy of each CDS disc to be kept in safe custody, so fresh copies can be made.

SEARCHING CD-ROM DATABASE

Conducting effective searches requires knowledge of a number of techniques. Users should not only have been an understanding of the nature, content and structure of the database, but also be familiar with the various option available in the search screen, the tools and techniques for searching, and the techniques and formats for display of the search output. The search features commonly available are Keyword Search, Phrase Search, Boolean Search, Truncation, Index and/or Thesaurus Support, Proximity Search, Field-Specific Searches, Free-Text Search, Combing Search Sets and Search Refinement, Limiting or Range Search, Searching through the Retrieved Records and they may vary from one CD-Rom to another.

SELECTION OF DATABASES FOR COMPARISON

Four CD-Rom Databases have been selected for a discussion on the various search and retrieval features available, 'Ulrich's on disc', 'Books in Print' from the category of general or ready reference sources, 'Ei Compendex', 'LISA plus' are Bibliographic databases containing details of documents including abstracts and Emerald full-text database of journal articles.

ULRICH'S ON DISC

Ulrich's on Disc from R. R. Bowker provides the ability to search and browse the entire Ulrich's family of databases.

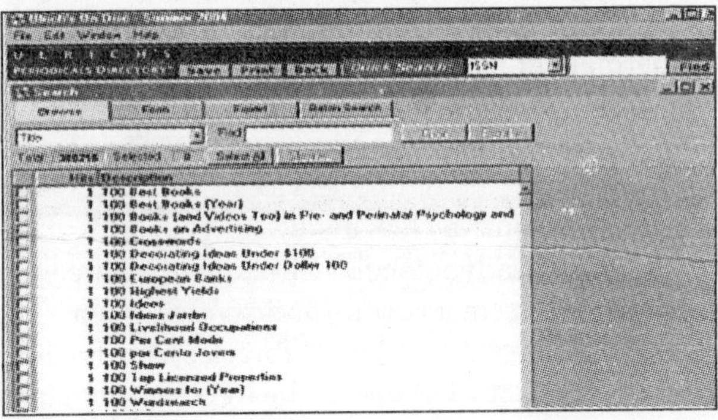

Fig 4.1. 'ULRICH'S on Disc' Main Screen

They included nearly 250,000 titles from over 200 countries, Information on about 11,000 new titles per year, annotations for almost 90,000 titles, full text reviews from *Magazines for Libraries* and *Library Journal* for over 8,700 publications, indicators for over 21,000 refereed publications and complete names and addresses for 80,000 serials publishers and distributors. The main screen of Ulrich's is shown in figure.

EI COMPENDEX BIBLOGRAPHIC DATABASE

Dialogue OnDisc® Compendex, produced by (Ei) Engineering Information Inc., provides coverage of the world's significant engineering and technical literature. Subject coverage includes but is not limited to the various disciplines of engineering, applied physics, electronics and instrumentation, light and optical technologies, and other areas of significant technology.

Compendex contains references to and abstracts from journals, technical reports, books, proceedings and conference papers, and more. Author-prepared abstracts are used when available. Publications from around the world are indexed, including approximately 4,500 journals and 2,000 conference proceedings per year. Approximately 10 per cent of the documents indexed are in a language other than English. Opening main Screen is like as figure.

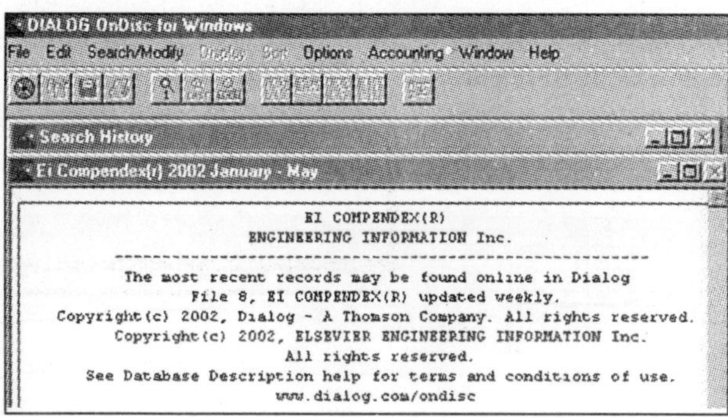

Fig 4.2.'Ei Compendex' Main Screen

LIBRARY AND INFORMATION SCIENCE ABSTRACTS (LISA PLUS)

LISA plus is the world's best known resource for the coverage of ongoing research in all aspects of library and information studies. Over 245,000 abstracts keep user well informed about such topics as artificial intelligence, information and knowledge management, publishing and copyright, World Wide Web resources and much more since, 1969. Lisa plus main screen is as figure

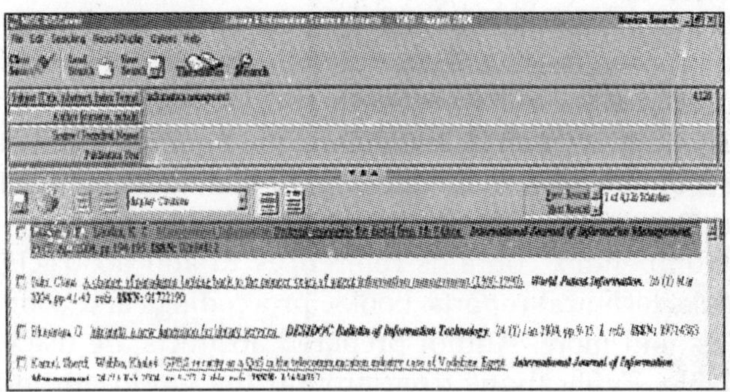

Fig 4.3 'LISA Plus' Main Screen

EMERALD FULL-TEXT DATABASE OF JOURNAL ARTICLES

Emerald is a full text database from MCB, covers more than 82 top journal across ten broad subject areas. It provides access to the full text of articles in PDF and HTML format published from 1994 to date.

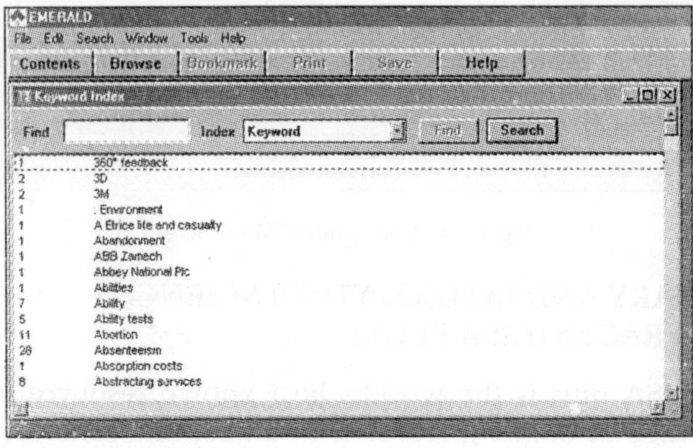

Fig 4.4. 'EMERALD (Full-Text Database)' First Screen

The subjects covered include Marketing, Human Resources, Quality Management, Information Management, Library and Information Services, Training and Education, General Management Property, Operations and Production Management, etc. Users can choose any subject and get a list of all the journals covered in that subject. First screen of Emerald is as figure.

ACCESSING DIFFERENT DATABASES

SEARCHING IN SPECIFIC FIELD OF SELECTED CD-ROM DATABASES

There are two forms of searching for information in CD-Rom databases—field-specific and free-text search. A user may know which field to search, or might like to restrict a given search to one or more fields. This is a field specific search. If the user are not sure of the field to be searched, they can conduct a free-text search, which means that the search is not restricted to any particular field.

While the free-text search is not universally available, field specific search is the simplest form of search, and CD-Rom databases offer various options to conduct searches on one or more specific fields.

The simplest option is the form search, where the user can select a specific box for a particular field as shown in figure and can key in the search term/phrase. Which search field can be searched in a database depends on the content and structure of the database concerned, and there fore they differ from one database to another.

Ulrich's on Disc

Search fields are Abstracting and Indexing Service, Area Code, Circulation, CODEN Number, Country, Dewey Number, Document Availability, Electronic Vendor, ISSN, Keyword, Keyword In Title, LC Class, Media Type, Personnel Name, Price (US Dollar), Publication Code, Publisher, Special Features, Special Index, Status Code, Subjects, Title, US State/ Zip, Year First Published. Search screen is shown by figure.

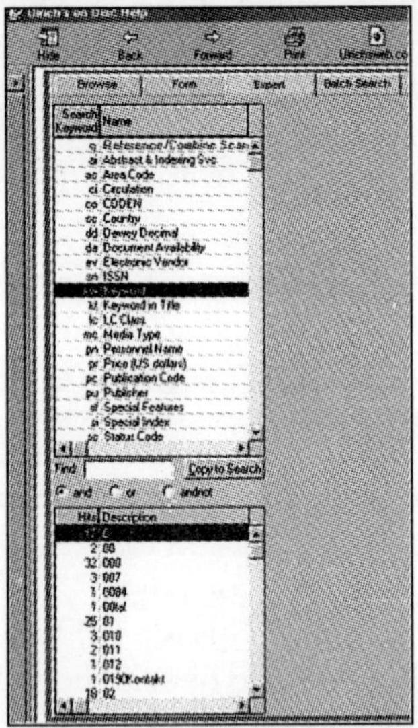

Fig 4.5 'ULRICH'S on Disc' Search Fields Screen

Ei Compendex

Under option 'Search/Modify' search fields are Word/ Phrase Index, EI Subject Headings, Author Name, Author Affiliation, Title Words, Journal Name, Conference Search Options (Conference Title, Conference Location, Conference Sponsor, Conference Year), Limit Options 'English…', (English only, Journal Articles Only, Conference Papers Only, Latest On Disc Records Only), Additional Search Options (Words/ Phrases, EI Classification Codes, Major Subject Headings, Treatment Codes, Year of Publications, Language) different fields and Search results screen shown in figure.

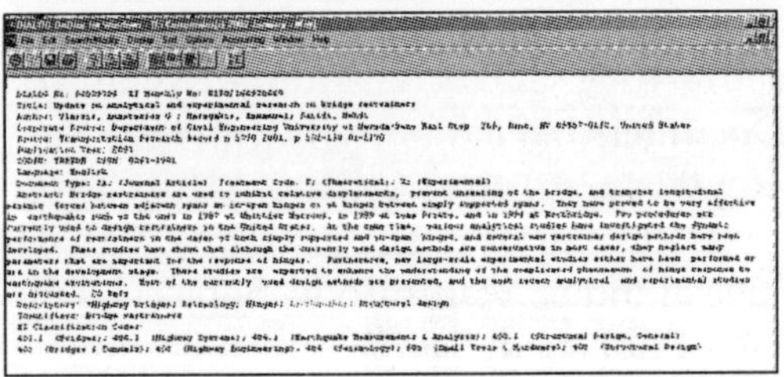

Fig 4.6 'Ei Compendex' Different Fields and Search Results Screen

LISA Plus

Subject, Title, Abstract, Index Term Or Keyword, Author, Source, Title Database Name,, Keyword, Language, Publication Date, Author Affiliation, Country Of Research, Record Number, CODEN, CATNI name, ISSN, Thesaurus term.

Emerald

Full Text, Author, Article Title, Keyword, Publication Year, Journal Title, Quality Indicators, Article Type Keyword search, author search subject search are most common search features. Search terms or phrases for the same or different fields can be combined using Boolean operators. Following table shows how searches on specific fields containing keywords and phrases can be conducted and what options are available in selected CD-Rom databases for searches on keywords or phrase.

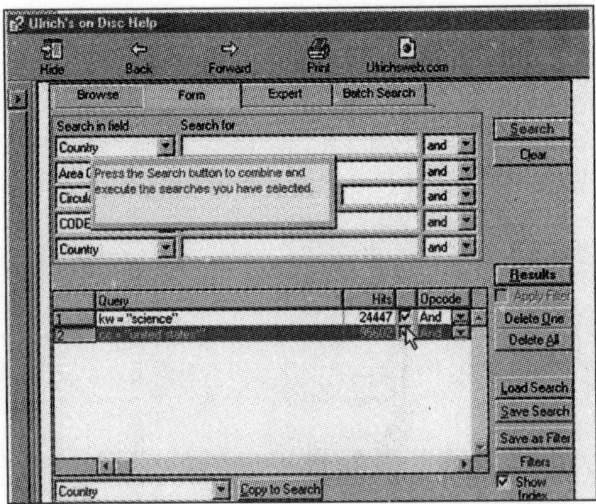

Fig 4.7 ULRICH'S on Disc' Form Search Screen

CD-ROM Databases	Option For Conducting Search On Words/Phrases	Method
Ulrich's on disc	Browse Index	Select a field, enter the search term in the appropriate box, and

(Contd...)

		search. Click on Find after entering the term
LISA plus	Browse	After entering and selecting the chosen term, click on view titles to see the results
Ulrich's on disc	Form Search	Select the particular field, enter the same term and search user can combine search terms, from the same or fields by Boolean operators. From Search Screen is shown in figure
LISA plus	Easy Search	Select any particular field and choose to view the index.select a term the index and search
Ulrich's on disc	Search	Enter the search term preceded by a field code (chosen from a list shown in the search fields box)and an equals sign, and then search
LISA plus	Expert Search	Select any particular field code and choose to view the index. Select the term from the index to search
Ei Compendex	Search/Modify	Click on 'search/modify' and then click on 'word/ phares' index. Enter the term in the small box after 'enter' and user will see the corresponding portion of the index. Select one or more terms and click OK. User will then see a search set with the given terms in the 'search history' window and the out put (the

(Contd...)

		then see a search set with the given terms in the 'search history' window and the out put (the complete record) in the output window) in the output window
Emerald	Basic Search	Enter the keyword in the box for search terms and click on the search, the system will then conduct the search and show the number of hits and brief information about each record (document number, title, author, document type, and quality indicator) will appear, double click on any record to see the full text. Multiple keywords can be joined by Boolean operator. Click on browse and click on any field (author, keyword, etc) and the correspon-ding index will be displayed, browse through the index and double click on any terms to select and search. Note that here keywords can be single words or phrases.
Emerald	Advanced Search	Select a field (eg. full text, author, and keyword) enter search terms and select search.

(*Contd...*)

	user can combine search terms with any other terms from the same or different field combined with Boolean operation (and, or, not)

BOOLEN SEARCH

Combine terms to make the search broader or narrower. How broad or narrow the search is depends on the search logic used to combine search terms. Three logical connectors, or Boolean operators, are used to define the relationship between search terms: 'and', 'or ', and 'not'. The Boolean operators may be used to join search terms within search fields in all search modes and to join search criteria between search fields in the Advanced and Expert search modes only.

Boolean searches can not be conducted in the 'browse index' mode of CD-Rom.

- *Ulrich's on Disc*: Operators are AND, OR, NOT/AND NOT and Options are, In the Form Search mode user can combine terms/phrases with Boolean operators in a chosen field box, or can type one term/phrase in each box and click on a Boolean operator in the box next to the box next to the term on the right. In the search mode user have to type the Boolean operator to combine terms/phares from the same or different fields.
- *Ei Compendex*: Operators are AND, OR, NOT and Options are: use these operators to combine search terms in the 'Modify Search Option'.
- *LISA Plus*: Operators are AND, OR, ANDNOT Options: In the Easy Search mode, user can combine terms/phrases with Boolean operators in a chosen field box, or can type one term/phrase in each box and click on a Boolean operators in the box next to the term on the right. In the Expert Search Mode, user has to type the Boolean operator to combine

terms/phases from the same or different fields. No nesting is possible.

- *Emerald*: Operators are And or, not and Options enter theses operators in the search in the search as well as Advanced Search Mode.

TRUNCATION SEARCH

Truncation of the three kinds of truncation, left truncation is not commonly available in CD-ROM databases.

The symbols for truncation and their syntax and effect vary, and the user has to learn these to conduct an effective search.

- *Ulrich's on Disc*: * or $ substitute for any number of characters and can be used for right truncation only. '?' Substitutes for one character, can be used anywhere in a word, or user can use multiple '?'Symbols.
- *LISA:* Truncation is the substitution of a wildcard symbol for any portion of a word to retrieve a group of words. Most often, truncation is used to abbreviate a word—to trim a term back to its stem, or root word. Truncating lets user search for word variants thereby broadening the search. The asterisk * is a multicharacter wildcard and the question mark ? is a single character wildcard. Wildcards are typically used at the end of a word but may be embedded within a word as well. Right and middle or internal truncation is allowed. Both the symbols can be used for right as well as middle truncation. User can enter the symbol as appropriate in the Easy Search as well as the Expert Search mode. Multiple ? can be used. Wildcards are typically used at the end of a word but may be embedded within a word as well. Avoid truncating words to less than five characters or user may retrieve unwanted results.
- *Ei Compendex:* '?' for any no. of characters. A combination of '?' and space can be used to conduct different types of truncation. To search on words that

start with a word stem and that have no more than one character after the stem, enter '? ?' For example, ROBOT? ? Retrieves robot and robots.to search on words that starts with a word stem and have no more than two characters after the stem. Enter '??' (two question marks) for example, Robot?? Retrieves: robot, robots, robotic.

- *Emerald:* Use a ? to find any single character in the position. Use an * to find any one or more characters in the position.

INDEX SEARCH AND THESAURUS SEARCH

The indexes allow users to select the search terms/ phrases from the term index, and a thesaurus allows users to consult a map of available terms to widen or narrow down a given search, as required. CD-Rom retrieval software provides index search facilities, ie users can select an index to browse and select from the index for searching. There may be an index file or a separate index for each searchable field so that the user can choose a field and then browse the corresponding index file. Index search facilities are more commonly available than thesaurus facilities. Thesauri are hierarchically structured.

This means that they go from broad terms to narrower, more specific, terms.

- *Ulrich's on Disc*: User can choose a field from either the search or the From Search mode. In each case user can display and browse the corresponding index and select a term/phrase from the index.
- *Ei Compendex:* In order to conduct a search, user need to choose an index: author, subject heading, keywords, etc, and then the corresponding index will be open for user to browse and to select the search term.
- *LISA Plus:* The thesaurus may be accessed via the Browse window by clicking on the Index drop-down list and selecting Thesaurus Term; highlight the required term and click View Titles. In the Expert Search mode enter the thesaurus term in the Search

Query Box, click on ok or press Enter. Press the 'View Brief' button to display the results of the search ie the thesaurus block. A thesaurus term can be selected to conduct a search in the database as shown in figure.

- *Emerald:* In the Advanced Search mode, user can choose one or more fields to search, and once users have entered a search term correspond to a field, they can click on the 'Thesaurus' button to get other words correspond to the search term.

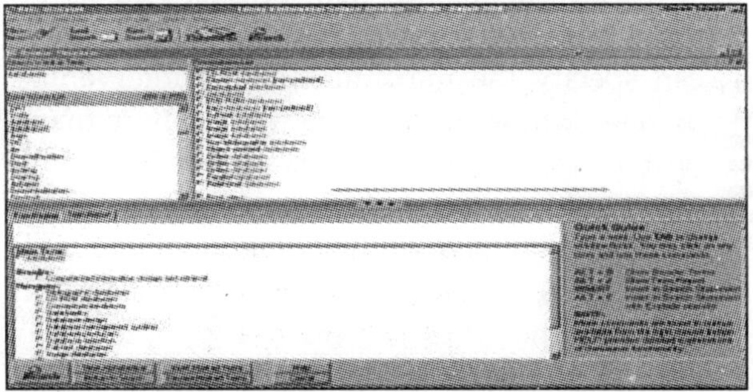

Fig 4.8. 'LISA Plus' Thesaurus Search

PROXIMITY SEARCH

With a proximity search, user can specify the number of words allowed between the search terms. In a general sense, there is a correlation between the number of intervening words and the topical relevance of users search results. The closer the distance between users search words, *e.g.*, 5 words, the more relevant but fewer the results may be. Likewise, the wider the distance between the search words, *e.g.*, 20 words, the less relevant but larger the CD-Rom results may be.

The type of proximity search operator to use depends upon whether user need search terms to be found in the same order as listed in the search statement or found in the same or reverse order of what user originally specified.

- *Ulrich's on Disc*: Not available.
- *Lisa Plus*: ANDx or NEARx locates both words, in any order within x words in the same field. NOTx locates the first word, but not the second within x

word in the same field. WITH: locates both words in adjacency, forward order only, in the same field. WITHx: locates both words, forward order only withx words in the same field. Option in proximity search is only allowed for the free text search. It can be used in both the Easy Search and Expert Search modes. Expert Search Screen of lISA is shown in figure.

- *EI Compendex*: Write two or more words consecu-tively to search as a phrase. Use periods (.) for on or more intervening words. Option for search expression 'artificial intelligence' will be searched as phrase, ie the word next to each other in the same order. User can specify the maximum no. of intervening words by one or more periods, eg information; management will retrieve both information management and information resource management.
- *Emerald:* Same document, same paragraph, word apart, exact order. In the Advanced Search mode, user can choose any of the four options to conduct a proximity search.

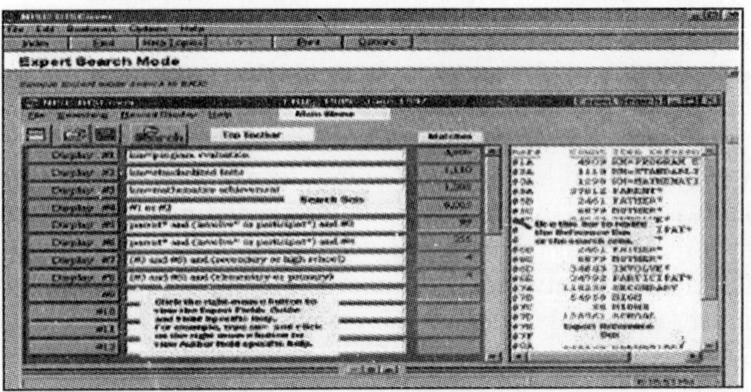

Fig 4.9. 'LISA Plus' Expert Search Screen

FREE-TEXT SEARCH

Free-Text Search enables the users to specify one or more search or phrases that are not limited to any particle field. There may also be index for free-text search terms. Instead of searching field, in some cases the user might like to conduct a search in all or many different fields. This is possible through what is known as the free search facility. In some cases, the default setting is the free text search, ie whenever a user enters a search term it is searched in all or a number of selected fields.

Free text option in selected databases as

- *Ulrich's on Disk*: No option is available for free-text searching.
- *Ei Compendex:* No free text search is possible; user have to choose an index to conduct a search.
- *LISA Plus:* Here a free-text term is any single word taken from any field in the record, with the exception of stop words (). Free text differs from keyword searching in that a space between two terms is treated as meaning true proximity in relative position and order. For example: ft = catalogue$ will retrieve all references that have 'catalog' as the first seven characters of the term; 'ft=line', will retrieve all references that contain the terms 'line' including 'line management', author/research worker 'Line Maurice B' ft=public libraries will retrieve all references where the term 'public libraries' occurs, but it will not retrieve records with the combinations. 'Libraries public' or with the phrase 'public and academic libraries'. If a term is entered in the Search mode' with out an operators a free text (ft) will be automatically carried out.
- *Emerald*: In the search option, or using the 'Full -text' option in the Advanced Search mode, user can conduct a full-text search, *i.e.,* a search on any part the document.

RESULTS

After the comparison we come to know that all databases have almost same basic accessing techniques as keyword search, Phrase Search, Boolean Search, Truncation, Index and/ or Thesaurus Support, Proximity Search, Field-Specific Searches, Free-Text Search, Combing Search Sets and Search

Refinement, Limiting or Range Search, Searching through the Retrieved Records and they may vary from one CD-Rom to another with a slight variation as given below:

- Boolean searching is possible in all the CD-Rom database, through how it is carried out varies. Boolean searches cannot be conducted in the 'browse index' mode of a CD-Rom database for the obvious reason that only one term/phrase can be keyed in to display the corresponding portion of the index.
- None of the sample databases provides left-truncations facilities. The symbols for truncation vary from one database to another.
- Search refinement of a given search can be refined by adding or dropping one or more search terms or criteria, such as limiting the output to a given language, year of publication, price range, and so on.
- Some CD-Rom products have more than one search interface, for example, Ulrich's on disc, while others have on search interface giving options for both - simple, novice and other advanced/ expert search.
- Some retrieval system such as EI Compedex show the result instantly, while in others the user has to chose the view/display option, as in LISA plus.
- Proximity search in CD-Rom databases allows users to conduct proximity searches in order to specify how closely the terms prescribed in a search expression.
- Two types of indexing practice are followed word index and phrase index.in the word index, each individual word in a field is indexed, while in the phrase index, a given phrase that may comprise several keyboard, is indexed. The user may need to check whether a field is a word- or phrase-indexed, by browsing through the index for the particular field, before entering a search term/phrase.
- CD-Rome databases do not usually provide facilities for ranking the search results according to relevance.

CONCLUSION

The mission of library services in the age of computer and electronic technologies is to provide information at the point and the moment of users' needs. Unquestionably, content is still the key to the success of a library electronic database. The medium of information delivery systems has evolved over the years from printed indexes to magnetic tapes, disks and compact discs. CD-Rom technology seems to be increasingly popular among library users. Users are not sophisticated searchers; their acceptance of the CD-Rom technology indicates that they are willing to learn. With initial training users may become less reliant on library staff, at least for routine database operations.

Improvements in the user-friendliness of software interfaces and standardisation of navigational functions should make CD-Rom databases easier to use and allow users to concentrate on developing good search strategies rather than such mundane activities as how to print. As the expertise of users increases, so do the expectations. With more databases containing abstracts and full text becoming available, user demand for immediate access to documents will grow. The availability and preference for the electronic version of documents will have an effect on print subscriptions and inter-library loan.

It is important that CD-Rom database developers and libraries keep abreast of the changing attitudes and use of CD-Rom by patrons in order to offer the services which will meet both present and future user information needs. The promise of new technology is for libraries to extend the reach of research and education, improve the quality of learning, and reshape scholarly communication. This is not an extravagant claim for the technology, but rather a declaration of an ambition shared by many who are developing and managing the technology. And the key to fulfilling that promise lies within the communities of higher education, science, and public policy responsible for applying the technology to those ends.

5

Bibliographic Displays

INTRODUCTION

Since, the introduction of the first Online Public Access Catalogues (OPACs) in the early 1980s, OPACs have revolutionised the operation of public, academic, and special libraries throughout the world and have generated a large body of related research. An OPAC is an automated, searchable bibliographic database which provides access to a library's collection. The bibliographic displays in an OPAC show information about items belonging to the library's collection.

Such items may include monographs, videocassettes, serials, sound recordings, etc. While the bibliographic information is entered into the database according to the standards established by the second edition of the *Anglo-American Cataloguing Rules* (*AACR2*), no such standard exists for the content or appearance of the bibliographic display. However, after fifteen years of OPAC development, interest in standardisation has been heightened as more and more people are exposed to the vast array of diverse OPAC systems in libraries, many of which are accessible on international computer networks, such as the Internet. The creation of a successful bibliographic display should include user participation in the design process.

Research is required to determine the most useful elements for a standard bibliographic display, and how they should appear on the screen. The choice of a particular bibliographic display format should take into consideration the opinions and needs of users, not just user performance. Figure shows a sample bibliographic display from an OPAC.

```
AUTHOR :    Garland, Henry Burnand.
TITLE :     The Oxford companion to German literature / by Henry and Mary
            Garland. --
EDITION :   2nd ed. / by Mary Garland. --
PUBLISHER :  Oxford [England] : Oxford University Press, 1986.
PHYSICAL DESCRIPTION  :  viii, 1020 p.
OTHER AUTHORS :  Garland, Mary.
SUBJECTS :  German literature -- Dictionaries.  * German literature --
            Bio-bibliography.
CATALOGUING SOURCE NUMBER  :  32755373
```

Fig 5.1. Sample Bibliographic Display

The characteristic which most clearly distinguishes most OPAC bibliographic displays from the format used on 3X5-inch cards in non-computerised catalogues is the use of labels. The words or phrases to the left of the colons (:) are labels. Labels identify the fields of a bibliographic record, such as Title and Author. In the sample bibliographic display shown in figure, all the labels are in uppercase and leftjustified. The words on the right side of the colons are the text or the values of the fields. The text in this display is in upper- and lowercase and is placed a few spaces away from the labels. The labels and the text are the main ingredients of a bibliographic display.

OPAC designers and librarians must decide which bibliographic information should be provided in a bibliographic display. In the display shown in figure, only eight bibliographic elements or fields are listed: Author, Title, Edition, Publisher, Physical Description, Other Authors, Subjects, and Cataloguing Source Number. After deciding on the elements to be displayed, designers have to think about the display format. Display format includes justification, typography, spacing, font, colour, and video effects, such as reverse video. Although omitted in this sample bibliographic display, instructions are usually included in the display to assist users in navigating in the system.

The instructions were not shown in the sample display because they were not of interest in the present project. Methods of collecting comments and opinions of users in research are numerous. The most frequently used techniques are questionnaires, interviews, and focus groups. The choice of technique is determined by the objectives and the scope of the study. Questionnaires are suitable for collecting representative information from a large number of people, while interviews provide detailed, in-depth opinions of a small number of people.

Focus groups usually involve more participants than interviews and fewer participants than questionnaires. Unlike interviews, participants in focus groups may help each other elicit and express their opinions as they discuss a topic together. In the field of library and information science, focus groups are generally used to study user satisfaction with library service. The present study used focus groups to investigate the bibliographic elements that users find more or less useful in bibliographic displays, the bibliographic information that users would like to add to displays, and the bibliographic display format users prefer.

One of the goals of the project was to explore the plausibility of using this qualitative research method in designing and assessing computer interfaces in general, as well as to investigate user opinions and suggestions regarding bibliographic displays. This study was the second phase of a larger project. The main objective of this study was to obtain information on content and screen design. In order to avoid any bias and influence on participants' opinions, the investigators of the larger project decided to select a student with no formal training in library science generally, and cataloguing, specifically, to be the researcher for this study. Thus, a student in the Master of Information Science programme was selected. The researcher also acted as the focus group moderator.

Possible similarities and differences between the English and Chinese (Cantonese) speaking OPAC users were of interest in order to take advantage of the researcher's language ability and because of the growing population of the Chinese community in the Greater Toronto Area. Therefore, library users of these two languages were asked to participate in the focus groups. Morgan pointed out that communication may be easier for participants of the same age group than for those of large age difference. In this case, different ages might imply differences in experience in using the computer catalogue system. As a result, age was used in grouping participants in the focus groups. Results collected from the focus group study may be used to design a standard bibliographic display which takes the opinions of users of different linguistic backgrounds and of different ages into consideration.

LITERATURE REVIEW

In the last 15 years, the OPAC has been the topic of a large body of research. This chapter presents a review of the studies that were pertaining to this project. The four sections describe the four aspects of this project: OPAC Interfaces covers a general overview of the development in OPAC design; Bibliographic Displays discusses guidelines on bibliographic display design in terms of bibliographic elements and display format; The Technique of Focus Groups describes focus groups as a research methodology; and The Use of Focus Groups in Library and Information Science summarises previous studies that used focus groups. The literature reviewed here served as the foundation of the present project in setting the objectives, shaping the methodology, and interpreting the results.

OPAC INTERFACES

The interface of an OPAC links users to the computerised catalogue using menus, commands, search screens, and messages. Designers of OPAC interfaces must take into consideration not only the purpose of the complete system, but of each individual screen. When making design decisions, interface designers should try to facilitate the achievement of the objectives that the library has set for its users and its catalogue.

Several researchers have developed guidelines for OPAC interfaces based on general guidelines for computer interfaces such as those provided by Galitz and on the results of user performance studies. While some researchers advocate increasing the involvement of users in the computer interface development process, few OPACs created in this manner have entered the market. Libraries searching for computerised library catalogues often meet with frustration since, most catalogues are designed by computer programmers, with little input from library professionals or users.

Based on previous studies which investigated features that facilitate user performance, Shires and Olszak developed guidelines on how to design an effective OPAC screen with respect to the overall screen layout, menu screens, and enquiry screens. The authors included checklists in the article for designers to use. OPAC screen designers were reminded to create an interface that puts the users in control. Users should not feel helpless and lost when using OPACs.

In order to ensure that user needs are dealt with during OPAC screen design, OPAC users, including librarians, should be informed of the latest developments in design and should be included in the design process. For screen appearance, Shires and Olszak recommended that information presented on the screen should have blank lines between different sets of information in order to improve user speed and accuracy in browsing the screen. Based on Galitz's book on computer interface screen design, Shires and Olszak concluded that an ideal screen should be orderly, clean, clutter-free, and the text on the screen should be balanced, symmetric, and in sequential order.

They provided the following suggestions to interface designers and librarians:

- Maintain a user orientation;
- Involve actual users in all phases of screen design: establishing, testing, and evaluating;
- Formalise the involvement of actual users;
- Establish a team or use other formal organisations to conduct the screen design process.

Shires and Olszak encouraged librarians to inform patrons about the development of the interface and to include them in the process as active participants. Instead of reacting to products or being tested for performance, patrons should have some input before prototypes are constructed. Yee reviewed a number of user studies that examined various OPAC features including vocabulary, arrangement of multiple entries, and display of a single record.

After she identified the problems with the existing designs, Yee suggested solutions with respect to bibliographic record display format design and the technical aspects of OPAC system design. She also provided pointers for future research. The studies she reviewed revealed that users encountered the following problems: unclear abbreviations and initials, difficulty in understanding codes, and ambiguous brief displays. She concluded that in order to improve the effectiveness of a bibliographic display, more research is required to study the vocabulary for the bibliographic labels.

O'Rourke pointed out that when librarians have to choose an OPAC to purchase, the information available about the systems is usually technical. Little attention has been paid to the appropriateness of the systems from the users' point of view. The design of an OPAC system should not be purely a computer programming enterprise. Crawford also reminded designers of OPAC user interfaces to understand their users' opinions. In other words, not only should the speed and accuracy of the users in locating information on a bibliographic display be taken into account when designing a new system, but users' opinions are worthy of researchers' and designers' attention.

BIBLIOGRAPHIC DISPLAYS

Bibliographic Content

The main purpose for using a library catalogue is to search for desired materials. Library clients determine whether they have found what they were looking for based on the information presented on the bibliographic display. According to the *AACR2*, bibliographic information, from title to physical description, is used in a library catalogue to identify an item. However, library catalogue designers do not usually include all of the bibliographic information in the catalogue record on the screen.

In order to ensure that library clients are provided with the information they need, the design of bibliographic displays should take into account users' preferences in using this information. Before computerised library catalogues, bibliographic information was printed on 3X5-inch cards which together comprised the whole catalogue. Arguments about the necessary elements and the presentation of bibliographic information on OPAC displays have questioned whether the card tradition should be kept or changed. If changes are to be made, the next question is what they should be. In the early stage of OPAC development, Aiyer, Hargrove, Mattison, and McPherson recommended the use of the conventional catalogue card format because users were familiar with it.

Compared to a display with labels for the bibliographic elements, card or citation format consumes less space. In spite of the familiarity and lower space consumption of the card format, the card-like presentation of bibliographic information has been generally rejected because computerised catalogues are regarded as fundamentally different from card catalogues with respect to capability and manipulability. The ease of modifying computerised catalogues provides library and information professionals with a chance to reform the old way of presenting bibliographic information. The large storage capability of computerised catalogues lets OPAC designers include information that could not have been available to users on 3X5-inch cards.

Crawford, Stovel, and Bales reminded designers that, while they have new ideas for displaying bibliographic information, the positive characteristics of the old card system should not be completely ignored. Crawford, Stovel, and Bales devoted an entire book to discuss the issues related to designing effective bibliographic displays. The basis of this book was the testing of RLIN (Research Libraries Information Network) MARC (Machine-Readable Cataloguing) records. The authors pointed out that different libraries have different needs, and researchers should not hope to create a single display to accommodate all libraries.

Decisions on bibliographic display design should be based on the needs of local users and the nature of the library collection. However, in general, a display designer should pay attention to the following: fields and subfields; field grouping and arrangement; labelled or cardlike displays; what the labels are and where they should be; typography; display modes; and additional information.

Crawford, Stovel, and Bales indicated that a successful bibliographic display should demonstrate the following characteristics:

- The display should provide an appropriate amount of information;
- Library users should understand the displayed information;
- The display should be readable and attractive;
- Library users should be able to locate necessary information on the screen rapidly; and
- All information should be displayed in a single screen.

Unlike card catalogues, OPACs usually present users with the option to obtain brief or long bibliographic displays. Crawford, Stovel, and Bales suggest that brief displays should provide users with sufficient information to identify an item. The elements in a brief display should include: main entry; title statement; publisher; date of publication; and physical description. A long or full display should give users as much information as they would find useful.

A survey of academic library users conducted by Seal, Bryant, and Hall showed that a bibliographic display with the following information should provide enough bibliographic information for the majority of users: Names; Title, Subtitle; Uniform Title; Subject Headings; Added Entries; Volume Number, Volume Title; Edition Statement; Date of Publication; Edition and History Note; References; ISBN or Control Number.

Additional information such as the location of the item, call number, circulation status, and presence of holds/reserves may also be included in a long bibliographic display. Stephens advocated the inclusion of holdings, locations, and circulation status in bibliographic displays. He pointed out that OPACs should not be forced to inherit the old problems and misunderstandings of the traditional card system. The display of holdings, locations, and circulation status can help users reduce the amount of screen scanning and get all the desired information from a minimal number of screens.

Cherry, Williamson, Jones-Simmons, and Gu evaluated twelve OPAC systems in Canadian universities. These researchers constructed an evaluation checklist to examine various aspects of the OPAC systems. The researchers assessed the systems with respect to database characteristics, operational control, subject search code, output control, user assistance, and usability via remote access. In the database characteristics checklist, the researchers included sixteen items to evaluate how much information the OPACs provided to users.

These sixteen items were:

- Call number;
- Author;
- Title;
- Subject heading(s);
- Edition information;
- Publication information;
- Copy information;
- Volume information;
- Location for current issues of serials;
- Name of the library where the item is located;
- Loan status;
- Document abstract;
- Table of contents;
- Citations within the text;
- Keywords from the book index; and
- Book review.

Although all the libraries received scores between 9 and 11, points were derived solely from items 1 to 11. None of the twelve libraries displayed information described in items 12 to 16 which previous researchers had suggested should be included in a bibliographic display.

Bibliographic Display Format

Once the list of elements to be displayed has been decided, designers have to consider various ways to arrange the elements on a screen. Although a screen is much larger than a 3X5-inch card, Hildreth pointed out that reading from the screen is more difficult than reading print material. To counter the problem, designers must be more liberal with the use of space in a display. Further, space on a computer screen is less expensive than that on print material. Despite the necessity of including plenty of white/black space in an OPAC bibliographic display, researchers warned designers not to overuse spacing to improve screen appearance.

Excessive use of space in bibliographic displays forces users to view the information on more than the necessary number of screens. In this case, designers face the risk that the users will view only the first screen and ignore the rest. Some of the design principles for OPACs suggested by Crawford are applicable to bibliographic displays. These principles refer to the text on the screen, screen density, and readability. In order to make the text displayed on the screen legible, the font used should be large and clear enough to make the information displayed stand out from the screen background.

The content of the screen should not take up every space available. He suggested that for bibliographic displays in a 25-line by 80-character screen, only 30 per cent of the screen should be used for content. Thirty percent of the screen translates to 600 characters or about 100 words. Matthews also suggested that readability can be improved by observing the following guidelines. The text in each line should occupy no more than 60 to 65 characters.

Enough space should be provided for labels to be spelled out. Blank lines and other white space should be used intelligently to enhance readability. However, the use of double spacing would lead to the loss of coherence in the text. Printing in all uppercase makes scanning difficult. Instead of using all capital letters, designers should effectively employ other different types of highlighting techniques like bold, italic, colours, and reverse video. However, Crawford advised designers not to use more than two or three different techniques in a single screen.

Designers should also keep in mind that the same highlighting technique should not be applied to different purposes. For example, if the labels are in bold, instructions should not be in bold as well. In addition to Crawford's suggestions, Matthews and Norman pointed out that bibliographic displays should only display information that users require and the information should be placed in a sequence users would expect. Fryser and Stirling investigated how a labelled format differed from the standard Library of Congress (LC) or card format in terms of time required for users to locate specific bibliographic information and in terms of users' preferences.

Using the data collected from 340 university students, Fryser and Stirling concluded that users could locate information faster with a labelled format than with the card format. In addition, users indicated preferences for displays with labels over the traditional card format. Fryser and Stirling attributed this preference to the fact that the labelled display was easily understood and required little effort to scan by the users. Hence, labels deserve special attention in their design and vocabulary. Matthews discussed format guidelines specifically for labels.

He asserted that labels should be:

- In uppercase;
- Spelled out as words, not abbreviations;
- Used for all fields;
- Right-justified;
- Separated from the text using a colon (:) and at least one blank space;
- Between 12 and 20 characters long; and
- Displayed in columns.

The objective of designing labels with the above guidelines is to ensure that the labels are distinguishable from the text. The choice of terms used in labels is as complex as the format used to display them. The labels used in bibliographic displays tend to mean something different from the usual meanings of the terms. The label 'TI' or 'Title' is often more than simply the title of the item because users can find title statement, collation, and imprint under this label. Not only would users be confused by the labels, but the vocabulary used in labels varies from catalogue to catalogue.

Users can be easily confused by the type of information grouped together by a system but treated separately in another. Many guidelines exist for designing bibliographic displays, some based on user performance and some based on user preference. Researchers have noted that the many variations in elements and formats in bibliographic displays require research to search for a standard that will facilitate user performance and improve user satisfaction.

Chan designed a checklist to evaluate OPAC bibliographic displays. The checklist consists of four sections to assess how well a bibliographic display follows the guidelines suggested by researchers including Crawford and Shires and Olszak : labels, text, instructional information, and screen layout. Chan applied the checklist to twelve academic and ten public OPACs in Canada. Her results demonstrated the wide gap between design guidelines and the existing displays.

The average score for the academic libraries was 59 per cent with a range of 49 per cent to 70 per cent. On the other hand, the public libraries averaged 55 per cent with a range of 52 per cent to 59 per cent. Among the four areas the checklist addressed, screen layout appeared to be the primary cause for such low scores. This checklist provides an evaluation tool and can also serve as a guide for designing new displays.

THE TECHNIQUE OF FOCUS GROUPS

Focus groups, a qualitative research method, have often been used by marketing professionals to learn about customers' attitudes towards a product. Compared to other qualitative methods like field studies, focus groups offer a better approach for studying people's attitudes and thoughts because participants have opportunities to elaborate on their opinions.

Results obtained through focus groups can be used as a self-contained study or part of a large project. Stewart and

Shamdasani suggested that focus groups can be used for: obtaining general background information about a topic; creating hypotheses to be tested with quantitative methods; generating new ideas and concepts; evaluating a product, a service, or a programme; developing questionnaires or other research tools using the information obtained; and interpreting previous quantitative results.

The validity of focus groups, like other research methods, depends on the research questions and the context. Several authors provide guidelines for conducting effective focus groups. The guidelines address the characteristics of the participants based on the research topic, the number of sessions, the number of participants per session, and the moderator's level of involvement. Morgan suggested six to eight participants for unstructured focus groups and three to four for structured ones.

Generally, the recommended number of participants per session falls within the range of four to ten. Too few participants may limit the diversity of discussion, while too many may prove hard for the moderator to control. The source of participants is also addressed by the guidelines. Although the sample does not have to be representative of the population because generalisation is not the goal of focus groups, participants should present a wide range of opinions regarding the topic. Depending on the topic of discussion, participants should be homogeneous in order to promote free discussion. For example, a discussion of health care policy should group participants by age because different age groups have different concerns regarding health care. In order to ensure that all opinions are exposed and discussed in depth, grouping by age is necessary.

Finally, the moderator's level of involvement in the focus group sessions must be selected. This will influence how the groups perform. A low level of involvement is important for exploratory type of research, whereas a high level of involvement is effective if the focus groups are conducted according to a clearly stated agenda. Compared to other qualitative research methods, focus groups are less expensive and more flexible because focus groups require fewer participants than surveys and less time than interviews.

THE USE OF FOCUS GROUPS IN LIBRARY AND INFORMATION SCIENCE

Both Baker and Widdows, Hensler, and Wyncott used focus groups to study user opinions about local library service. Baker used twelve questions to probe for opinions regarding Iowa City Public Library's special service for the business community. Participants recruited from the business community provided suggestions with respect to equipment and facilities to the library in order to assist the library to better serve the business community. This focus group project served as an opportunity not only to collect opinions from clients, but also to spread the news of this special service to the community and to promote the library's public relations.

Widdows, Hensler, and Wyncott used focus groups to investigate the attitudes of Purdue University students concerning the quality of the library service. Data collected from the focus groups supplemented the data obtained earlier in a questionnaire survey. Students expressed opinions pertaining to the library's long term planning such as catalogue system centralisation and to its current services including the availability of photocopiers.

The researchers from both studies recommended the method of focus groups as a research tool in the field of library science. As part of the Council of Library Resources (CLR) nationwide study of OPACs and their use, Kaske used focus groups to validate and expand the data previously obtained from a questionnaire survey. In the CLR study, researchers recruited 440 OPAC users and non-users from six different libraries. After interviewing 70 groups of library clients, the researchers discovered about 60 themes concerning OPACs.

These themes were grouped into four categories:

- Existing system(s);
- Card to computer transition;
- Database; and
- User assistance.

After reviewing Kaske's study, Drabenstott concluded that focus groups are "an effective method for identifying people's feelings and beliefs about situations, products, and services and how these shape their behaviour.' The advantages of focus groups have not been fully exploited by the OPAC researchers. One could say that OPAC is a service that a library provides to its clients. Therefore, the opinions and comments of the clients regarding the OPAC system can be obtained through focus groups. These opinions and comments, like those discussed by Baker; Widdows, Hensler, and Wyncott; and Drabenstott , can be used to improve the quality of OPAC for users.

METHODOLOGY

RESEARCH DESIGN

This project focused on the similarities and differences between English and Chinese speaking OPAC users for two reasons. Since, the majority of the population in Canada speaks English, the opinions of English OPAC users were pertinent to this study. Chinese speaking OPAC users were also studied because the first language of the researcher is Chinese, and the Chinese population is growing in Canada, particularly in the Greater Toronto Area.

Table 5.1. Design for Focus Group Study

	Language	
Age	**Chinese**	**English**
18-30	n = 5-10	n = 5-10
31-49	n = 5-10	n = 5-10
50+	n = 5-10	n = 5-10

The need of OPACs in different languages was assessed. Following guidelines provided by Morgan and Krueger , three age groups were formed: 18-30, 31-49, and 50+. This grouping by age was intended to ensure that the participants would feel comfortable during the discussion. The researcher tried to balance the gender of the participants. Other possible factors such as socioeconomic status and educational level were not manipulated and thus assumed random. Hence, this project employed a 2 (Language) by 3 (Age) design. Within each cell, we planned to recruit at least five and no more than ten participants.

Each focus group session consisted of the following parts:

- A structured discussion using the researcher's questions;
- Two response forms to elicit the participants' preferences of different bibliographic displays and the participants' perceived importance of various bibliographic elements; and
- An unstructured discussion during which the participants designed an 'ideal' bibliographic display using the elements they deemed as important in the previous questionnaire.

The researcher served as the moderator for the focus group sessions. In order to familiarise herself with facilitating focus group sessions and to refine the procedure, the researcher conducted two practice sessions in the Faculty of Information Studies at the University of Toronto. Two additional sessions were carried out at the University as pilot sessions to finalise the procedures and the questionnaire.

Details of the practice and pilot sessions, including participant recruitment and subsequent changes to the procedure. For the Chinese sessions, three different master's students from the Faculty of Information Studies at the University of Toronto were moderator assistants.

A doctoral student from the same faculty acted as moderator assistant for all the English sessions. The assistants helped prepare the rooms for the sessions, arrange refreshments, greet the participants, monitor the taperecorder, distribute debriefing and honorarium receipt forms at the end of the sessions, and hand out honoraria to the participants when they returned the completed receipts. The researcher gave each assistant a moderator assistant checklist providing guidelines on an assistant's duties.

HOST LIBRARY

Scarborough Public Library was chosen as the site for the study because Scarborough has a large Chinese population. About 10 per cent of Scarborough residents speak Chinese as their first language; Chinese is the fastest growing language group in Scarborough, resulting in a 137.8 per cent increase since, 1986. The previous contact that the Faculty of Information Studies had with Scarborough Public Library was another incentive to propose this project to them. The English-speaking population in Scarborough constitutes 66.4 per cent of the Scarborough population.

Statistics Canada's Census '91 showed that Scarborough is inhabited by 524,598 people. The city of Scarborough is at the east end of Metropolitan Toronto; its neighbouring cities include Toronto, North York, Markham, and Pickering. Scarborough Public Library consists of 19 branch libraries, including 3 district libraries. The collection of over 1.5 million items, including both printed and non-print material, can be searched with the aid of an OPAC, which is a Geac system.

The library accommodates the diverse cultural background of Scarborough's residents by offering multilingual resources. The host library provided a meeting room in a branch library in the northern district of the city for the Chinese focus group sessions. The moderator and her assistant placed four rectangular tables together in the middle of the room to form a large 'table' with enough chairs around the tables. Refreshments were placed in the middle of the tables. The English sessions were conducted in two different branches in the southeastern district. The rooms were set up similarly for the English sessions.

APPARATUS

A Bell and Howell Educator Series Model 3191C tape recorder equipped with a Crown microphone and ten Maxell 90-minute blank audiotapes were used to audio record the focus group sessions. A Sharp tape recorder and a pair of Koss earphones were used during transcription for tape playback. Two matting boards were used to mount the sample bibliographic displays used in the focus group sessions.

A 24" X 36" whiteboard was the canvas for display construction while four colour dry-erase markers served as paint brushes. During the display design discussion, the whiteboard was supported by a small coffee table found in the room. A Polaroid Impulse Portrait camera was used to capture the displays created in the sessions.

MATERIAL

Questionnaire and Forms

Participants were asked to complete two forms and one questionnaire prior to the focus group sessions: These included a Consent Form, an Audio Recording Release Form, and a Background Questionnaire. Two additional forms were used during the focus group sessions. These forms were used to collect written responses from the participants. The first form asked the participants to choose the display they preferred from five given displays.

The second form listed the bibliographic elements that could be included in a display and asked the participants to choose and rank their importance. Session number, time, date, location of the focus groups, and the questions were printed on the forms. The participants' names were not recorded on the forms. Figure shows the bibliographic element list on the Bibliographic Element Ranking Form. This list was a compilation of the elements listed in the *AACR2* second level of description. The names of the elements used in the *AACR2* were modified from library jargon to simpler and more descriptive terms.

In addition to the *AACR2* elements, the elements used in Cherry, Williamson, Jones-Simmons, and Gu's database characteristics checklist, and additional elements compiled from research studies by Diodato , Pejtersen, Hancock-Beaulieu, Robertson, and Neilson , and Drabenstott and Vizine-Goetz , were also included.

Evaluating Bibliographic Displays from the Users' Point of View:
A Focus Group Study

Part 2 - Question 2

Session # ____________ Date: ____________
Time: ____________ Location: ____________

Here is a List of Elements that we could put on a Bibliographic Display. We would Like you to Pick and Rank the Elements in Order of Importance in Selecting the Book you want. Number only those you Think are Important and Omit the Ones you Consider Unimportant. Then the Most Important One should be 1, the Second Most Important 2, and so on.

Element	Rank	Element	Rank
Author(s)		Title	
Type of Material (e.g., Videocassette, etc.)		Main Title in a Second or other Language	
Subtitle		Author or Editor Information	
Other Authors or Editors		Edition Information (e.g., 1st; Revised; etc.)	
Editor of the Edition		Place of Publication	
Name of Publisher		Date of Publication	
Number of Pages or Parts		Illustration or other Physical Details	
Size of Item		Series Title	
Editor of the Series		Standard Number for the Series (ISSN)	
Series Number		Title of Subseries	
Subseries Number		Target Audience	
Standard Number for the Book (ISBN)		Document Abstract	
Table of Contents		Bibliography	
Keywords from the Book Index		Book Review(s)	
Book Index to the Book		Contents Note	
Summary		Language of Text	
Nature of Contents (e.g., Reviews, Filmographies, Legal Cases)		Notes about the Item (e.g., Includes Index; Includes Bibliography; etc.)	
Genre		Reading Level	
Typography		Call Number	
Subjects			

Fig 5.2. Bibliographic Element Ranking Form

The new elements extracted from the above research projects are:

- 'Target Audience' which would inform users for whom the authors had intended the item.
- Document Abstract' which would provide a peek into the content of the item.
- 'Keywords from the Book Index' would list important terms from the index that would convey the main themes of the book.
- Contents Notes" would let users learn about the content of the book.
- 'Reading Level' tells users the reading level required to understand the book.

- 'Genre' classifies an item into a general category such as mystery novel or encyclopaedic handbook.
- 'Typography' describes the print or type size of the book.

Sample Displays

For Part 1 of the focus group session, three records used in Chan's study were used because these records contained different amounts of information and both this and Chan's studies were parts of a larger project by Cherry and Howarth. A copy of the display for each of these records was captured from a Dynix system used by a Canadian public library.

This system was chosen because the bibliographic elements and display format which it used were distinctly different from that used by the host library OPAC system. For Part 2 of the session, five different displays of the same record were used. The record chosen was the shortest of the three records in Part 1. Since, the participants had to examine five displays, we chose the shortest record in order to minimize the amount of information the participants had to process. The five displays included one from a Dynix system, one from a Data Research Associates (DRA) system, one from a Geac system, one from the Library of Congress system, and a prototype display.

The prototype display was constructed as follows. The display which received the highest score in Chan's study was used as the basis. Various features of this display were modified so that they complied with Chan's checklist. For example, text was displayed in bold, labels were displayed in uppercase, and periods were placed at the end of each field text.

Four elements were added to compose the prototype display:

- Summary;
- Genre;
- Reading Level; and
- Typography.

These new elements were suggested by Book House, a graphical OPAC system developed in Denmark. Information for the Summary was extracted from the Preface of the book, while Reading Level was assumed as Average. Typography was added to indicate the size of print.

Other modifications to the display, such as placing Author and Other Author together, including edition information at the end of the title, and eliminating some of the publication information were based on the opinions of the researcher and the English assistant on how to improve the bibliographic display.

The five displays were printed on different coloured paper in order to help the participants distinguish among them. Identifiers and the colour of the paper were randomly assigned to the five displays in the focus group sessions to avoid any order effect on display preferences. Order effect results from participants preferring a particular display because they saw it first or last or because it gained an exaggerated advantage being seen before or after an inferior display. For all the displays in Parts 1 and 2, only the bibliographic parts of screens were used; *i.e.,* instructions to the users, command lines, etc., were omitted.

The displays were produced using WordPerfect for Windows 6.1. All screen breaks and spacing were preserved as in original screens except in the Library of Congress system. The LC system displayed all the information on one screen; but, when being retyped in WordPerfect, an additional screen was required to accommodate all the information.

None of the systems or sites was identified on the displays. The forms and questionnaire and the three displays required for Part 1 were placed in the left pocket of a duo-tang folder whereas the five displays and the two forms were placed in the right pocket of the folder.

Focus Group Script

The questions in the focus group script were formulated to elicit OPAC users' opinions about bibliographic displays.

The purpose of the first question was for the participants to get to know each other and to provide an opportunity for each participant to talk.

The next three questions focused on bibliographic elements:

- The elements that participants would use to decide whether they found what they wanted;
- The elements that the participants believed to be unimportant or unnecessary; and
- The information that the participants would like to see in bibliographic displays but that was not available on the sample displays.

Welcome: The Participants were Welcomed and Thanked for taking Part in the Project. The Moderator Introduced herself and her Assistant to the Participants and Briefly Explained the Purpose of the Project. Then the Moderator asked the Participants to Introduce themselves and Talk about what they were Looking for the Last Time they Used the Library Catalogue.

Part 1: The Following Questions Refer to Displays of Three Different Records taken from One System

1. What Information in these Displays Helps you Choose the Book you want?
2. What Information do you Think should be Removed from the Displays and why?
3. What Information would you Add to the Displays and why?
4. What Features of the Displays make Reading the Screen Easy and why?
5. What Parts of the Bibliographic Displays are Confusing to you and why?
6. Comment on Display B in Terms of Bibliographic Information and Display Format
7. Comment on Display C in Terms of Bibliographic Information and Display Format

Part 2: The Following Questions Refer to the Same Record from Five Different Systems

1. Please Write Down which Display you Prefer and List the Features (for Example, Labels, Text, Content, Appearance, and Overall Layout) you Like and why.
2. Here is a List of Elements that we could Put on a Bibliographic Display. We would Like you to Pick Out the Elements you want to See on a Bibliographic Display. Then Rank these Elements in Order of Importance. Number only those you Think are Important and Omit the Ones you Consider Unimportant. Then the Most Important One should be 1, the Second Most Important 2, and so on.

Part 3: Now you have a List of Elements you would Like to See on a Display. Let's Try to make Our own Iideal Display with the Elements you Consider as Important. (The Participants Engaged in a Free, Unstructured Discussion to Design an ideal Bibliographic Display.)

Fig 5.3. Focus Group Script

Then the participants' attention was directed to the display format. The last two questions in Part 1 of the session prompted the participants for comments related to Display B and Display C in terms of bibliographic element and display format.

Part 2 involved two forms in which the participants were asked to indicate their preferences among the five displays of the same record and the perceived importance of each bibliographic element. The moderator explained the questions to the participants. Part 3 of the focus group session was an unstructured discussion. Therefore, only a single instruction was included.

PROCEDURE

Participant Recruitment

At the request of, and with instructions from, the researchers, librarians at the Scarborough Public Library branches approached adult library users. The study required that these users should visit the library regularly and have experience with OPACs. If the librarians found the users suitable, they would ask the users if they would be interested in participating in the focus groups. The librarians also asked to which of the three age groups the users belonged. The librarians also recruited book club members using the same procedure. Names and telephone numbers of the interested library users were collected by the librarians and given to the researcher.

The researcher phoned each individual to check that he or she was suitable for the project. The researcher checked with each interested library user to see if they were in the appropriate age group, if they visited the library at least once a month, and if they were familiar with the library catalogue system. In cases where time permitted, confirmation letters were sent to the participants prior to the focus group sessions. The researcher also telephoned the participants the day before the focus group sessions to remind them of the time and location of the sessions.

Focus Group Sessions

Before the session began, a duo-tang folder containing the forms, questionnaire, and the displays for both Part 1 and Part 2 was placed at each seat. The participants were asked to sign a Consent Form to indicate their agreement to participate in the study, and an Audio Recording Release Form to authorise the recording of the focus group sessions. The participants also completed a Background Questionnaire that was used to collect demographic information for the purpose of participant description. These forms and questionnaire were found in the left pocket of the folder.

In a welcome speech, the moderator introduced herself and the assistant to the participants and thanked the participants for taking the time to come. The participants were informed about the purpose of the project. After the welcome speech, the focus group session began. The participants were asked to take out the three displays from the left pocket of the folder. Questions listed in the interview script were used to lead the discussion.

Part 1 of the session used three bibliographic records extracted from a Dynix system as the basis of the discussion. The moderator went through questions 1 to 5 using Display A as the basis of discussion. Then the participants were prompted for comments regarding the different characteristics in Display B and Display C including Series and the information written in French. Throughout the discussion in Part 1, the moderator put up the mounted displays on the table in front of the participants to guide the discussion. This part took about 50 minutes.

The participants had a break for 10 to 15 minutes. The moderator invited the participants to have refreshments and informed them of the locations of washrooms. In Part 2, each participant took out the copies of the five bibliographic displays of the same record including displays from the corresponding display used in Part 1, a DRA system, a Geac system, the Library of Congress citation style display, and a prototype display from the right pocket of the folder. The participants were asked to write down on the Display Preference Form found in the same pocket, which of the five displays they preferred, the features they liked in the preferred display, and the reasons for their preferences.

A list of elements that could be placed on a bibliographic display was given to the participants on the Bibliographic Element Ranking Form which was stapled to the Display Preference Form.

The participants were asked to choose those elements they considered important. Then they were asked to rank the elements according to their importance. The participants needed about 10 to 15 minutes to complete Part 2. For Part 3, the moderator asked the participants to form a design team who would use the elements they had selected from the list and create an 'ideal' display on a whiteboard.

The participants' creation was captured with a Polaroid camera. This part required about 40 to 45 minutes. At the end of the session, the assistant handed out the Debriefing Form and the Honorarium Receipt Form to the participants. The Debriefing Form gave information about the researcher and her supervisor whom the participants could contact should they have questions or concerns about the project. After the participants completed the Honorarium Receipt Forms and returned them to the assistant, the participants received an honorarium of $20. The whole session lasted for about 2 hours.

RESULTS

DATA ANALYSIS

The audiotapes were transcribed and saved as ASCII text files by the researcher using MS-DOS Editor, Microsoft Notepad, and Microsoft Write. The transcripts were later checked for errors by either the researcher or her assistant. For the Chinese sessions, the researcher translated the speakers' meanings into English. In other words, the Chinese sessions were not translated literally into English. After transcription, the researcher scanned all the transcripts for emerging themes which were used as nodes in Q.S.R. Nud•ist. As a qualitative data analysis tool, Nud•ist helps organise the data into an index system. Parts of the transcripts can be 'cut-and-pasted' to different indices to show their different implications in the project. Data can be retrieved according to their themes from the index system.

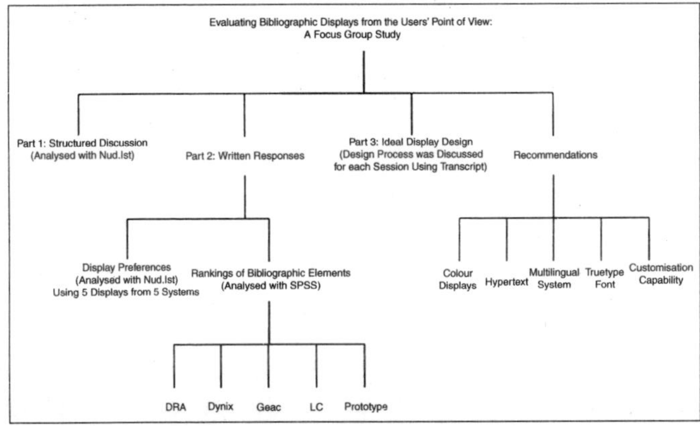

Fig 5.4. Overview of Data Analysis

As shown in figure, the data collected in this project were analysed as follows:

- *Part 1*: Nud•ist was used to group the data that were related. For example, the comments on the importance of Title were gathered from all the sessions and placed under one node. Figure presents a summary of results obtained from Part 1.
- *Part 2:* The written responses collected by the Display Preference Form were analysed using Nud•ist in order to group comments according to systems. The selection and rankings of important bibliographic elements collected from the Bibliographic Element Ranking Form were analysed with SPSS for Windows 6.0. Scores for the bibliographic elements were calculated and sorted in descending order by the software package. The rankings that the participants assigned to each of the bibliographic elements were listed as well.

- *Part 3*: Transcript of the display design process of each session was used to describe how each group created their design.

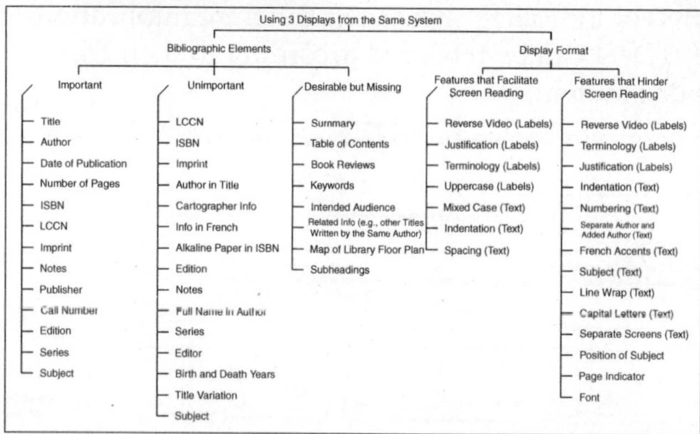

Fig 5.5. Structured Discussion

Nud•ist was used to organise the comments related to the recommendations for future design of bibliographic displays and OPAC systems.

PARTICIPANT PROFILE

Sixteen adults with Chinese as their first language and thirteen adults with English as their first language were participants in the focus group sessions in this project. All participants visited the library regularly and were familiar with online library catalogues. The distribution of gender was almost equal between male (*N*=13) and female (*N*=16). The composition of the six focus group sessions is shown in table.

Table 5.2. Composition of Focus Group Sessions

	Language		
Age Group	Chinese	English	Total
18-30	8 (6F, 2M)	6 (2F, 4M)	14 (8F, 6M)
31-49	6 (4F, 2M)	4 (2F, 2M)	10 (6F, 4M)
50+	2 (0F, 2M)	3 (2F, 1M)	5 (2F, 3M)
Total	16 (10F, 6M)	13 (6F, 7M)	29 (16F, 13M)

Notes: F=Females; M=Males

The participants had combined experience with a total of seventeen OPAC systems. The number of different OPACs the participants had used ranged from one to seven, with an average of about three (M=2.66) systems per participant. These systems included those from public and academic libraries. Eighty-six percent had experience with the OPAC at Scarborough Public Library.

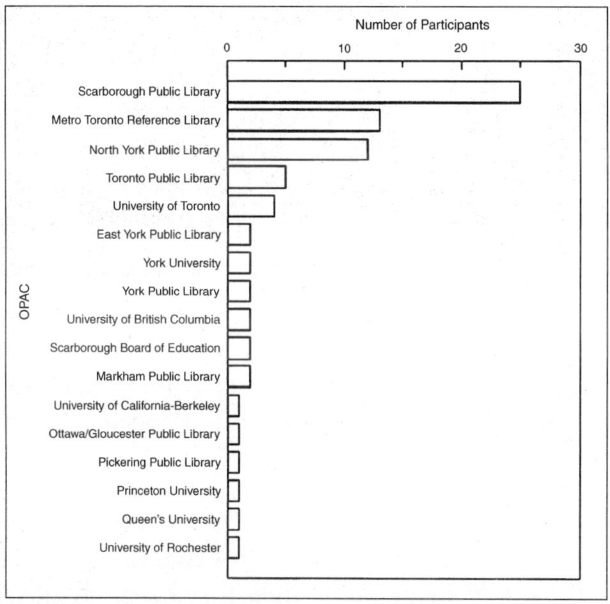

Fig 5.6. OPACS Used by Participants

Systems from other municipalities, the Scarborough Board of Education, and universities were also used by these participants. Thirteen of the participants reported that they had previously used Metropolitan Toronto Reference Library OPAC system. The OPAC at North York Public Library was used by 12 of the participants as well.

CHINESE PARTICIPANTS

Bibliographic Information for Decision Making

In all three of the Chinese sessions, the participants agreed that they would use Title because a book could be identified with this field. Title would be used when participants wanted to clarify the title they were looking for: *'Sometimes I look for a book that I already know the title....'* A number of participants noted that title would be the first piece of information they would use when they saw a bibliographic display: *'I think I would look at the title first.'*; *'Title....'*. Author was also regarded as an important field by the participants in all three sessions who pointed out that during the course of research, they would usually come across a number of authors that were specialised in the area of interest.

Thus, Author was a useful source of information to decide whether the book shown on the bibliographic display would be appropriate. One participant noted, *'I think author is important too. Say if the author is very famous for a particular topic.'* Except for those who were from the Age 50+ group, when participants were asked what information they would use to decide whether they had found a book they wanted, Subject was the third most frequently mentioned bibliographic element.

Nevertheless, some participants complained that the information presented in Subject did not specify the content matter of the item:

- *MC*: Subject, I think, is too brief.
- *Moderator*: Too brief?
- *MC:* I've tried to look for an Economics book and it says only Economics. Then it doesn't say anything. Like I was looking for development and it doesn't say anything like that. Doesn't say what field. I would still need to go.

In addition to Title, Author, and Subject, the Chinese participants mentioned that information contained in the Imprint and Collation fields was useful for deciding whether they would actually go to the shelf and check the book. Date of Publication was considered the most important piece of information found in these two fields.

Participants would use this to find out if they had found the most recent edition or the edition they were looking for:

- *AT:* "That depends how I do my search. If I want to get something on history, I'd find something older.

If I want something recent, I'd try something newer, not some archives."

Another participant said that Publisher would influence whether or not she would like to look up a book: *'If this book is about German literature, I would look for a German press [publisher].'* When one of the participants suggested that Number of Pages be removed, another participant responded that it was an important element:

- *CC:* I think page number and length are not really Moderator: So collation....
- *CMC*: Well, I prefer more pictures and more text.
- *CMC*:... [T]he number of pages would be quite useful. necessary. If you really need the book, you don'tcare how big the book is.. The bigger it is the better. I don't like getting out small books.

The participants in all of the Chinese sessions mentioned that Call Number would not play a part in their decision concerning whether they had found a book they were looking for. Nevertheless, Call Number was recognised as an important piece of information because without it, the book could not be located in the library. This is shown later in the Users' Ideal Display section. With respect to International Standard Book Number (ISBN), one of the participants described the following experience:

- *PC*: "I was in London, England. Before I had to board the plane to Canada, I was looking for this book that's really important. The title was quite confusing. It had several editions but the ISBN number is unchanged. I know that with ISBN, I would be able to find the book, right? And when it changes edition, the ISBN is not changed. And then you have to log on [to the library catalogue system]."

Another participant from the Age 50+ group noted that if "some people would decide to buy [the book]...., [they] would go to the book store to give the ISBN and the large bookstores would be able to locate the book right away."

Participants in only one group agreed that Series was a useful element:

- *DH:* "I think in [Display] B, series is important. Not every book has this series. It's good to know the book is part of a series. I don't think that it's taking up space. But with this series, I get this book called A Course on Mandarin, which has beginner, intermediate, and advanced. It's published in Hong Kong. Some books have even five components. I would like to know how many I need to go through. I got the first one then the second one, and I can find out if there's a third one. The course can be complete."

Bibliographic Information Considered Unnecessary

While a few participants knew what ISBN was, none knew what LCCN represented. Most of the participants in the three Chinese sessions commented that this number was of no use to them:

- *EC:* 'LCCN? I don't even know what it is.'
- *AT*: 'ISBN and LCCN. They're useless to me.'

On the other hand, ISBN was regarded as useless explicitly only by one participant in the Age 50+ group: *"ISBN and LCCN. They're useless to me."* Some of the information found in Imprint and Collation was not considered as important by participants from two of the sessions.

This information included number of pages and the dimension of the item:

- *CC*: "I think number of pages and length [dimension] are not really necessary. If you really need the book, you don't care how big the book is."
- *PC*: The number of pages isn't useful either. The hell
- *Moderator*: Anyone like to borrow books of a lot of pages?
- *EC*: Some students might avoid books with a lot of with that. pages. It depends who uses this.
- *EC*: Say in imprint collation, the 24 centimetres. I don't know what it's for. I don't understand. That it's so thick?

- *Moderator*: It's the height of the book. That's how tall the book is, from the top to the bottom.
- *EC*: Okay, but then so. It doesn't help to decide on the book.
- *Moderator*: Anyone think that it's important to know?
- *AN*: Not really.

However, some participants felt that the number of pages could be useful:

- *CMC*: "The bigger [the book] is, the better. I don't like getting out small books."
- *JS*: "The number of pages can tell you how complete the book is because if it's an extensive subject. A small book would indicate something fairly basic. A big book would be something more comprehensive."

Another piece of information that the participants thought should be removed was the repetition of author names in Title.

Participants commented that the title field should consist of only the title:

- *KW*: I think that in title, there're more names.
- *Moderator*: Here 'by Michael Peterman'?
- *KW*: I think it's a little too confusing.
- *Moderator*: So putting the author after the title is a little.
- *KW*: Yes, but I think this may not be. The author confusing. names could sometimes be part of the title. But sometimes authors should be separated.

The bilingual display in Part 1 caused much discussion in two of the Chinese sessions. In general, the participants would prefer to have the information in French displayed separately. They suggested that users should be provided with an option to choose the language they want the display to be in, then all the displays would be only in the selected language.

To include both languages on a single display, in the participants' opinion, only made the display extremely hard to read.

- *CMC*: Very messy, especially in title. Too big. If it has French and English, there should be a 1 in front of English and 2 for French.
- *Moderator:* So they should be separated and 1 is English and 2 French?

- *CMC:* That's right. So if you want to see French it gives you a function to switch to French.
- *Moderator*: So you'd have another screen to have only French.
- *JL*: Actually for French, it should ask users right from the start whether they want English or French. If the person doesn't understand English and only knows French, he wouldn't be able to read it anyway.
- *Moderator:* So you're saying if I picked English, it'd be all in English. If I picked French, everything would be in French.
- *JL*: Because French isn't really that important.
- *Moderator*: Anyone think that French is important? Anyone know French here?
- *JL*: There're so many languages. Can you put all the languages in there?
- *CMC*: I think there must be both English and French because in Canada these two languages are official. But adding in too many other languages would be too messy in the library system.
- *Moderator*: So you're saying if the book is in two languages. Both languages should be there?
- *CMC:* I think English should come first and then there could be an option 'other' or an asterisk to take users to French.
- *Moderator*: But here in this display, everything would be in English. If you need French, you could go to a French display.
- *CMC:* That's right. If the book is available in French, I think it should state in here somewhere that it's available in French as well. Like in other information including call number of the French book. Then you would know where the book is.

On the other hand, the Age 31-49 group decided to remove all the bibliographic information in French:

- *BY*: Shouldn't have French.
- *PC*: That's right.

- *Moderator*: Take away all the French? Do you want to put it.
- *BY*: Well, I don't know. Some people study at French somewhere so people can find it or take it off completely? schools, but they know English. You don't have to show French to them. That's not necessary.

The participants in the Age 18-30 group noted that the editor and cartographer information should not be placed with Title. They suggested that it should be included in Notes. In the Series field in Display B, three separate lines with 'Twayne's world authors series; Canadian literature TWAS 780.", 'Twayne's world authors series; TWAS 780.', and 'Twayne's world author series. Canadian literature.' were displayed.

The participants in the Age 31-49 group recommended the removal of the last two lines of the series. They considered these two lines repetitive, unnecessary, and *'too much of a waste'* of space and computer memory.

The same group also viewed the inclusion of the author's full name in the author field confusing and redundant:

- *EC:* I think that Henry Burnand in brackets is a little.
- *JS*: Redundant.
- *EC:* It is redundant.
- *Moderator:* Spell out the whole name?
- *EC*: Yes, just that is enough.
- *Moderator:* Anyone think that the initial is better?
- *JS:* That depends on the book because some authors
- *Moderator*: So that depends on the author. But you don't.
- *PC*: I think full name is better because if they have the confusing. would only have the initial on the book. On the cover of the book, it's only an initial. Sometimes, you don't even know what the full name is. need both? same name, like same initial, then it would be confusing. So Henry B is not necessary. Just put Garland Henry Burnand.

Some participants in the Age 18-30 group suggested removing Edition; however, one of the participants disagreed:

- *JC*: I think edition is [not important] to someone.

- *Moderator*: So there's not much difference between different.
- *CMC*: No, I think it's useless too.
- *Moderator*: Anyone think that edition is useful?
- *JL*: Edition should be quite useful. Sometimes you mean to people who are looking for this book, it wouldn't make any difference. You only need to get the resources from the book. It doesn't really matter. editions?... Anyone think that edition is useful? You [CMC]? might find things that are only in the second edition. They weren't there in the first edition. Something newer.

Desirable but Missing Bibliographic Information

Only two additions were mentioned in more than one group: Summary and Circulation Status. Except for the participants in the Age 50+ group, the Chinese participants would like to be able to read a brief summary of the item before going to the shelf:

- *MC*: But I think if there's a description of the book.
- *PC*: Yeah, yeah.
- *MC*: Like a brief description. Then when you look for.
- *Moderator:* So you mean.
- *MC*: Say I need to search for a book, I search on the.
- *Moderator*: Yeah, so like a summary.
- *MC*: Yeah, something brief. A couple of paragraphs the book, you know what the book is about without going to go through the book. screen. I jot down the name [title] and I might not know if it's right. Like on the screen, this book is like about what. Then I wouldn't have to go to the book and look it up. Don't need to walk up and down. I can know before going to the shelf. to tell you.

Nevertheless, one of the participants expressed concern about how this could be accomplished: *"How many books do you think there are in the library?... Way too many books. You can't do that to every book except for the special books."*

One of the participants in the Age 18-30 group would like to know the chapter titles of the book as in a table of contents. It was also recommended by a participant in the Age 31-49 group: *"Chapter title is good too. Yeah, like 12 chapters. You just need a couple of lines to show them all like Chapter 1 is cell structure, Chapter 2 is tissue, Chapter 3. You know, just for example."*

While several participants were concerned about whether the book was in the library or not, only those in the Age 31-49 group wanted to know at which branch the book could be found. This group also suggested the capability to start a search using the information found on the bibliographic display. Instead of having to memorise or write the information and return to the search menu, these users would like to utilise the information on the bibliographic display directly.

The only additional suggestion made by the participants in the Age 50+ group was to further break down the subject headings and create subheadings:

- *AT*: "Okay, there was this time when I was looking for a topic: psychiatry. All the books I got weren't what I wanted. So I went to the librarian and told her that I used psychiatry to search. She asked me whether I wanted clinical psychiatry or theoretical psychiatry. What I wanted was on children, early childhood psychoanalysis. Even the library couldn't help me. So I think there's a problem with the catalogue. So if I got in and wanted psychiatry, I should get something like clinical psychiatry and so on."

Display Features that Facilitate Screen Reading

None of the Chinese participants found any of the features in Part 1 particularly pleasant or easy to read. Although the participants did not particularly like the display features, some commented that when all the limitations of the computer screen were taken into consideration, the system did *'pretty much'* all it could do and the users *'can't ask for more.'*

Display Features that Hinder Screen Reading

The participants from the Age 18-30 and Age 31-49 groups complained about the extensive use of abbreviation in the bibliographic displays. They had trouble understanding what ISBN and LCCN stand for. The participants in the Age 31-49 and Age 50+ groups mentioned that the separation of author and additional authors on the display was also confusing. The participants recommended placing the authors together because it was a more logical decision than placing them separately. The youngest group of participants discussed three other display features that they found confusing.

The indentation of text made the display unclear. In the participants' opinion, the text should be aligned to the left. The numbers used in Author and Subject were deemed unnecessary. They felt that commas should suffice as separators between the names and subject headings. The last confusing feature noted by the participants in this group was the position of Subject on the displays that included Series and Notes.

Subject was positioned after these two elements, and the participants judged that this piece of information was more important than the other two. In other words, the more important elements should be displayed on the first screen while the less important ones on subsequent screens. The Age 31-49 group discussed two different display features that they found confusing.

The words or vocabulary, especially Imprint and Collation, used in the labels were not clear enough:

- *PC*: "I think the word collation is redundant. Imprint is enough, no need for collation. This collation. Because the information is staring right at your face anyway, right? I mean it's very formal. Imprint collation but that's redundant."

Display Preferences

Participants were presented with five different displays of the same record and were requested to choose the one they liked best and describe the features they liked. Of the total 16

Chinese participants, 13 preferred the prototype display. Of the remaining participants, one preferred the DRA display, one preferred the Dynix display, and one preferred the Library of Congress display.

Table 5.3. Chinese Participants—Display Preferences

Display	Number of Participants	Percentage
Dynix	1	6
DRA	1	6
Geac	—	—
Library of Congress	1	6
Prototype	13	81

The reasons for choosing the DRA display included the presence of 'Material' as an element. The placement of this element was also appreciated. The participant who was in the Age 18-30 group wrote, *"I think I like [the DRA display] more than other. It shows the material first to let me know if it is a book or a video. Then all information is very important and very simple."* Although it was selected as the preferred display by one participant, the DRA display was considered as *'not bad'* and *'OK'* by two other participants.

The participant in the Age 50+ group who preferred the Dynix Display indicated that the labels were clear because of the highlighting effect. He also thought that the content in the Dynix display was *'concise and meets most readers' needs [because there was] not much repetition.'* However, other comments regarding the Dynix display were not as positive as this one. Two participants from the Age 31-49 group thought the Dynix display looked *'funny'* and *'busy looking'* which would *'[take] too long to scan.'* Among the 13 participants who chose the prototype over the other displays, eight commented on the inclusion of Summary.

They wrote:

- "[I chose the prototype] because it includes all necessary information to access the work with a brief summary of what the book is about."

- "I think the summary will be useful for the users to determine whether the book is useful or not."
- "...the user can observe [scan] all the summary in a short time from the computer."
- "I would like to choose 'display 3' [Prototype] because it shows a lot of information and details for the book. For example, it shows the brief summary for the book."
- "Summary is helpful to get to know the book."
- "Nice summary."
- "Especially it states out the summary and reading level."
- "It is better than display 5 [Dynix] because it ... has a 'summary'."

Regardless of the overwhelming support for the inclusion of a summary, one participant considered that the prototype had *'too much'* information. Genre, Reading Level, and Typography were also welcomed by the participants:

- 'It also indicates the book is an encyclopaedic version.'
- "It shows the brief summary, what subject it belongs to, what grade for the reading level. It can manage by the reader in their reading level. Also it can make give more understanding and study hints for the book."
- 'Reading level/typography useful'

Most of the participants concluded that the amount of information presented in the prototype display was appropriate:

- 'I prefer Display 3 [Prototype] because it is very detailed and clear'
- 'Clear and informative'
- 'Information useful to most readers'

Most of the comments made with respect to the prototype concerned the display format. The use of 'Screen 1 of 2' as an indicator of the number of screens and the placement in relation to the screens was complimented: *'It tells me there are 2 screens so that I don't overlook the 2nd screen even if I am in a hurry.'*

Bold text was rated as an effective tool to help distinguish the text and the labels: *"Bold word [text] would give us a clear vision [view] while our skimming [of the] information."*; *"The different fonts used for label and content makes [make] it easy to distinguish the 2 sets of information.... The bold face fonts for the content portion makes [make] it easier to read."*

In general, the prototype display was:

- 'In a really neat format'
- 'Very detailed and clear'
- 'Easy to read [and] clean'
- 'Clear and informative'
- 'Clear and good screen space usage'

Despite the positive responses, one participant provided some pointers to improve the prototype display:

- Instead of opening new column [field] for indicating other author, we can put it in the bracket after the major author.
- Physical Description can be described after the published [publishing] companies.
- Keyword should be highlighted in the summary.

In addition to suggestions for improvement, there were also criticisms: *'I cannot understand the call number."*; and the prototype presented *'too much'* information. Although the Geac display was not selected as a preferred display by any participant, comments concerning this display were abundant.

As all the comments were directed at the format of the display, it seems that participants were very dissatisfied with the display format:

- 'Those [The] information are [is] too close.'
- '[The display is] not clear, poorly organised.'
- '[The display] is really hard to read. The cramp spacing is confusing to the user.'
- '[The display is] too simple.'
- '[The display is] busy looking [and] takes too long to scan.'

Besides the positive comment about the LC display from the person who preferred this display, another participant from the Age 31-49 group thought that the LC display was *'OK.'*

However, three participants from the Age 18-30 group were critical of this display:

- '[The display] puts everything together like author, title.'
- '[The display is] difficult to understand.'
- 'Display 4 [LC] has very little labels for necessary info.'

Rankings of Bibliographic Elements on a Display

Given a list of possible bibliographic elements which could be included in a display, the participants chose those they would like to see and ranked the importance of each bibliographic element. The most important element was ranked first and so on. Each element was assigned a unique ranking; *i.e.,* no ties were allowed. Scores for each of the 39 elements were calculated by assigning 39 points to each first ranking, 38 points to second, and so on. The scores for the bibliographic elements selected by the Chinese participants are listed in figure.

All the bibliographic elements will be discussed in descending order: from the element with the highest score to the one with the lowest score and the elements that were not chosen by any participant. Title, Author, and Call Number were the bibliographic elements that the Chinese participants ranked as the first, second, and third most important, respectively. These three elements placed the same in the three age groups as well.

Title was ranked first by eleven participants, third by three, and fourth by two. Although Author was not ranked as first by any participant, it was ranked second by eleven, third by three, fourth by one, and fifth by one. Call Number was ranked in the top five by ten participants. The lowest ranking Call Number received was 19. All the Chinese participants selected and ranked Title, Author, and Call Number as important.

Name of Publisher, ranked fourth overall in importance, scored the sixth, fourth, and fifth highest in the Age 18-30, Age

31-49, and Age 50+ groups, respectively. The highest ranking Name of Publisher received was third and the lowest eighteenth while the most frequently assigned ranking was fifth, given by four participants. Two of the participants did not select Name of Publisher as an important bibliographic element.

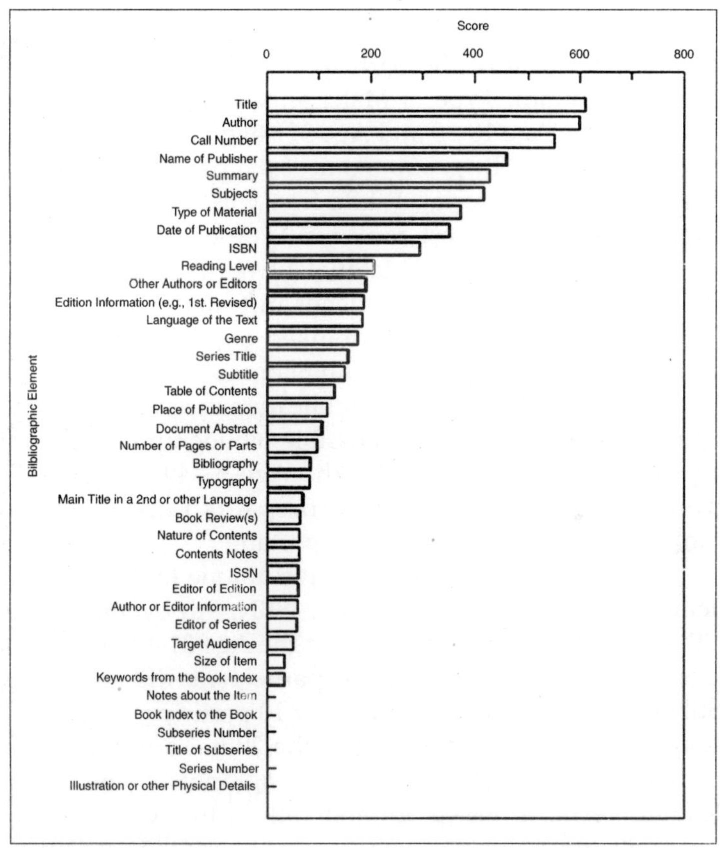

Fig 5.7. Chinese Participants - Ranking of Bibliographic Elements

The fifth overall was Summary, which placed fifth in the Age 18-30 group, tenth in the Age 31-49 group, and sixth in the Age 50+ group. Three of the participants did not select and rank this bibliographic element. The highest and lowest ranks for Summary were fourth and eleventh. Four participants ranked it seventh. Subjects was sixth overall on the important bibliographic elements ranking list. Subjects received different scores in the three different age groups: in the Age 18-30 group it placed fourth, in the Age 31-49 group eighth, and in the Age 50+ group tenth. It was not selected as important by four of the sixteen participants.

However, seven participants gave it third, fourth, and fifth rankings. The rest of the participants ranked subjects sixth, eighth, and ninth. Type of Material, seventh overall, placed seventh in the Age 18-30 and Age 31- 49 groups, but it scored ninth by the Age 50+ group. Four of the participants did not choose Type of Material. While first was the highest rank, fifteenth was the lowest rank for Type of Material. Three participants gave Type of Material a twelfth ranking.

Usually part of the publisher information in existing displays, Date of Publication ranked eighth overall on the Chinese participants' important bibliographic element list. In the Age 18-30 group, Date of Publication received the eighth highest score among the 39 possible bibliographic elements. It placed sixth and fourth by the Age 31-49 and Age 50+ groups, respectively. Four participants ranked Date of Publication as the fourth most important.

The rest of the participants gave unique rankings to this element ranging from 6th to 21st. ISBN, 9th overall, placed 19th in the Age 18-30 group, 5th in the Age 31-49 group, and seventh in the Age 50+ group. Six participants did not include ISBN in their ranking list. The other 10 participants ranked it from the third most important to the 20th. To round up the overall top ten most important bibliographic elements was Reading Level. It placed 9th and 13th in the Age 18-30 and Age 31-49 groups, respectively, while none of the participants in the Age 50+ group selected this element.

Over half of the participants did not select and rank Reading Level as an important element. One participant ranked it 5th and 3 ranked it 10th. The others ranked it 11th and 14th. Other Authors Or Editors ranked 11th overall. In the Age 18-30 group, it scored the 10th highest. In the Age 31-49 group, it placed 27th while in the Age 50+ group, it placed twelfth. The majority of the Chinese participants did not choose this element. The rankings given to other authors or editors ranged from 3rd to 16th. The 12th most important element overall was Editor Information. Editor Information placed 24th in the Age 18-30 group.

On the other hand, in the Age 31-49 group, it placed 11th. In the Age 50+ group, it placed higher, 8th. Ten participants did not include this element in their important bibliographic element list. However, four participants ranked it fifth or eighth. The rest ranked it 11th and 17th. Language of the Text, the 13th overall most important bibliographic element, scored 11th in the Age 18-30 group, 26th in the Age 31-49 group, and 13th in the Age 50+ group.

Only six participants gave the element rankings. The highest rank was 2nd and the lowest 14th. Genre was 14th on the overall list. In the Age 18-30 group, it placed 12th while in the Age 31-49 group it placed 17th. None of the participants in the Age 50+ group selected it. The six participants selected Genre and ranked it from 9th to 13th. Series Title followed Genre to be the 15th on the overall list. In the Age 18-30 and Age 31-49 groups, it scored 16th and 12th, respectively.

None of the participants in the Age 50+ group, on the other hand, included this bibliographic element as an important element. Selected only by five participants, Series Title ranked from fourth to twelfth. The 16th most important bibliographic element overall was Subtitle. Although it was not chosen by any of the participants in the Age 50+ group, it placed 13th and 18th in the Age 18-30 and Age 31-49 groups, respectively. Although it was only chosen by four participants, Subtitle was either at the second or third place. Table of Contents, was selected as the 17th most important overall.

The rankings the participants gave placed Table of Contents as the 14th and 23rd most important bibliographic element on the Age 18-30 and Age 31-49 groups' lists, respectively. Ignored by 12 participants, Table of Contents was ranked 6th, 7th, and 9th by the remaining 4 participants. None of these four participants was from the Age 50+ group. Place of Publication, usually part of the publisher information, was ranked 18th overall. In the Age 18-30 group, it placed 15th while in the Age 31-49 group, it scored 28th. This bibliographic element was not selected by any of the participants in the Age 50+ group. The four participants who chose this element gave it the 5th, 7th, 9th, and 22nd rankings.

Document Abstract was at the 19th place overall. Document Abstract was selected by only three participants who ranked it as the 3rd, 5th, and 6th most important. All of these participants were from the Age 31-49 group; for this group, Document Abstract scored the 9th highest. While the 20th overall bibliographic element, Number of Pages Or Parts, was not selected by any of the participants in the Age 31-49 group, it was 21st and 11th on the Age 18-30 and Age 50+ groups' lists, respectively. The three participants ranked it 5th, 6th, and 12th.

Bibliography ranked 21st on the overall most important bibliographic element list. Only participants from the Age 18-30 group selected this element; in this group, Bibliography placed 17th. The rankings received by Bibliography were 8th, 13th, and 15th.

Typography was ranked 11th, 12th, and 15th by the three participants from the Age 18-30 group. Main Title in A Second Or Foreign Language ranked by one participant from each of the Age 18-30 and Age 31-49 groups who ranked it 4th and 7th, respectively. Book Review ranked 24th overall on the important bibliographic element list.

One participant from each of the Age 18-30 and Age 31-49 groups gave this element the 6th and 10th rankings, respectively. The next most important bibliographic element, Nature of Contents, was selected by two participants who gave the 8th and 10th rankings.

Contents Notes tied with Nature of Contents at the 25/26th place overall and was ranked 9th by two of participants in the Age 18-30 group. Inter-national Standard Serial Number (ISSN) for the series and Editor of Edition were tied at the 27/28th place overall. The score of 61 for ISSN came from the 9th and 10th rankings from the participants in the Age 31-49 group.

One of the participants in the Age 18-30 group gave Editor of Edition a 6th rank while another in the Age 31-49 group rated it 13th. Only selected by two participants from the Age 31-49 group who ranked it 9th and 11th, Author Or Editor Information ranked 29th overall. Although Editor of Series was ranked 11th by two participants from the Age 18-30 and Age 31-49 groups, it was 30th overall. Target Audience came after Editor of Series as the 31st. Rankings of 12th and 16th were given by two participants who were in the Age 18-30 and Age 31- 49 groups.

Size of the Item and Keywords From the Book Index were the second last and last bibliographic elements, respectively, selected by the participants. Size of the Item was ranked 6th by a participant in the Age 18-30 group while Keywords. From the Book Index was selected and ranked 7th by a participant who was in the Age 31-49 group. Six of the bibliographic elements on the ranking form were not selected by any of the Chinese participants: Notes About the Item, Book Index to the Book, Subseries Title, Subseries Number, Series Number, and Illustration Or Other Physical Details.

The Age 18-30 group selected 28 out of the 39 bibliographic elements. In addition to the above six bibliographic elements, the participants in the Age 18-30 group did not choose and rank: Nature of Contents, Keywords From the Book, Document Abstract, ISSN, and Author Or Editor Information. On the other hand, five extra bibliographic elements were not selected as important bibliographic elements by the participants in the Age 31-49 group: Typography, Contents Notes, Bibliography, Size of Item, and Number of Pages Or Parts.

The selection resulted in 28 chosen bibliographic elements. Due to the small size of the Age 50+ group, a large number of the bibliographic elements on the questionnaire were not selected by the participants. The thirteen elements that were chosen included Title, Author, Call Number, Date of Publication, Name of Publisher, Summary, ISBN, Editor Information, Type of Material, Subject Headings, Number of Pages, Other Authors Or Editors, and Language of the Text.

Users' Ideal Display

After the participants selected and ranked the bibliographic elements on the questionnaire, they were asked to design an ideal display with the selected elements. Since, the whole group would create one display and the participants had different element selection and rankings, discussion was rigourous.

The ideal displays that were designed by the Age 18-30 and Age 31-49 groups were reproduced in WordPerfect and included in this section as figures. The Age 50+ group could not agree on one ideal display thus none will be presented in this report. The discussion that led to the final design will show further what the users want in a bibliographic display.

CHINESE: AGE 18-30

The display designed by this group resembled the sample displays they had seen in this project or other OPAC systems. The bibliographic elements they decided to use were displayed in a text-based format with labels on the left and the text on the right.

The group voted to determine which bibliographic elements should be included in the display and where they should be positioned. The participants in this group indicated that they would like the system to employ touch screen or a mouse as a part of the input device.

In order to fully utilise the touch screen or mouse, the participants designed option buttons on the bottom of the screen. These buttons consisted of 'MORE INFO', 'LOCATION', 'MAIN MENU', and 'HELP'. 'MORE INFO' would provide users with the whole list of bibliographic elements as in the ranking form of the questionnaire from which they could choose to obtain further information.

'LOCATION' would take users to an information screen which would give users the information on where the items are located. Users could return to the main menu or the search screen by touching or clicking on the 'MAIN MENU' button. If a touch screen was used instead of a mouse, 'HELP' would *'tell you what these functions are.'* With a mouse, *'you can just move the mouse to point at the function then you get a brief description on what the function is.'*

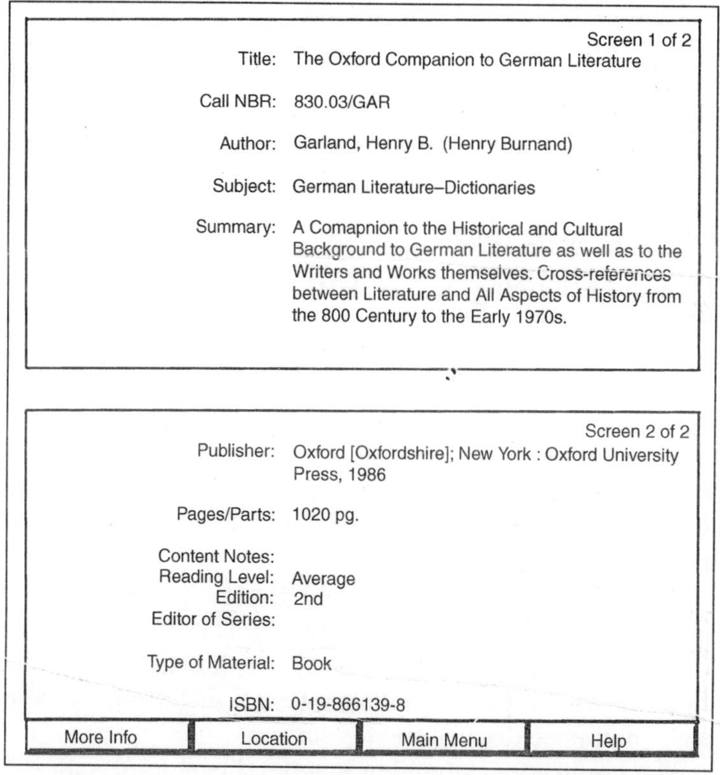

Fig 5.8. Chinese Participants, Age 18-30 - Ideal Display Design

The elements chosen by the participants to place on the display were: Title, Call Number, Author, Subject, Summary, Publisher, Pages/Parts, Content Notes, Reading Level, Edition, Editor of Series, Type of Material, and ISBN. Of these thirteen bibliographic elements, three were new: Summary, Content Notes, and Reading Level. The labels employed the reverse video technique to ensure that they stand out from the rest of the text.

One of the participants suggested using point form in displaying Summary; however, another participant pointed out that the display *'would be messy.'* The participants would also like to see the field they search highlighted. For example, *"if you search by author, author should be highlighted. If it's by title, it should be highlighted.'*

In addition to highlighting the search field, the participants wanted important keywords in Summary highlighted. One participant also suggested using a graphic to indicate *'what the category the book belongs to.'* Finally, the participants wanted to add the pagination indicator on the display.

CHINESE: AGE 31-49

In the beginning of this design session, this group of participants were a little reserved about what features they could use in the bibliographic display because they were concerned about how much the design would cost. After they were told that budget was not an issue about which they had to be concerned, they came up with more ideas. One of the ideas was to use a colour monitor for the OPAC system. The display would be shown using black text on a green background.

The nine elements on the ideal display designed by this group included Title, Author, Publisher/Date, Call Number, Location/Status, Subjects, Additional Info, ISBN, and Material. When one of the participants suggested including Reading Level, an intense discussion was started.

The implications of giving Reading Level information in a bibliographic display were discussed. Some participants were concerned that such information would discourage readers from expanding their horizon because they might think that they were not up to the level prescribed.

On the other hand, the participants who favoured inclusion of the element believed that users could more effectively use the library because they could save time by avoiding books that they could not understand. In the end, the group decided to dismiss the idea of including reading level on the bibliographic display:

	Screen 1
Title	The Oxford Companion to German Literature
Author	1) Garland, Henry Burnand 2) Garland, Mary
Publisher/Date	Oxford University Press, 1986. 2nd Ed.
Call Number	PT41 .G3 1986
Location/Status	Bridlewood/ On Loan Woodside/ In Library
Subjects	German Literature-Dictionary German Literature-Bio-bibliography

	Screen 2
Additional Info (Summary/Document Abstract)	A Companion to the Historical and Cultural Background to German Literature as well as to the Writers and Works themselves. Cross-references between Literature and All Aspects of History from the 800 Century to the Early 1970s.
ISBN	0-19-866139-8
Material	Book

Fig 5.9. Chinese Participants, Age 31-49-Ideal Display Design

- *AN*: And then I think reading level.
- *Moderator*: Reading level.
- *AN*: Yes, looking at this, if the reading level is not
- *Moderator*: Not suitable then.
- *AN*: Don't have to go through again. Don't waste
- *PC*: That's true.
- *AN*: People have different standards.
- *EC*: So how to describe this? My level is really low.
- *AN:* That.
- *BY*: See if the book is suitable for children or adults.
- *EC*: Or use grade school level.
- *BY:* Are they classified already in the library?
- *EC*: No, no.

- *PC*: It's really difficult by classify by grade.
- *Moderator*: Basically now it's children and adults. That's it.
- *PC*: That's really difficult. Like a novel, Mill on the.
- *BY*: Does that depend on what reading level the book
- *Moderator*: But sometimes you have novels that you can read.
- *AN:* I don't think so. Just put down the minimal.
- *Moderator*: The basic minimum.
- *AN:* Yes, say grade 12.
- *BY:* Yeah, grade 11 or 12.
- *AN*: You can choose that. If I can understand that,
- *PC*: That's social engineering because you go to the suitable, you skip it. time. When you choose books, there are many different types of people. How to do this? For illiterate? But sometimes you might want to read a children's book because it's useful. Floss. I read it when I was 12 then I read it again at 18. How would you classify this? is published for? What age? from as a child to an adult. grade level to understand this book. Able to understand. that's suitable. library for many purposes. You narrow, you narrow yourself. At the back of your mind, you shouldn't. You keep thinking that you can't read it, but maybe you can. You can't limit yourself.
- *Moderator*: You might look down yourself. So an eighth-
- *MC*: Everyone's different, right?
- *PC*: Yeah.
- *EC:* The reading progress.
- *PC*: When you read the book, you'd know.
- *AN*: But I think.
- *PC*: At some point, you have to read the book, right?
- *EC:* But say for the general public.
- *PC*: Say Batman Forever. Everyone can see that.
- *EC*: I think her [AN's] meaning of reading level is.
- *PC:* Hmmm.
- *PC*: First, not all books can fit into this academic.

- *BY:* I feel that if you have this book, you read through
- *PC*: Yes, that's right. grader might try too hard to stay away from something that's been designated for grade 12. When you read the book. You've read it since, your childhood, so what grade is that? like Toronto Star is for grade 12 and Toronto Sun, well, we don't know. I think her meaning is like that. Is that right?...
- *Category*: Like encyclopaedia. You can use it for a project in grade 10.... Say for printing, even for a job interview at a printing firm, you can get information from there. Up to the professional level. So where do you gauge that? I got this encyclopaedia of science and technology so what is the reading level? You can't gauge that. You really can't. it. If you can't understand up the fifth word, then don't read this book. You keep reading and realise that you don't understand it, then you should put the book down. That's what I think. Shouldn't be scared by the reading level.
- *PC:* If you put it in there, you discourage people to expand their minds. Like here [pointing to the poster on the wall in the meeting room], the more you read, the smarter you grow. That's the definition of library. You want to expand your mind.

The choice of vocabulary for Additional Info also sparked a discussion. One participant felt that the word, Summary or Document Abstract, seemed too restrictive and did not exactly convey the nature of the information. Consequently, Additional Info was used which could be replaced by Summary or Document Abstract or other relevant bibliographic element as appropriate for the particular record.

As for display format, the participants recommended the use of 'Screen 1' and 'Screen 2' to indicate at which page the user was reading. The participants decided to display the labels in their bibliographic display in reverse video so the labels could be clearly distinguished from the text.

Call Number would be shown in a larger type so it could be easily located on the bibliographic display. The family names of the authors in the author field were in uppercase in order to distinguish the family names from the rest of the name.

CHINESE: AGE 50+

Since, the Age 50+ group consisted only of two participants, agreement on what bibliographic elements to include and the display format to use on a display was hard to achieve. Therefore, for this group only the agreed features will be discussed in this paper. Both participants agreed that the sequence of the first three elements should be Title, Author, and Call Number. The labels should also be highlighted with either reverse video or bold, and blank lines should be placed between bibliographic elements.

RECAPITULATION

The common bibliographic elements chosen by the first two groups of participants included Title, Author, Call Number, Subject, Summary, Type of Material, Publisher and Year of Publication, Edition, Location, and ISBN. The characteristic that made these two displays and the idea of the Age 50+ group different from most of the existing displays was that Call Number was placed after at least one other bibliographic element while the majority of the existing displays displayed Call Number first.

The logic was that users have to decide whether the book was useful before obtaining the Call Number information which could be used to locate the book in the library. The reverse video highlighting technique was appreciated by both groups, and the need to visually separate the labels and the text was apparent.

ENGLISH PARTICIPANTS

Bibliographic Information for Decision Making

Among the bibliographic elements identified as useful for decision making by the English participants, Title and Author were the first mentioned. The purpose of using Title was to confirm that they had found the item: *'...just look at the title just to make sure this is the right book.'* Although one other participant indicated that she would choose to use other elements before Title, Title was acknowledged as one of the most useful elements: *'[Answering moderator's question] The author.... Sometimes the title.'*

Some participants pointed out that Title and Author are the only two pieces of information they would need to decide whether they wanted the book or not: *'I think just take the title and author and go check out the book.'*; *'To me, all I need is author and title.'*

Apart from Title and Author, participants in all three age groups agreed that Subjects is useful in determining whether they have found a book they want. One participant explained that in order to know whether she had found a book she wanted, she could *'see if [the area she's interested in is] listed under subjects.'*

However, one participant from the Age 18-30 group thought that Subjects could be more informative if the headings were more specific:

- *KA*: Yeah, I wouldn't be [going through all the
- *Moderator:* So that's too brief?
- *KA:* Yeah, it depends on, like, if you know, it depends subject headings]. It's probably not narrowed down very much here. what you're looking for.... If you only had words or subjects... it depends how many things are under German Literature though, I guess. But yeah, you'd probably be able to narrow it down further, with more words.

Except for the Age 50+ group, the English participants found the Notes in Display B and Display C useful because knowing that the book has an index and bibliography could help them judge how useful the book would be to them. However, one participant pointed out that the usefulness of Notes depended on the purpose of the search: *"... if I'm doing research I can probably think of something but I personally. What's on there right now, I can't really see them as useful. In research, I don't really see that."*

A Ph.D. student in the Age 31-49 group explained the importance of Notes:

- *FB*: In research, yes, it's important to have an index
- *RG*: But it's not giving you any information there.
- *FB*: That there's an index. That's important.
- *RG*: Okay.
- *FB:* If you have a theme, you can go to the book and
- *RG:* Oh, yes.
- *AT:* Yeah, that's pretty important too. That's true. and to have a bibliography.
- What do you gather from there? From what you see. see very quickly whether the theme is in the book. But you would rather choose books with index. And bibliography.
- *RG*: But not everybody's in research. It might not be
- *FB*: It won't be relevant for [the general users]. relevant.

Other bibliographic elements that did not receive support from all the groups included Date of Publication, Publisher, and Call Number.

The currency of a book was considered essential by a participant from the Age 18-30 group:

- *KA*: "The other thing I find useful is the year. When it listed the year, when I go through a book, a listing of books, I'd like to know if I'm, if I've got a dead-on book that I really want but I find that it's from 1950 then it's not as relevant."

Publisher and Call Number were regarded as useful by the participants in the Age 50+ group. The Publisher was considered as something *'you should know.'* The Call Number is important *'when you look for it.'*

Bibliographic Information Considered Unnecessary

When the participants were asked to name the bibliographic elements they thought were unnecessary, all chose ISBN and LCCN. None of the participants had used these identification numbers before in a library catalogue. In fact, the participants pointed out that they would not search for a book by any of these two numbers. One of the participants in the Age 18-30 group simply said that *'they're a waste of space on my screen.'* Other bibliographic elements that some participants found unnecessary were Imprint and Collation.

The dimension of the book was not regarded as useful in the process of searching for the desired book:

- *II:* What about the 27, 24 centimetres?
- *CW:* I don't think it is [useful].
- *KA*: I don't know what it's for.

Other participants stated that Number of Pages was the most useful information in Collation. One of the participants in the Age 18-30 group pointed out that the usefulness of Number of Pages could be determined by the purpose of the search: *'If you're looking for a research or something, maybe more pages would help you to find something more specific. If you're reading a novel, you don't want to spend two years reading a novel."*

The participants in the Age 31-49 group decided that the information presented in both Imprint and Collation was not helpful in determining whether a desired book has been found:

- *RG*: How about imprint collation? We can eliminate
- *FB*: Oh, yes, I can't stand that. It should be.
- *Moderator*: Imprint is publisher.
- *FB*: That's why it's there.
- *Moderator:* Collation is just number of pages and the size of
- *RG*: Yeah, that's very important!!
- *FB*: That shouldn't be on the first screen. that.. the book.

The participants in the Age 50+ group also *'doubt[ed] that [they] would be worried about the imprint collation..."* In all the three English groups, the inclusion of author names in Title was discussed.

The participants agreed that it was redundant and repetitive:

- *KA*: The title. By Henry and Mary Garland. I
- *Moderator*: So take off the authors?

- *KA*: Yes.
- *Moderator:* The authors in the title should go?...
- *SJ*: If you remove the authors from the title, you've
- *Moderator:* I think it's, okay, I think what it is that this book.
- *SJ*: Yeah, why would they put additional author down.
- *SJ:* If you want to remove it from the title because already know that. only got the one author up there. And there's the additional author. But is that additional author just mean that one book or does it mean there could be additional authors for that German literature? has two autnors but the arrangement is. here and also have it in the title?.. you've got the one here and leave the additional author. Why not put it all in the title then you know that both authors are there.
- *FB*: Somehow the title has by Henry and Mary.
- *FB:* It doesn't make sense.
- *RG:* But it doesn't make sense. It doesn't.
- *FB:* I mean it's four lines. I mean if you take Garland. You must be kidding they just say it. Why do they repeat?.. Garland, Henry. By Henry and Mary Garland. Garland, Mary. It's four lines for one piece of information.

The editor and map information in Display C was discussed by the participants in all three groups. The participants in the Age 18-30 group believed that the map information was not useful at all whereas the editor information may be more important, especially if the book is an edited work:

- *CW:* No one cares about the editor.
- *KA:* But if it's a compilation of things and there're.
- *Moderator*: So the editor is important.
- *KA:* Yes, in this case.
- *Moderator:* Okay, and the cartographer is.
- *CW:* That's you're more interested in the authors.

- *KA:* But if you're looking for a book, if you see this several authors, you would only get an editor. Like if you get a book of readings, it's only. They don't list in the library search you don't get. Yes, it's a compilation of works but you. book in a bibliography, and you see a work. When you cite a reference in a bibliography, you cite that. You cite the author of the particular piece within the book but then they cite the book. If you're picking out the author, do you know what I mean? You go to a reading within a book, you reference the author of the reading and the book. You go to the bibliography and you look for the book. The editor not the author of the piece. You're not gonna find it. You're gonna find the book that has the piece in it.

The participants in the Age 31-49 group came to a similar conclusion regarding the map and editor information. They suggested that this information could be placed in Notes instead of Title: *"They could be in notes. I'm not a map reader but if you're looking for a specific map or a specific map designer, you would need that information. So notes."*

The editor was also considered to be more important than the cartographer:

- *FB:* "Maybe Brereton is well known. So many times the editor is like has a title like an author because he's editing and introducing. It would be very important if he works as a commentator, for example."

On the other hand, the participants in the Age 50+ group were only concerned that the additional information would clutter Title. While one participant thought that *"it's just too much there in the title area"*, another was *'trying to read the title in there.'* All the participants in the English sessions agreed that the French information such as translated Title, Series, and Title Variation in Display C should be removed.

The participants suggested that library users should be given the choice of language before starting a search:

- *II*: 'Can you ask first do you want to search in English or French and you just have one?'

- *RG*: 'Doesn't make any sense to have it like that. You should just be able to push it, F, Alt-F, Alternate F, Alternate French, a button and the whole screen becomes French.'
- *CM:* "It's like an instant teller, you should get to choose French or English. And if you want French you get the same information in French, and English will be just English. I don't think they should be together."

The English participants also noticed that the full name of the author was placed in brackets after his middle initial. The participants considered this arrangement redundant: "... *that's redundant. Should just do Henry Burnand. That's it. Why Henry B.?'* However, while the Age 50+ group agreed to display only Henry Burnand, they noted the exception when the author *'[is] usually known as Henry B.'* The usefulness of Edition generated discussion in all three age groups. The participants in the Age 18-30 and Age 31-49 groups held different opinions regarding this bibliographic element whereas those in the Age 50+ group did not think that it was useful to them at all.

One participant in the Age 18-30 group suggested that the edition information should not be included as a separate bibliographic element; however, another participant disagreed:

- *SJ*: Can they put the edition in the imprint, collation
- *Moderator:* So you don't think it's necessary to have
- *SJ*: Not separate.
- *KY:* I disagree. I think, I find that edition is a very
- *KA*: Yeah, I think it's useful information.
- *SJ*: But when you look at the year, you would look at
- *KY*: Not necessarily. I don't know if it's. You don't part? separate. important thing. I always look at it. To keep it separate is clear. the edition too, wouldn't you? At the same time. know what year it's first printed.

One participant of the Age 31-49 group suggested removing the edition information, but objections were expressed:

- *RG*: Probably eliminate edition.

- *Moderator:* Eliminate edition as well?
- *RG*: Yeah, 'cos.
- *FB*: No.
- *RG*: No? I've never used that.
- *FB*: It's very important because generally you want a
- *RG*: Yeah, two copies of the same book. I always
- *LG*: No, no. They might have more than one edition in
- *RG*: Yeah, that's true.
- *LG:* So theoretically you would want the newest, the
- *FB:* Well, sometimes it's actually interesting to have
- *LG:* That's true.

The participants in the Age 31-49 and Age 50+ groups noticed that in Display B, 'alk. paper' was shown after the ISBN number in the field labelled ISBN. They did not consider this an important piece of information unless as one participant suggested that *'when you try to conserve the library, that's probably important.'* Other suggestions were made concerning the removal of other bibliographic elements from the displays but with less agreement.

The participants in the Age 18-30 group believed that the information in the Series field in Display B was *'very repetitive'*, and that only the first line was necessary to convey the information. The Series field in Display B consisted of three lines which were variation of the same title: 'Twayne's world authors series; Canadian literature TWAS 780.'; 'Twayne's world authors series; TWAS 780.'; and 'Twayne's world authors series. Canadian literature.'

This group also discussed the inclusion of the birth and death years of the authors. At first, these participants could not understand the meaning of the dates in the names. After they realised the meaning, they could not see the purpose. The Age 50+ group noticed that Subjects used in Display C did not provide any additional information at all. The information found in Subjects was already indicated indirectly elsewhere such as through the title.

Desirable but Missing Bibliographic Information

None of the additional information was common to all three groups. The Age 50+ group did not suggest any additional information while the other groups provided more recommendations.

Both the Age 18-30 and Age 31-49 groups would like to have some description of the book such as Summary:

- *SRJ*: Is there another screen that gives a little.
- *Moderator*: You mean.
- *SRJ*: Beyond that a brief description about the content
- *Moderator*: Like what kind of content? Like summary?
- *SRJ*: Yeah, a basic summary. description of the book? of the book.

While discussing the addition of a summary, the participants in the Age 18-30 group also suggested adding *'annotation notes'* and *'review'*. One participant from this group would like a map or layout of the library so he could locate the physical book easily. He complained that *"even if [he] got the call number and everything, [he had] to ask the library because [he did not] exactly know where.'* The Age 31-49 group proposed two unique pieces of information. They suggested that Keywords be included in a bibliographic display because they can help *'find something specific.'*

These participants would also like to have the power to search for related material using the information found on a bibliographic display:

- *RG:* "If the author did another book in the same subject matter, like other than going to the other area and tab it or. Right on there you have all three, you know, then you don't have to go around fiddling other sections.'

Display Features that Facilitate Screen Reading

One of the participants in the Age 18-30 group liked the indentation of the text on the display:

- *II*: I like how the titles [labels] are indented Moderator: So all the labels are aligned to the right.

- *II*: And then title is indented one more time. [aligned].

The participants in the Age 31-49 group did not identify any features that they liked in the displays used in Part 1. The participants in the Age 50+ group expressed their preference of the use of reverse video in the labels: *'[The labels] stand out from the rest. Anything that would make it stand out is preferable.'*

Display Features that Hinder Screen Reading

The participants had trouble understanding the abbreviations used in the three displays in Part 1. These abbreviations included: 'ISBN', 'LCCN', 'CALLNO', 'ADD AUTHOR', 'port.', and 'DSS Cat.'. They also had trouble recognising the roman numerals in Imprint and understanding their purpose. One participant simply said that *'it's very weird that it's so much gibberish.'* The participants noted that the names of authors were separated into two different fields: Author and Add Author. They could not understand why Additional Authors would be placed on the bottom of the display while Author is the second field on the display:

- *KA*: Yeah, because if you're looking by author, and
- *II:* Author.
- *KA:* Just combine the two. it's only in title, you're not gonna find the author. I would move additional author up into Yeah, or just take author and put both names in author. I don't know why it's additional.
- *AT:* What's a-d-d author?
- *FB*: Added author.
- *Moderator:* Yeah.
- *FB:* She's his wife.
- *Moderator:* Yeah.
- *FB:* Gee, look at him. She's a co-author. She's right
- *Moderator*: So you're saying this one should go with the
- *FB:* I mean this is not logical. I would put ISBN and at the end of this. I've got to write to the Library of Congress about this. author. imprint, collation there and add author on the first [screen].

The participants did not like to have one piece of information split across two screens:

- *CM*: "Another thing that annoys me is that in imprint, one line is in section [screen] one and the second line are in section [screen] two with continued. You would think that you wouldn't get the second line on the first one. Or if they can't put both lines on the second one."

The participants from both the Age 31-49 and Age 50+ groups found the rightjustification of the labels to be confusing. The screen looked too busy and was hard to read:

- *CM*: This surprised me. The labels are this side.
- *Moderator:* You mean the labels are aligned to the right.
- *CM:* You know what I mean.
- *RB:* Doesn't look neat and tidy, does it?
- *CM:* No, doesn't look neat. Should be to the left.

In the displays used in Part 1, the labels were right-justified while the text was not justified.

These two groups pointed out that the indentation of the text was messy and confusing:

- *RG*: "But then the body copy [text] should be flushed left too. Now you're having this Oxford sticking out indented. That just throws off the whole thing. If you're gonna have numbers like 2nd [in edition], that should all lined up to the seam. That adds up to the busy-ness too."
- *NS:* "What I can't understand is in the top display [screen], everything's lined up except the number which is off line and the title is offline. Because it's very easy to misread it."

Unlike the participants in the Age 50+ group, the participants in the Age 31-49 group did not think reverse video was an effective way to display the labels: *"Don't like it. It's too. It adds to the busy-ness of the screen. But I know you need something. You need something to highlight it. I'd probably go a bolded type..."* One of the participants in the Age 31-49 group suggested that the display of text did not need to wrap at the right-hand edge of the screen. Library users could continue to read the text by pressing the left arrow key. This could reduce the amount of text or information display on the screen.

The same group proposed deleting the second German Literature in Subjects in Display A because it took up too much space and was repetitive:

- *FB:* About the subject, why do they have two?
- *AT:* Slash.
- *FB:* Bio-bibliography. German literature dictionaries and German literature. Why not only one subject? German literature dictionaries.

In the displays used in Part 1, numbers were placed next to the names in the Author, Subjects, and Add Author fields. For example, in Display A, the text in Author looked like this: '1) Garland, Henry B.".

The participants in the Age 31-49 group expressed their objections to having numbers in Author. They thought that these numbers in Display A were confusing because there were only 1's, no 2's or 3's, in both Author and Add Author.

Moreover, they were considered the numbers irrelevant. These participants also complained about the lack of French accents in OPACs. They pointed out that without the accents, the French information was barely intelligible. A participant in the Age 50+ group was annoyed by the lack of capital letters in Title: '*This annoys me. The words in title should all begin with capital letters.*'

Display Preferences

The participants chose a preferred display among the five given to them in Part 2. In addition to the preferences, the participants were asked to provide brief reasons why they selected a particular display. They were encouraged to write any comments regarding other displays as well. Table shows that nine of the thirteen English participants preferred the prototype display. Two participants selected the Dynix display while the DRA and Geac displays were each chosen by one participant.

Table 5.4. English Participants—Display Preferences

Display	Number of Participants	Percentage
Dynix	2	15
DRA	1	8
Geac	1	8
Library of Congress	—	—
Prototype	9	69

One of the two participants that selected the Dynix display believed that this display was superior to others with respect to text, overall layout, appearances, and content.

The other participant preferred this display because:

- The labels—dark w/ light stands out better.
- All pertinent info is on the 1st screen. Any more info I would need to see the book, but I would need to have used the book anyway, *i.e.*) in a reference for an essay:
  - If I am looking for a book to read for pleasure, I would likely already know the author and title
  - Overall layout is good

  Text is good and simple"

The participant in the Age 50+ group who chose the DRA display did not give any reason in the Display Preference Form. Another participant from the Age 18-30 group questioned the need to display Type of Material: *'did you really need to put material: book listed'*

RECAPITULATION

The three display designs demonstrated one difference among ages groups: The use of graphics was significantly less in the Age 50+ group as compared to the Age 18-30 and Age 31-49 groups. Nevertheless, the common bibliographic elements chosen by these groups were Title, Author, Call Number, Edition, and Availability.

6

Pre-Coordinate Indexes

INTRODUCTION

In the era of card catalogues, user searches by subject were not as frequent as known item searches and thus received little academic or practical attention. However, the introduction of on-line catalogues (OPAC's) renewed users' interest in subject searches. With the new OPAC's, users searched by subject more often than any other search method but were frustrated by the various limitations of the early OPAC's cited in Drabenstott. In response to users' demands for better subject access, researchers have proposed a series of rather elaborate online public access catalogue (OPAC) designs, containing, among other things, on-line thesauri, syndetic structures, class schedules, and document clustering.

A promising development is the combination of probabilistic and Boolean retrieval in the Okapi and Cheshire systems. Nevertheless, subject searching still leaves much room for improvemens. Many of these proposals remain in an experimental stage, and some place new burdens on users who have to master advanced system features for effective use, where it is known that even traditional Boolean queries are difficult for most users cited in. For these and other reasons, subject searching remains difficult for users.

The recent special issue of JASIS dedicated to OPAC's began with Borgman's paper entitled 'Why are Online Catalogues Still Hard to Use?' The editors of the special issue accepted the premise that "despite the advances in technology, research continues to show that these systems are ineffective and hard to use". The frequency of subject search failures, *i.e.,* subject queries which return zero hits or a very high average number of hits per query are the most frequently cited search failures. Taken together, these results imply that users are either getting few useful results or are overloaded with results in response to a given query.

As the costs of digital publishing fall, inexpensive online and Internet publishing is rapidly expanding the available number and types of searchable documents. However, for a given level of search precision, increasing the size of the searchable world of documents means a corresponding increase in the size of the result set, confronting users with an information overload problem. Users increasingly discover that queries to search engines like Alta Vista that index a large part of the public Internet result in unmanageably large response sets.

To make matters worse, Internet indexing methods have heavily favoured full text over other types of indexing. While there are some results to the contrary, the overwhelming evidence is that full text search results in lower precision ratios than keyword search for large databases. Moreover, as databases grow the problem of low precision in full-text search is *proportional* worse. Thus we can assume that the increasing size of result sets will render full text search of documents published on the Internet or other very large electronic document collections increasingly impractical and inefficient.

In this introductory paper we propose a new method which we call partial coordination that combines the strengths of two subject cataloging and search methods for documents —pre-coordination, as in traditional card catalogues, and post-coordination, as in computerised keyword search. We propose this method will result in greater precision for a given level of recall. The proposal is made in the spirit of Lynch's belief that librarians can help computers bring order to the digital world.

PRE-COORDINATION AND POST-COORDINATION CRITICALLY REVIEWED

Historically, library science focused on providing good subject access to documents using pre-coordination of subject terms. Fixing the citation order of each subject heading, *e.g.*, United States—History—Civil War in a card catalogue system is known as pre-coordination.

For a user of the catalogue system to successfully find relevant information on the history of the US Civil War, they would have to:

- Choose the right terms from the many possible synonyms which refer to a given concept, and
- Choose the correct ordering from the many terms in a compound subject. For example, know to look under United States—History—Civil War in an alphabetical catalogue to find relevant documents.

The latter requirement is obviated by the introduction of computers and OPAC's. Using a keyword search, the computer would find documents labeled with the subject heading United States—History—Civil War, even if the user input the query terms in the 'wrong order'—*e.g.*, a query 'Civil War History United States'. Allowing the terms of a compound subject heading to be effectively re-ordered to match any query is known as post-coordination.

In some communities such as the World Wide Web, post coordination is generally accepted as more practical and useful, and its costs and effectiveness relative to pre-coordination have been largely unquestioned.

However, there are substantial benefits and limitations to both methods which are reviewed below. We refer to pre-coordination as a method of indexing *and* retrieval. When discussing pre-coordination, then, we intend a situation in which the cataloguers supply terms and an order among them, and this order is then actually used in the process of retrieval.

Similarly, when discussing post-coordination we intend a situation in which subject terms are not given an order, nor are users anticipating any such ordering of terms. We focus our analysis at a level that allows meaningful comparisons without getting distracted by the specific implementation of a particular system.

PRE-COORDINATION STRENGTHS AND WEAKNESSES

The enhanced precision and recall benefits of pre-coordination arise from the standardisation of term orderings, and from the selection of intelligent term orderings.

Standardisation of Order imposes a specific term ordering in the catalogue "to ensure that the same composite subject is always treated in the same way, no matter how it may be expressed in natural language". This ordering enhances *recall* when the *same idea* can be expressed with different syntaxes using the same natural language subject terms.

Standardised term ordering reduces the variability from different syntaxes, and provides a consistent way for users to find documents regardless of variety of ways of combining natural language terms to express the same idea. This particular benefit is also realised in post-coordination, since, postcoordination ensure a topic can be repeatedly found regardless of the cataloguer's or user's selection of a citation order of subject terms for the topic.

A second, often overlooked advantage of pre-co-ordination, is that standardisation of order enhances *precision* when the same terms can express *diferent ideas* through different syntaxes. For example, 'Wars Economic Crises' is different from 'Economic Crises Wars'. In both cases the same terms are related by a different cause-effect relationship.

Theoretically, pre-coordination can define a standardised ordering of concepts when two terms are related in such a semantic relationship. For example, where the terms are related by the 'cause-effect' relationship, it may be standardised that the 'effect' term must always precede the 'causef term. This standardisation would allow 'Wars-Economics' to have an entirely different meaning from 'Economics-Wars', and appropriately assigns documents to distant parts of the card catalogue, to avoid confusion on the subject.

In post-coordination the unordered list of query terms 'war, economics' matches documents on both subjects.

Moreover, with postcoordination search a query term can match any subset of the document's subject terms, regardless of those terms' position in the subject heading. An arbitrary subset of the subject heading's terms can represent a very different meaning from the original heading.

Thus the *precision enhancing benefit* of pre-coordinated standard orderings is totally lost in post-coordination. This precision enhancing benefit of pre-coordination is generally underemphasised in most comparisons of pre- and post-coordination. All these benefits are somewhat diminished in a dictionary catalogue with a rule of specific entry as opposed to an alphabetico-classed catalogue. However, even dictionary catalogues such as LCSH are strongly influenced by the principles of classed catalogues because of "the decided advantage of the alphabetico-classed catalogue for grouping related objects together" which has proved too much for the 'keepers of LCSH' to resist.

In summary, for every relationship among terms—syntactic or semantic—a cataloging formalism can be defined to standardise term ordering and thus enhance precision. Various pre-coordinate schemes differ in the number and kind of relationships for which they standardise a citation order among the terms. One ambitious scheme of this kind is PRECIS. While selection of any standardised citation order can achieve the aforementioned benefits, selection of *intelligent term orderings* further enhances the precision of pre-coordination.

Regarding recall, consider a document on the 'religious aspects of dreams'. This document should be grouped with other books on dreams rather than with other books on 'religious aspects '. This reasonable grouping is achieved by ordering the 'dreams' term before the 'religious aspects' term. This intelligent decision by a cataloguer enhances recall by making it easier for a user to correctly guess the citation order. Intelligent term orderings also enhance precision by grouping together like documents and un-grouping un-like ones. This means that once a user has found the complete, and correct subject heading, he or she will find mostly related and relevant documents.

A second precision enhancing mechanism of intelligent ordering is the *avoidance* of *improper partial matches* by clearly defining the *context* of each heading term. In pre-coordination a partial match occurs when the user has guessed the first terms of a subject heading in the correct order, but he or she has not guessed all the terms. By not completing the subject heading, the user must now browse the various subdivisions. An intelligent ordering will help ensure that users will not achieve partial matches which require them to browse through mostly irrelevant material.

The ordering ensures that if the user matches the subject's outer terms in a partial match, he will be browsing in the right ballpark; at the same time, it ensures that the inner terms are hidden, and cannot be the basis for a partial match. In the example book on religious aspects of dreams, the enhanced precision is clear. Suppose this book were catalogued under the subject heading Religious Aspects—Dreams. Then a user interested in this aspect of dreams, who partially matched by looking under 'Religious Aspects' would find himself browsing through numerous documents and subdivisions related to Religious Aspects of Everything, and totally unrelated to his area of interest.

In this sense, he would have partially matched the term Religious Aspects out of context, It is better for precision if the term Religious Aspects is only found as a subdivision of the more substantive Dreams term. In that case, the Religious Aspects term would be matched only in the context of Dreams, and an inappropriate partial match would be avoided. Pre-coordinate schemes use two mechanisms to establish the context for a term. Citation order is one mechanism, term phrasing is another. For example, the LCSH heading 'Art, Asian' uses a term phrase to ensure that the term Asian matches only in the context of Art.

With a compound subject, the cataloguer prevents spurious partial matches by either forming a phgrase or using citation order between terms. While standardised and intelligent selection of term orderings provide a number of precision enhancing benefits, there are numerous limitations to traditional pre-coordination. First, there is a limit to the precision with which documents can be cataloged using pre-coordination.

Most LCSH authority subject headings contain a single main heading with no topical subdivisions; only 'occassionally' is there an authority heading with two or more topical subdivisions. This is a necessary—not incidental—limitation with pre-coordination, since, users of pre-coordinated search are required to correctly guess each term in its correct order, in order to locate the intended subject heading. Only a fairly shallow subject heading has any chance of being properly guessed at by the user. But this limit on the number of subdivisions directly limits the potential precision of search results.

Related to this, not only is the number of subdivisions limited, but only a limited *kind* of semantic relationships is represented in LCSH subdivisions. There is only a small number of subdivision types, *e.g.,* form, location, sub-topic. And even the topical subdivisions often represent one of a limited number of relationships, often established in a pattern, *e.g.,*—Economic Aspects. Here again, this limitation is not incidental to LCSH, but is a necessary limitation of a pre-coordinated approach. Second, ordinary users cannot be expected to encode their queries according to elaborate rules.

Even in the relatively simple LCSH scheme, users find it difficult to guess the citation order of compound subjects. Steinberg and Metz found that only 28.2 per cent of the users even knew the subject heading needed to be an authorised LC heading. Perhaps for reason of these difficulties, subject searches were less common than know nitem searches in the era of pre-coordinated card catalogues. These results suggest that attempts to improve subject search results should introduce no new burdens on users.

POST-COORDINATION
STRENGTHS AND WEAKNESSES

The primary benefit of post coordination is to reduce the users' effort of learning any formalisms, including rules governing citation order, to construct queries. However, the benefits of standard or intelligent orderings are thereby lost. The most significant loss in performance in contrast to pre-coordination is the loss of *precision* arising from *intelligent* orderings to prevent inappropriate partial matches. This is doubly unfortunate because partial matches are an even more significant issue in the post-coordinate document retrieval. With pre-coordination, a partial match only occurs to the extent the user guesses the first terms in their proper order; the match is then partial with respect to the later terms which he has omitted.

In this partial match the user does not immediately retrieve documents but instead, is presented with a pre-coordinated hierarchy of subject headings. The topic and documents the user desires is somewhere below the subject heading fragment which the user has guessed. In post-coordinate systems, on the other hand, a partial match of one or more keywords actually retrieves lists of documents, and furthermore, any document is retrieved if any of its uncoordinated subject terms matches any term in the uncoordinated list of query terms. This large number of inappropriate partial matches may be reflected in lowered precision and large retrieval sets of post-coordinate keyword search.

Revisiting our previous example, suppose a user is interested in the religious aspects of dreams. He would like to specify the two keywords Dreams and Religious Aspects is of no interest, while a book about dreams which is not about its religious aspects has some relevance. But the user's query vector will retrieve documents of both sorts with an equal partial match. The subject term 'Religious Aspects' from the document about religious aspects of war, will match the Religious Aspects term in the query about dreams.

Yet this match is totally out of context, and represents a false drop. In this way, the loss of an intelligent ordering of terms may result in many false drops. Post-coordinated search may therefore result in lower precision than precoordinated search, *given* the *identical subject terms*. But because the process of keyword selection is different when assigning an authorised precoordinated subject heading and when selecting post-coordinated keyword terms, the two retrieval methods typically do *not* operate on the identical subject terms. We indicate that the differences in keyword selection may actually exacerbate the problems of false drops in postcoordinated retrieval.

In contrast to Library of Congress style pre-coordination, the *lack of a theory* for selecting postcoordinate keywords encourages the use of more subject keyword terms and more narrowly specialised keyword terms. With full-text indexing, these tendencies are automated. For manually assigned subject terms, reports of these tendencies are anecdotal but appear widespread.

In post-coordination it is assumed the user can only benefit from the application of more keyword terms to a document. The user is not penalised in post-coordination for missing the citation ordering or for missing an additional subject term, so the additional terms can only lead to more matches, which is assumed to benefit the user.

Adding more keyword terms seems reasonable. But if the additional keyword terms would rightfully be ordered after another term if term coordination were employed, then adding the term without coordination creates more opportunity for an out of context post-coordinate match. The addition of *narrow* keyword terms can also exacerbate out of context matches.

Despite the LCSH rule of specific entry, pre-coordinated subject heading terms describe a category rather than its instances. Fuggman refers to these as general concepts. For example, 'Insects' is an authorised subject heading, while the names of particular kinds of insects are not. This example was originally introduced by Fuggman as demonstrating the need for controlled vocabulary to enhance recall through 'representational predicatability'.

But the use of general concepts in a controlled vocabulary actually enhances precision, especially in a post-coordinated environment. The reason for this is that a specific instance of a category may simultaneously be an instance of many other categories potentially causing false drops. For example, 'Tarantula' may be considered by some as a poisonous insect, and by others as a horror film prop.

The categorical subject term 'Insect' will not cause an out of context match, but the additional narrower term 'Tarantula' may indeed cause out of context matches, as a user may intend biological research and the document may be about B-movies. For example, an Infoseek search produced in the top 10 documents, some which regard tarantulas as pets, and one of a Native American folk story of creation.

To some authors, a tarantula is an instance of a house pet, while to others it is an instance of a Native American mythical figure. The problem of non-categorical subject terms can be stated generally as follows: Non-categorical terms that are the instance of a specific category can simultaneously be instances of other categories. The addition of such narrow terms can thus further exacerbates the problem of out of context partial matches. The two described characteristics of post-coordinate keyword selection versus pre-coordinate LC heading term selection—*i.e.,* more and narrower terms—are not necessarily misguided.

The addition of more and narrower terms for post-coordinated keyword search does indeed have some benefits. But these may be offset by reductions in precision. An empirical study of these tradeoffs is a target for future research. Our point here is not to resolve these issues but to indicate that the problems of false hits in post-coordinated search may be exacerbated by the subject term selection process. In summary, pre-coordination enhances precision by specifying both so*me* order and an *intelligent* order on terms. In contrast, post coordination reduces the user's and cataloguer's efforts to select and order terms.

However, post coordination does not recognise the benefits of term ordering and thus gives rise to spurious partial matches. As the volume of material increases in a post coordinate system, the number of false drops continues to rise. In an ideal post-coordinate system, users would not receive spurious partial matches, but would still be relieved from the need to specify term orderings, or the need to think about synonym and hierarchy control. We critically examine and further classify the types of out-of-context partial matches. Partial coordination which we propose later in this paper overcomes many types of out-of-context partial matches, and aims to reintroduce the precision-enhancing benefits of term coordination to the postcoordinated online environment of OPAC's.

OUT OF CONTEXT MATCHES *TYPES AND ISSUES*

Out of context matches are a primary source of false drops. Understanding the types of out-of-context matching is critical to improving search methods. Our analysis identified five distinct and major types of out-of-context matches. Some of these false drops are particularly problematic in full text search.

ORDERED RELATIONSHIP AMONG TERMS

In our previous example on "Dreams—Religious Aspects' false drops can occur if a query term matches 'Religious Aspects'. The term 'Religious Aspects' has *matched out of context of its* relationship to another term in the heading.

POLYSEMY

Out of context false drops can also occur when a term in the document index differ in meaning from the same term in the query. Anyone searching the WWW with a full-text search engine such as Lycos or Infoseek will have encountered any number of surprising—and sometimes very amusing—false drops which result from a polysemous term. For example anyone searching for articles on the birth of Andromeda may get articles on both the birth of starfish or a galaxy.

Unlike the previous out-of context problem, this occurs because an identical term has different meanings in the document and the query. Polysemy is worst in the case of full-text indexing, since, cataloguing schemes would generally make some effort to avoid including polysemous words through a controlled vocabulary. This is consider a problem of 'context' in the sense that a human reader—or intelligent machine—could identify the *various meanings from* the context in which they appear.

OUT OF PHRASE TERMS

These false drops occur when a query or document phrase is not treated as a single unit. For example, query #I59 from the TREC3 conference asks about electric cars under development, and the full-text retrieval we studied ranked as 36th an AP newswire about a couple whose *car* was hit by lightning in an *electrical* storm. In the newswire, the terms electric and car both appear, but not in the phrase 'electric car'. In these types of false drops, an individual term may occur within a phrase in the document heading, and in a very different phrase or as an individual term in the query. A false match occurs when a term matches *out of context of its term phrase.* This problem has been extensively addressed in IR research.

EXHAUSTIVITY—SECONDARY TOPIC KEYWORDS

A fourth sort of out-of-context matches occurs when the matching term in the document and query can be said to have an identical meaning, yet the document term does not represent a primary topic of the document. Manual assignment of subject headings can avoid this problem by not including keywords of secondary importance, but then a certain degree of recall and precision would be lost, as only the broadest topic of each document would be indexed.

In the case of full-text indexing, much research effort has gone into this challenge of automatically identifying the 'aboutness' of documents. The goal of these efforts is to rank documents which are very 'about' the query topic. In spite of those efforts, many of the false drops we studied from TREC3 were a result of this sort of error. This problem is essentially one of reduced precision from increased exhaustivity of indexing".

This problem may be viewed as a document matching 'out of context' in the sense that the matching terms are assigned unwarranted prominence by an algorithm which does not understand the primary topic or 'context' of the *document.* This problem is also addressed by partial coordination.

DEPTH—NON-CATEGORICAL TERMS

As discussed in the earlier review of post coordination, the use of non-categorical terms as subject heading keywords poses problems because a query or document subject term which is an instance of one category can simultaneously be an instance of one or many other categories. This problem is essentially one of reduced precision due to increased depth in indexing. A false drop may occur when the narrower term matches out of the context of its intended broader category.

Users have two strategies where the document subject terms are non-categorical: To use the appropriate categorical term in the query despite its likely absence from the document headings, or to use in the query the narrower terms he expects to find in the document headings. However both strategies are vulnerable to problems of recall and precision. These five types of out-of-context matches reduce the effectiveness of post-coordinate searches. They are partly responsible for the phenomenon of WWW search engines returning thousands or even hundreds of thousands of irrelevant documents in response to queries. The partial coordination method which we propose below can alleviate all the problems except for polysemy.

PARTIAL COORDINATION

We propose partial coordination as a new method to inhibit inappropriate partial matches of keyword searches through the use of context. Partial coordination differs from pre-coordination by replacing term orderings with term dependencies, and from post coordination by using the dependency information to achieve better in-context matches between queries and documents. Partial coordination improves precision by defining high relevance scores for documents when particular *combinations of dependent terms* match in the query and document in contrast to independent matches of individual terms in both the query and document.

In this way, a term might contribute to the match in the right context but nothing or little in the absence of that context. There are a number different approaches to defining term dependencies and document scores. The term dependency information must accompany either the documents' subject headings or the users' queries. A user can define the query terms, and then further specify term dependencies which determine the score a document has as a function of which query terms it matches. In the extreme case, for n query terms the user specifies a score for each of the possible 2"-1 partial matches.

Alternatively, a cataloguer can specify a *document's* keywords, and further specify term dependencies which determine the score this document will have in terms of potential queries. In the extreme case of the latter approach, for n keywords, the cataloguer has to specify document scores with respect to each of the 2^{n-1} queries which partially match the document's keywords. We adopt the latter approach in the sense that the dependency information accompanies each document's subject heading, rather than each user's query. This approach imposes the least effort on the user. In our approach the cataloguer does not need to explicitly define 2^{n-1} possible scores.

Instead, he/she supplies term dependency information. A scoring function is then applied to each document during retrieval which calculates the score of the document as a function of the particular subject terms included in the user query. For each partially coordinated document, the cataloguer defines a list of index terms. The list of index terms remains similar to pre-or post-coordinate terms. In pre-coordination the cataloguer then forms *term phrases* and *term orderings* to prevent spurious partial matches. In contrast, with partial coordination the cataloguer specifies *term dependencies* instead of term phrases and term ordering.

Specifically, the cataloguer defines each subject term in the document subject heading to depend on zero, one, or more other 'dependency' terms. If subject term A is specified by the cataloguer to depend on dependency term B in a particular document, then term A in this document will match a corresponding term A in a query *only if the query also includes the term B.* Only subject terms can match query terms. Dependency terms are not access points to the document, and cannot match query terms. But a term can be used as a dependency term and also as a subject term. For example, suppose the cataloguer has specified that subject term A has the single dependency term B.

The cataloguer can then independently decide whether to include term B as a subject term, and what its dependencies should be. If the cataloguer in this case decides to include subject term B, and specifies that it depends on term A, then he/she would effectively form a phrase consisting of both terms A and B in no particular order. A cataloguer thus has the usual freedom regarding what terms to include as subject terms for a document. In addition, by specifying term dependencies, a document subject term *will n*ot automatically form a partial match with every query which contains it. Rather, it will form a partial match only with queries which contain that term and also contain that term's dependencies.

A PARTIAL COORDINATION EXAMPLE
DEPENDENCIES AND SCORES

Consider a Wall Street Journal article about the government takeover of an oil spill cleanup effort. Suppose we use the post-coordinated subject terms: 'government takeover oil spill cleanup'. Then, a user submitting the query 'government takeover banks', for example, will get a partial match and retrieve this document with a positive score in a post coordinate system. However, the score zero would seem more appropriate in this case as the query term 'takeover' ought not to match 'takeover' in the document subject term.

This is an example of the out-of-context match, in which an individual term matches out of the context of a topic/subtopic relationship between the terms 'cleanup' and 'takeover'. Similarly, any query regarding a spill of anything or regarding the oil industry would retrieve this document if each query term is treated independently, unless the user knew to specify that the two terms form the phrase 'oil spill'. This is an example of two terms which would match out of the context of a phrase.

By partially coordinating the document subject terms 'oil' and 'spill' to depend on one another; and by partially coordinating the document's subject term 'takeover' to depend on the term 'cleanup', and the term 'government' to depend on both 'oil' and 'spill', the cataloguer can solve the problems. With these dependencies, the subject terms 'oil ' and 'spill' are hidden behind one another—something that is not possible where genuine ordering are required—so that neither of those document terms will match any query unless the query contains both of those terms. The term 'takeover' is hidden behind the term 'cleanup'.

This dependency captures the topic/subtopic relationship between 'cleanup' and 'takeover', so that takeover does not match except where the query regards a 'cleanup'. And the term 'government' is hidden behind the phrase 'oil spill'. This dependency also represents a topic/sub-topic relationship, so that the term 'government' does not match out of the context of its dependency—*i.e.*, oil spill. A user entering the query 'government takeovers banks' will not retrieve this document at all, as the document terms 'government' and 'takeover' will not match with respect to this query.

The flexibility of partial coordination can be seen in the nuances of this example. First, the number of coordinated terms is more than could be reflected in the limited number of LCSH subdivisions allowed in an entry. Second, we identified two dependencies as reflecting a topic/sub-topic relationship, yet these are not the sort of topicical subdivisions we would ordinarily expect in LCSH. For example, we would not expect to see a heading such as 'Oil Spill--GovernmentM But with partial coordination, subject terms which would not be expected in a pre-coordinated heading can be included and related to one another. A partially coordinated subject heading can be expressed by the cataloguer using a simple table notation.

Table is an example of the subject heading for the example document on government takeovers of oil spill cleanup efforts:

Subject Terms for Document WSJ990123-1234	Dependency
Oil	Spill
Spill	Oil
Government	Oil, Spill, Cleanup
Takeover	Cleanup
Cleanup	Oil, Spill

A table such as this is created for each document. The only access points into the document are the terms listed in the first column. These are the document's subject heading terms. Each subject heading term can then be assigned zero, one, or more terms which serve as dependencies to specify the context in which that document term will match a corresponding query term. The document subject term of the first column will match a corrsponding query term only if the query additionally contains that document term's dependencies as specified in the rightmost column.

Any term may appear as a subject term only, as a dependency term only, or as both. A subject term cannot depend on itself. Table shows that the terms 'takeover' and 'government' each depend on the term 'cleanup', while the term 'cleanup' depends on the two terms 'oil' and 'spill'. Then, even if a query contains the term 'takeover', for example, this document will not match that query term unless the query also contains the term 'cleanup'.

The cataloguer has thus indexed the document with a list of terms, and has further specified dependencies among the terms. If a term has two or more dependencies, then it is dependent on all those terms for its context, and matches only if the query contained all those terms. *Note that the order of terms in a query never matters.* A dependency requires that the dependent term occur somewhere—anywhere—in the query.

Given dependencies, the document scoring for each query is computed from the following rule:

- For each query term q, if q appears in the document's subject terms, and if *all* that term's dependent terms as specified for that document appear somewhere in the query, then q matches, and we add one point to the score; otherwise, q is no match and we go on to the next query term

Table shows the scores of this document with respect to some of the possible queries containing one or more terms from the document's five subject terms. Unit query and document term weights are assumed.

Query	Traditional Post-Coordination	Partial Coordination
Government	1	0
Takeover	1	0
Cleanup	1	0
Oil	1	0
Spill	1	0
Oil Spill	2	2
Government takeover	2	0
Government cleanup	2	0
Government oil spill	3	2
Takeover oil spill	3	2
Cleanup oil spill	3	3
Government takeover cleanup	3	1
Government cleanup oil spill	4	4
Government takeover cleanup oil spill	5	5

Reconsider the query 'government takeover banks' to represent an interest in government takeovers of failing banks. The term 'government' appears. among the document's terms, but its dependent term—*i.e.,* the phrase 'oil spill'—does not appear in the query. The term 'government' is therefore prevented from matching out of context and adds nothing to the score. We go to the next query term, 'takeover'.

This term also appears in the document's index, but again, its dependent term—*i.e.,* cleanup—does not, so this query term is also prevented from matching out of context. Lastly, the query term 'banks' does not appear in the document index at all. So under partial coordination the score of this document with respect to this query is zero, as it clearly should be.

Dependencies in partial coordination are not transitive. For example if a user interested in a private company's takeover of a toxic waste cleanup program enters the keywords 'private sector takeover cleanup toxic waste' the example document receives a score of 1.

Two of the query's keywords, 'takeover' and 'cleanup' appear as subject terms. 'Takeover' is considered a match, because both it and its dependent term—*i.e.*, cleanup—appear in the query. However, the query term 'cleanup' itself is not a match, because although it appears in the document index as a subject term, its dependency term—*i.e.*, the phrase 'oil spill'—does not. Thus, the term dependencies are not transitive, so while 'takeover' depends on 'cleanup' and 'cleanup' on 'oil spill', nevertheless 'takeover' does not depend on 'oil spill' unless the cataloguer expressly adds dependency arrows directly from 'takeover' to 'oil' and 'spill'.

The reasoning here is that the term 'takeover' is not matching out of context, in this cataloger's opinion, as long as both document and query regard takeover of a cleanup effort, and so a point will be added to this document's score for being about the right sort of takeover. But this cleanup is not the same sort of cleanup in the query and document, so the term 'cleanup' is not considered to have matched. There are two major benefits to omitting transitivity.

First, it helps ensure the scores of *this document with respect to various queries* make sense by scoring higher for someone interested in takeovers of a cleanup than for someone interested in another unrelated sort of takeover. Next the *scores of various documents with respect to a given query* also make sense as this document on the takeover of a toxic waste cleanup effort scores higher for this query than documents on takeovers of other kinds.

PARTIAL COORDINATION BENEFITS

Partial coordination increases precision, thereby reducing information overload from spurious partial matches. Most of the thirty-one possible queries using only terms from the document index, result in lower scores under partial coordination compared with post-coordination. For example the query 'government takeover', gives a score of zero under partial coordination, but a score of two under post-coordination. Given a set of index terms, the addition of dependencies can only serve to lower scores. The hope, of course, is that the dependencies will lower scores of relatively less relevant documents, thereby increasing precision.

Thus all of these score reductions appear beneficial at first glance. A possible objection to this supposed improvement is that the cataloguer's choice of subject terms 'government takeover' lends itself to out-of-context partial matches. A good cataloguer would never include such terms in a post-coordinate environment for fear of such poor matches. This argument actually illuminates an additional benefit of introducing term dependencies. We agree that cataloguers choosing keywords for a post-coordinate environment ought to hesitate before including such terms in a document's index.

But the document is, after all, primarily about a government takeover of the cleanup effort, not about the cleanup effort itself. Certainly the terms 'government' and 'takeover' ought to be included in the document index to enhance recall, were it not for fear of those terms matching out of context. Partial coordination allows the cataloguer to add these terms which may enhance recall, by eliminating the fear that they will decrease precision by matching out of context.

Thus, partial coordination should be viewed not only as enhancing precision, but also as enhancing recall by allowing cataloguers the freedom to include additional relevant terms without fear of poor precision. The meaning of a term dependency is identified with the reason for its use, which is one of the following: an ordered relationship, a phrase, a secondary topic, a narrow term.

Partial coordination dependencies effectively substitute for ordered relationships such as topic/sub-topic relationships among the index terms, without the user having to guess a correct citation order. This resolves out-of-context matches due to lack of term ordering as in the case of pre-coordination. Partial coordination does not directly address the problem of polysemy.

However, other sorts of context provided by partial coordination may help ensure that even if an irrelevant document may achieve a non-zero score because of a polysemous word, the document is not likely to achieve a high ranking. Outof- context matches from a single term matching out of the context of its phrase is resolved by establishing term inter-dependencies between the many words of a phrase. Again in this case the user does not have to form specific phrases in his query.

Partial coordination also allows the cataloguer to include index terms to represent secondary topics or other details with greater exhaustivity, without fear that those terms will match out of context. This is simply accomplished by defining dependencies in which the secondary terms depend on the primary ones for their context. Within that context, these secondary terms come into play, to help distinguish the best among the broadly-relevant documents.

Finally, partial coordination allows the cataloguer to resolve problems caused by non-categorical terms by including narrow terms together with the broader terms for increased depth, with the narrow terms depending on the broader terms. For example, if the document is about tarantulas as horror movie props, then the cataloguer may have the term "tarantulaff depend on a term such as 'movie' or 'prop'; a different document, in which tarantulas are an example of a poisonous insect, would be cataloged differently, with the term 'tarantula' dependent on a term such as 'Insect'.

We believe the scores in the example of table one, as well as the analysis of out-of-context matches, highlight the potential of partial coordination to shift out the recall/precision curve for post-coordinate keyword indexing. Partial coordination is a powerful way to prevent out of context matches, capturing the ability of pre-coordination to enhance precision without requiring the user to order his query terms. Partial coordination also indirectly improves recall.

If the fear of matching out of context is removed, cataloguers can include more details, *i.e.*, more terms, or narrower terms. Where the query includes both the broader and narrower terms, precision is enhanced by including the narrow term in the document's subject heading. Where the user query included only the narrower term, its inclusion in the document heading enhances recall. Finally, the appropriately lowered scores of irrelevant or partially relevant documents with respect to the various queries will serve to improve the rank ordering of documents.

PARTIAL COORDINATION AND OTHER APPROACHES TO CONTEXT

Partial coordination differs from pre-coordination and other methods of reducing out-of-context matches. We enumerate other methods with some applicability to reducing out of context matches, and indicate the possible advantages of partial coordination over these methods.

PARTIAL COORDINATION IN CONTRAST TO PRE-COORDINATION

Partial coordination differs from full pre-coordination in five ways. *First,* a subject term may be hidden behind another term which is not itself an access point, *i.e.,* it is not itself a subject term. This is accomplished by introducing a dependency term which is not itself a subject term. *Second,* unlike one linear citation order for all the document terms in pre-coordination, a cataloguer can specify a set of individual restrictions on that order.

Many complete orderings may satisfy the individual restrictions defined by the cataloguer on a document's terms. For example, the cataloguer may specify '*A* after *B*, *D* after *E*, and no restrictions on *B*, *C*, or *E*' allowing many complete orderings to meet these restrictions. *Third,* partial co-ordination can reflect any number of arbitrary topic/sub-topic relationships between terms.

Precoordination can reflect only a limited number and kind of such relationships. *Fourth,* like the post-coordinate environment, partial coordination permits partial matches to be recognised, such that the greater the match, the higher the document's score with respect to the query.

So if any term, from anywhere in the ordering, matches a query term and fulfills all its dependencies, that term will contribute to a partial match. *Fifth,* orderings are replaced by existential dependencies. Thus the actual ordering of query terms never matters, and the user does not even have to specify partial orderings. What matters is whether a contextual term appears somewhere in the query or is totally absent from it. There is one circumstance in which existential dependencies are not quite as precise as actual orderings.

In the case where two or more terms are related in multiple ways and a query includes all the terms involved in both documents' dependency relationships, then an irrelevant document may be retrieved. This is because in our scheme, a query with the terms *A B C* is equivalent to a query with the terms *C B A*.

The small price paid for not requiring the user to order his query terms, is that the scheme does not distinguish between these two queries. The differences between traditional pre-coordination and partial coordination, interact to create a powerful yet simple cataloguing and retrieval mechanism. Each term may contribute to a partial match with respect to the query as in post-coordinate search, but only if that term is requested in the context of other terms.

PARTIAL COORDINATION *VS.* EXTENDED BOOLEAN

If we are willing to shift the burden of specifying context from the cataloguer to the user, extended Boolean queries may also able to provide the basis for an alternative context-sensitive model. In traditional Boolean logic, a user my express '*B* depends on *A*' with the Boolean expression '*A AND B*'. The problem with this formulation is that, *A* also depends on *B*, contrary to the user's intentions.

In pre-coordination terms, this is like giving lead status to neither term alone. If the user tries '*OR A*' to indicate that B is of interest only in the context of *A*, but that *A* is of interest in any case, the expression simplifies to just '*A*'. This simplification occurs due to the binary nature of Boolean logic.

Some proposals extend the definition of Boolean operators to the non-binary case. In order to achieve a ranking of documents, document or query terms must be assigned weights. The definition of Boolean operators is then extended to the non-binary case, or a ranking function which can account for term weights is added to a traditional Boolean retrieval.

Theoretically, it is conceivable that under some definition of *AND* and *OR*, a user could express his contextual dependencies, but it is not clear what definition of AND and OR would allow this. Suppose the user is interested in *B* only in the context of *A*, and in *A* in any case.

Then, according to a contextsensitive ranking principle, we would like the following ranking:

- For a document with *A* and *B* as index terms, rank is highest.
- For a document with only *A* as an index term, rank is medium.
- For a document with only *B* as an index term, rank is lowest.

However, it is impossible to achieve these desired rankings for the most common extended Boolean definition of *AND* as *MIN* and *OR* as *MAX*, even if query term weights are also supplied.

In general, it is an open research question to find definitions of extended Boolean operators which would follow an intuitive context-sensitive ranking principle in arbitrarily complex cases, or how complex these user queries would have to become to achieve the desired rankings.

Given the difficulty users have with traditional Boolean queries, it seems unreasonable to expect user to formulate complex extended Boolean queries with query term weights to express context and to result in the intended document rankings. Partial coordination in contrast does not encumber the user in this way.

PARTIAL COORDINATION AND TERM WEIGHTING

Weighting of document and/or query terms may enhance precision. But assigning weights to individual terms cannot be used to adequately represent context. Term weights for individual terms represent a linear scheme, which alone cannot achieve the non-linearity of dependencies.

Term weights would have to be specified to every pair, triple, etc., of terms, either for each query or for each document in order to achieve the notion of context such that the document score depends on the particular combination of document terms matching the query terms. Thus single term weights alone cannot be used to establish the sort of context achievable with partial coordination.

PARTIAL COORDINATION AND FULL TEXT INDEXING

In recent years full text indexing has dominated information retrieval research. As discussed earlier in this paper, the problem of false drops seems to be greater in the case of full text.

But few studies have directly compared full-text to non-full-text indexing, and we know of no study which experimentally compares the effectiveness of state of the art full-text indexing and retrieval with manually assigned controlled vocabulary subject headings.

Full text does allow for new techniques which enhance recall and/or precision. These techniques are the focus of much research attention. Two methods applicable with full-text indexing that are most closely related to the notion of context, are term phrases and the probabilistic term dependence models.

In any case, despite the potential of full-text retrieval, given large paper document collections, no libraries currently provide it, nor are they likely to provide it in the foreseeable future for their paper collections. Partial coordination in contrast is a feasible enhancement to current OPAC's, as it does not require full text availability.

PARTIAL COORDINATION AND TERM PHRASES

The extensive research into term phrases is closely related to our proposal. Term phrase construction allows the retrieval engine to account not only for individual terms, but for particular combinations of terms. Experimental results indicate a modest improvement in retrieval results when phrases are manually identified in the query but this poses an extra burden on the user.

Results were not encouraging for automatic phrase identification without manual help. Fagan reviews the difficulties of automatic phrase formation. The statistical approaches use co-occurence data as a very imperfect surrogate for identifying phrases.

The syntactic approaches which can theoretically help avoid improper phrases, have generally been even less successful than the statistical ones. A second and much more important reason why partial coordination is expected to enhance retrieval beyond the success of phrases, is that term phrase construction is only one special use of partial coordination.

Partial coordination can be used to represent arbitrary syntactic and semantic relationships. Indeed Croft concludes "...in Boolean queries, experts often form the *AND* of two concepts which are not phrase components. This implies a strong relationship between those concepts... but it is not clear what type of relationship".

We clarified what types of relationship may induce experts to *AND* two together two terms. We identified a set of contextual relationships which require two or more terms to be treated together.

Partial coordination was proposed as a means of expressing all these contextual relationships. Thus, phrase formation is just one of many uses of partial coordination, which can also express the other relationships hinted at in and identified in this work. Moreover, with partial coordination the burden is shifted from the user query to the one-effort of the cataloguer.

PARTIAL COORDINATION AND GENERALISED PROBABILISTIC MODEL

The most relevant work to the proposal put forward in this paper is the generalised probabilistic model which is possible in full-text and non-full-text environments. In this model the probability of relevance to a query is estimated on the basis of the particular *corn bina t ion* of index terms in each document. The extent to which each document index term indicates probabilistic relevance to a query, is considered to depend on the presence or absence in the document index of every other term in the vocabulary or at least in the query.

Thus, for example, joint probability estimates are used to assess the relevance of a document with index terms *A* and *B*, separate from the estimation of relevance for the documents indexed with only one or the other term. This approach can theoretically incorporate all notions of context, not only term phrases. although it does so implicitly. In this sense, the probabilistic model is most closely related to our partial coordination. However, this approach theoretically requires relevance data to estimate parameters of the relevant and irrelevant documents separately.

Even with feedback data, this general model has been considered impractical because of the exponential number of parameters involved. The tree term dependence model is a limited version of this model which strictly limits the number of parameters. In this model, each term is considered to depend on at most one other term in the vocabulary or query. This approach is not only feasible, but has been shown to considerably improve precision for given levels of recall. Nevertheless this approach still requires feedback data for parameter estimation.

The favourable experimental results in utilised feedback data. In the absence of feedback data, Croft suggests heuristics for estimating a subset of these parameters. However, these heuristics require Boolean queries, and were only very marginally effective. Only manual phrase construction by the users was again shown to supply enough information for real improvement in retrieval effectiveness. In contrast to these approaches, partial coordination aims to increase precision even in the first iteration of search—prior to feedback—so users are not initially discouraged by a large number of hits. Our approach also relieves the user of any responsibility for phrase formation.

PARTIAL COORDINATION AND 'MIXED APPROACHES'

Our literature review identified only one attempt to directly combine the strengths of pre-and post-coordination within the traditional non-full-text environment. Gary Lawrence reviews the limitations of both pre-and post-coordination, and follows with a brief section entitled Mixed Approaches. One approach, attributed to Mischo is to "selectively manipulate subject headings and titles to present important words and word pairs at the beginning of the index entry in a heading-based retrieval system".

In other words, he suggests retaining the basic pre-coordinated environment, but including index entries for many possible citation orderings, depending on "the contents of defined subfields". In this way, the precision of pre-coordination is not lost, while not requiring that the user to guess the one correct citation order. While cross-references already provide indirect access through multiple citation orderings, Lawrence suggests providing actual index entries instead of just cross-references. But it is unclear how rotations are selected. And his method of selectively-rotated subject headings does not include the ability of post-coordination to provide partial matches. His proposal is appropriate for addressing the well-known problem of which and how many ordering permutations to include in a card catalogue.

PRECIS

Related to Lawrence's ideas on intelligent rotations, is PRECIS, a cataloging system developed for the paper card catalogue environment. While PRECIS is concerned with selectively-rotated entries, and also includes a notion of context, it nevertheless offers no help in avoiding out-of-context partial matches in the online environment.

PRECIS'S primary goals were:

- To allow the cataloguer to enter one encoded string to represent each document; the string includes document subject terms and PRECIS codes.
- To automatically produce catalogue entries for a number of possible rotations of the document terms. A 'heading' is the access point for each automatically produced entry. A heading contains one or more of the document's subject terms.
- To ensure that entries are produced only for headings which 'make sense', that all headings which make sense have an entry, and to ensure that the presentation of each entry makes clear the meaning of the whole subject heading assigned to the document.

A concept of 'context dependency' was developed to allow the PRECIS system to produce any and only meaningful entries, and to ensure that the presentation of each entry makes clear the meaning of the whole subject heading, "This principle requires that... each term in the entry is related to the one immediately preceding and the one immediately following it. Each term sets the next term into its obvious context."

PRECIS codes, which represent a limited number of facets are embedded by the cataloguer into each subject heading, so that each term is explicitly assigned to one role. Using this role information, and following the principle of context dependency, the PRECIS algorithm determines which catalogue entries to generate, and how each should be presented. The meaning of the whole heading is made clear through adherence to the principle of context dependency.

The importance of automatically creating rotated subject headings with transparent meaning is particular to the mechanics of pre-coordinate search. On the one hand, contrary to post-coordinate search, additional access points are necessary through the use of rotations; on the other hand, the process of pre-coordinate search is a two-step process as described in, the first step of which requires the user to understand and identify the intended subject heading. In this way, the philospohy of PRECIS assumes a pre-coordinated environment, and facilitates selection of meaningful rotations.

PRECIS requires cataloguers to specify the role played by each term in a heading. This explicit role information may be used in an algorithm to help avoid bad partial post-coordinate matches, but we know of no such algorithm, and PRECIS itself does not include such an algorithm. We know of no discussion regarding the application of PRECIS in a post-coordinate environment to limit bad partial matches.

Indeed, there exists an online version of PRECIS called COMPASS, and in this system, the role operators have been eliminated in favour of traditional post-coordinate term matching. Why not use all the valuable PRECIS role information to limit bad partial matches in the post-coordinated version COMPASS? Presumably, an algorithm to do so has not yet been developed, and promises to be highly complex. We agree with earlier reviews of this work, that the PRECIS role operators would seem to provide valuable information which might be somehow used to prevent false drops.

This possibility has not been addressed by the developers of PRECIS or COMPASS. We, too, leave this for future work, and view the utilisation of PRECIS codes as a possible means of formalising the process by which cataloguers specify term dependencies. As PRECIS and COMPASS are being phased out of use, such future work ought to focus more generally on exploiting available role information in whatever form it takes. In summary, PRECIS as it has been developed to date does not help solve the problem of spurious partial matches in an online post-coordinate retrieval environment.

FEASIBILITY

Partial coordination is proposed as an extension to non-full-text OPAC's, as well as to full-text available databases such as the WWW. In the case of OPAC's which rely on LC or other pre-coordinated subject headings, the additional manual effort required to provide partially coordinated keywords, seems very small compared to the effort already required to produce the LC heading. Moreover, cataloguers are already asked to include additional non-controlled subject terms.

The incremental effort required to instead include partially coordinated terms is small. If an OPAC were extended to rank documents using partially coordinated subject terms, existing MARC records with subject headings would not require revision, because a document with no term dependencies is just a special case of a partially coordinated heading. The ordering of terms in the LC heading would just be ignored as in traditional keyword search.

One issue which does require resolution, however, is that the rank order of documents for a query would need to fairly integrate the scores of partially coordinated documents with those unrevisied records which lacked partial coordination. In the full text environment, the additional effort required to assign partially coordinated subject terms is great, since, the full text indexing requires no manual effort at all.

We envision our proposal as relating to full text indexing in two ways:

- First, automatic techniques may be pursued which will automatically create some term dependencies.
- Second, the labour of adding additional subject terms with partial coordination may be distributed among the documents' readers. We are currently working on both these proposals.

CONCLUSIONS

The partial coordination proposal in this paper combines the advantages of intelligent pre-coordination—*i.e.,* greater precision—with the chief advantages of post-coordination—*i.e.,* the user is relieved of the burden of learning cataloguing rules such as citation order, and partial matches are supported. The technique we propose concentrates on the benefits of *intelligent* ordering, which can be realised in an OPAC environment without any additional effort on the part of the user; the user enters his keywords as before, but the intelligent coordination of documents' keywords prevents inappropriate partial matches.

Our critical analysis of out-of-context matches and review of partial coordination in the context of alternate techniques suggests that this is a promising technique for improving precision and recall in OPAC and other emerging information retrieval contexts such as the WWW.

Bibliography

Aaron, E.: *Abstracts Produced Using Computer Assistance,* Washington: National Academy Press, 2000.

Austin, Derek: *PRECIS: A Manual of Concept Analysis and Subject Indexing,* London: The British Library, 1984.

Balkus, R.: *Writing Abstracts for Free-text Searching,* Washington: Social Security Administration, 2009.

Bonura, Larry S.: *The Art of Indexing,* New York: John Wiley & Sons, 1994.

Borko, Horald, and Bernier, Charles L.: *Abstracting Concepts and Methods,* New York: Academic Press, 1975.

Borko, Horald, and Bernier, Charles L.: *Indexing Concepts and Methods,* New York: Academic Press, 1978.

Brenner, Diane, and Rowland, Marilyn: *Beyond Book Indexing,* NJ: Information Today, 2000.

Brian, R.: *Documentary Abstracting: Toward a Methodological Model,* London: Macmillan, 2004.

Burton, A.: *The Role of Information Competency and Skills in Learning to Abstract,* Berkeley: University of California Press, 2003.

Cleveland, Donald B., and Cleveland, Ana D.: *Introduction to Indexing and Abstracting,* Englewood, CO: Libraries Unlimited, 2001.

Craven, Timothy C.: *String Indexing,* New York: Academic Press, 1986.

Cremmins, Edward T.: *The Art of Abstracting,* Arlington, VA: Information Resources Press, 1996.

Ellen, A.: *Abstracts and Abstracting in Knowledge Discovery,* New York: Academic Press, 1998.

Ellen, J.: *Quality of Abstracts*, New Haven: Yale University Press, 1999.

George, R.: *String Indexing*, Expanded, Baltimore, MD: Johns Hopkins University Press, 2003.

Gerhard, A.: *Citation Indexing: Its Theory and Applications in Science*, Technology and Humanities, New York: Berg, 2007.

Hamilton, C.: *Automatic Indexing and Abstracting of Document Texts*, Chapel Hill: University of North Carolina Press, 2004.

Henman, P.: *Indexing and Abstracting on the World Wide Web*, New York: E. Sharpe, 1998.

Hollingsworth, J.: *Information Representation and Retrieval in the Digital Age*, Philadelphia: University of Pennsylvania Press 2005.

Howard, S.: *Construction and Maintenance of Indexing Languages & Thesauri*, New York: Academic Press 2008.

Jepsen, M.: *Indexing Specialized Formats and Subjects*, New Haven: Yale University Press, 2005.

Joel, F.: *Challenges in Indexing Electronic Text and Images*, Cambridge University Press, 2005.

Meyers, William P.: *Indexing Books: Lessons in Language Computations*, UK: British Library, 2005.

Index